The
Panoramic Bible

The Storyline of Scripture

William Hollberg

The Panoramic Bible: The Storyline of Scripture

Written by William Hollberg
Illustrations by Catherine C. Anderson

© Copyright 2018 William Bealer Hollberg

ISBN 978-1-63393-442-9 Softcover
ISBN 978-1-63393-443-6 Ebook

Front cover: God's wisdom is a tree of life to those who embrace it and hold it tightly (Proverbs 3:18, author's paraphrase).

Cover and interior design: Köehler Studios, Kellie Emery

Published by William Bealer Hollberg
in association with

◣ köehlerstudios™
www.koehlerstudios.com

For Spencer, William, and Laine,
my thoughtful and inspiring grandchildren.

Table of Contents

FOREWORD 1

INTRODUCTION 3

WHY I WROTE *THE PANORAMIC BIBLE* 7

PART ONE
God Created the World and Began His Special People 8

1. God Created Everything
[from Genesis 1 and 2] 10

2. Adam and Eve Were the First People God Created
[from Genesis 1 and 2] 10

3. God Wanted Adam and Eve to Remain Good and Pure
[from Genesis 2:15–17] 11

4. Adam and Eve Disobeyed God and Were Punished
[from Genesis 3] 11

Illustration 1: Adam and Eve Expelled from Garden 12

5. God Made a Promise of Love to Adam and Eve
[from Genesis 3] 13

REFLECTION 1: God's Promise of Love Is for Us 14

6. Cain Dishonored God and Then Killed Abel
[from Genesis 4] 14

7. More People Dishonored and Rejected God
[from Genesis 6:1–7] 15

8. Noah Was True and Faithful
   [from Genesis 6:8–9] 16

9. God's Flood Killed Wicked People, but His Love Saved Noah
   [from Genesis 6:14–8:12] 16

Illustration 2: Noah: The Flood, the Rainbow, the Promise 17

10. God's Promise of Love to Noah Was a Covenant of Life
   [from Genesis 8:13–9:17] 17

11. After the Flood, Many Rejected God and Built the Tower of Babel
   [from Genesis 11:1–9] 18

12. One Man Who Honored God Was Job
   [from Job] 19

13. God Had a Special Plan for One Part of Noah's Family
   [from Genesis 11:10–12:7 and 22:17–18] 19

Map 1: Journeys of Abraham 20

14. God's Special Plan for Abram Was a Covenant of Land and Family
   [from Genesis 15–18] 21

15. Abraham and Sarah Had a Son, Isaac
   [from Genesis 17:9–14 and 21:1–8] 21

16. God Used Isaac to Test Abraham's Heart
   [from Genesis 22:1–18] 22

REFLECTION 2: Obedience and a Substitute Sacrifice 23

17. Abraham Had Confidence That God Would Fulfill His Promise
   [from Genesis 24:1–10] 23

18. Isaac Married Rebekah
   [from Genesis 24:11–27:41] 24

19. Jacob Ran Away from Esau and Met God
   [from Genesis 27:41–28:22] 24

20. Jacob Married Rachel and Wrestled with God
[from Genesis 29–32] 25

Illustration 3: Jacob Wrestled with God 26

21. Jacob Had Twelve Sons
[from Genesis 37] .27

22. Joseph Became a Slave in Egypt
[from Genesis 39–40] 27

23. Joseph Met Pharaoh, the King
[from Genesis 41] .28

Illustration 4: Joseph: From Slave to Officer in Charge 29

24. Joseph's Brothers Went to Egypt for Food
[from Genesis 42:1–43:15] 30

25. Joseph and His Brothers Were Reunited
[from Genesis 43:16–50:21] 31

REFLECTION 3: God's Sovereignty 32

26. Jacob's Whole Family Moved to Egypt
[from Genesis 43:1–47:12] 32

27. Jacob's Family Stayed in Egypt after the Famine
[from Genesis 50:1–Exodus 1:14] 33

28. Moses' Mother Saved Him from Being Killed
[from Exodus 1:15–2:25] 33

Illustration 5: Moses' Mother Was in Anguish 34

29. God Called Moses to Save His People
[from Exodus 3:1–4:23] 35

30. Moses Told Pharaoh to Let God's People Go
[from Exodus 4:27–10:29] 36

31. God Protected His Covenant People
[from Exodus 11:1–13:16] 37

REFLECTION 4: Passover 38

32. God Made Dry Land in the Red Sea
[from Exodus 13:17–14:31] 38

33. God Gave His People Food and Water in the Wilderness
[from Exodus 16:1–17:7] 39

34. God Led Israel Out of Egypt as Part of His Covenant Plan
[from Exodus 19:1–8] 39

REFLECTION 5: The Promise 40

35. God Gave His People His Good Law in the Wilderness
[from Exodus 19:9–20:26] 40

36. God's People Wanted a God They Could See
[from Exodus 31:18–33:17 and 34:1–28] 41

Illustration 6: The Calf Idol: A God the People Could See 42

37. The Tabernacle Was Built for Worshiping God in the Wilderness
[from Exodus 25:1–31:11 and 35:4–40:38] 43

38. God's Priest, Aaron, Led the People in Offering Sacrifices to God
[from Leviticus 1:1–9:24 and 16:1–17:16] 44

REFLECTION 6: The Sacrifice 45

CONNECTION 1: Preparation to Enter the Promised Land 45

39. God Wanted His People Joined Together by Tribal Families
[from Numbers 2:1–34] 46

40. God Wanted His People to See the Promised Land
[from Numbers 13:1–14:38] 46

41. God Gave Phinehas a Covenant of Peace for a Perpetual Priesthood
[from Numbers 22:1–25:18] 47

42. Moses Gave Israel a Farewell Address and a Serious Warning
[from Deuteronomy 31:1–33:29] 48

PART TWO

A Homeland for God's People 50

43. God Appointed Joshua to Lead His People into the Promised Land
    [from Deuteronomy 34 and Joshua 1] 52

44. Joshua Met God before the Battle of Jericho
    [from Joshua 1:1–6:27] 52

Illustration 7: Joshua: Who Was the Commander? 53

45. After Many Years and Battles, the Land Was Divided
    among the Tribes of Israel
    [from Joshua 13:1–24:20] .53

Map 2: Twelve Tribes of Israel 54

46. God Gave Israel New Leaders
    [from Judges] 54

47. Ruth Became an Adopted Daughter of Israel and Ancestor of Jesus
    [from Ruth] 55

48. Samuel Was Israel's Last Effective Judge
    [from 1 Samuel 1:1–8:9] 56

CONNECTION 2: The History of Israel When Kings Ruled 57

49. God Chose Saul as Israel's First King
    [from 1 Samuel 8:22–15:35] .57

50. God Told Samuel to Anoint David as Israel's New King
    [from 1 Samuel 16:1–33] 58

51. Before Becoming King, David Killed Goliath
    [from 1 Samuel 17:1–18:9] .59

52. After David Killed Goliath, Saul Tried to Kill David
    [from 1 Samuel 18:10–31:13] 60

53. David Became the King and Kept Singing
    [from the Psalms] 61

Illustration 8: David: Shepherd Boy and King 62

54. David Wanted to Build a Temple for God
[from 2 Samuel 7:1–13a and 1 Chronicles 28:1–21] 63

**55. God Intended to Build an Eternal Kingdom
through David's Family**
[from 2 Samuel 7:13b–29 and 1 Chronicles 28:4–29:20] 63

56. Solomon Became King and Prayed for Wisdom
[from 1 Kings 3:3–28 and 2 Chronicles 1:7–13] 64

57. Solomon Wrote Wise Sayings Collected as Proverbs
[from Proverbs] 65

58. Solomon Built the Temple
[from 1 Kings 9:1–9 and 2 Chronicles 2:1–3:2; 7:11–18] 66

CONNECTION 3: Solomon Wrote Two Unique Books—Ecclesiastes and
Song of Solomon 66

**59. Solomon Said Life Is Vanity, but God's Plan Implements
His Sovereignty**
[from Ecclesiastes] 67

60. Solomon's Most Beautiful Song Teaches about Real Love
[from Song of Solomon] 68

61. Solomon Turned from God, and His Son Divided the Nation
[from 1 Kings 11:1–12:33] 69

Illustration 9: Solomon: Worshiping Idols—a Divided Heart 70

PART THREE
God's People Rejected Him and Went into Exile 72

CONNECTION 4: Divided into Two Nations, Israel Heads
toward Captivity 74

Map 3: Kingdom Divided 75

SECTION A. ISRAEL—The Northern Kingdom from King Jeroboam
to the Assyrian Captivity 76

62. Elijah Called Israel to Repentance
[from 1 Kings 18:1–46 and 21:1–29] 76

63. Elijah Was Taken to Heaven in a Whirlwind of Fiery Chariots
[from 2 Kings 2:1–18] 77

**64. A Young Girl Knew of Elisha, Trusted God, and Acted
with Courage**
[from 2 Kings 5:1–3] 77

65. Elisha Healed the General of Israel's Enemy from Leprosy
[from 2 Kings 5:4–19] 78

66. God Sent Jonah to Tell Foreigners about God, and They Repented
[from Jonah] 79

67. Israel Refused to Repent When Amos Preached
[from Amos] 80

**68. Hosea Was God's Last Prophet to Israel before Its Conquest
by Assyria**
[from Hosea] 81

CONNECTION 5: The Southern Portion of the Nation of Israel
Became Known as Samaria 81

SECTION B. JUDAH—The Southern Kingdom from King Rehoboam
to the Babylonian Captivity 82

CONNECTION 6: Judah Heads toward Exile 82

**69. Joel Told Judah the Locust Plague Was Nothing Compared
to the Future**
[from Joel] 83

Illustration 10: A Locust Plague Devours Judah 83

**70. Micah Was God's Prophet in Judah When Hosea
Was a Prophet in Israel**
[from Micah] 84

71. Isaiah Was God's Prophet to the Leaders in Judah
[from Isaiah] 85

72. Isaiah Said God's Messiah Would Come as the True Ruler
[from Isaiah] 86

73. Nahum Told Judah That Assyria Would Soon Be Conquered
[from Nahum] 86

74. Zephaniah Told Judah to Prepare for God's Judgment Day
[from Zephaniah] 87

75. Habakkuk Couldn't Believe God Would Use the Evil Babylonians
to Punish Judah
[from Habakkuk] 87

76. Obadiah Spoke to Edom and Judah about What It Means
to Be Family
[from Obadiah] 88

77. Jeremiah Was the Last Prophet to Judah before
the Babylonian Captivity
[from Jeremiah] 89

CONNECTION 7: Jerusalem Was Destroyed and Judah Went
into Exile in Babylon 90

78. All That Remained of Jerusalem Was a Lament
[from Lamentations] 91

Illustration 11: The Temple Was Destroyed 92

79. God Promised to Make a New Covenant with Israel and Judah
[from Jeremiah] 93

80. Ezekiel Was a Priest Taken Captive in Babylon
[from Ezekiel] 93

81. Daniel and His Three Friends Were Captives in Babylon but
Stayed Faithful to God
[from Daniel 1–2] 94

82. **Daniel's Three Friends Served the King, but Other Officials Hated Them**
[from Daniel 3] 95

83. **Daniel Served the King, but Other Officials Hated Him**
[from Daniel 5:31–6:28] 96

Illustration 12: Daniel Was Persecuted .97

PART FOUR
God Restored His People to the Homeland 98

CONNECTION 8: A Remnant of God's People
Returned to Jerusalem after Exile 100

84. **Ezra and Daniel Wrote about the First Group to Return to Judah**
[from Ezra 1–2 and Daniel 5:31–11:1] 100

85. **Zerubbabel Led in Building the Temple's Foundation, but Then Work Stopped**
[from Ezra 3–6] 101

86. **Haggai Told the Israelites to Get Back to Work on the Temple**
[from Haggai] 102

87. **Zechariah Encouraged the People to Build the Temple**
[from Zechariah] 103

88. **Esther Served God in Babylon and Saved God's People through Obedience**
[from Esther] 103

89. **Ezra Became the Teacher in Jerusalem**
[from Ezra 7–10] 104

90. **Nehemiah Anguished over the Disgrace of God's People**
[from Nehemiah 1:1–2:10] 105

91. **God Used Nehemiah to Rebuild Jerusalem's Walls**
[from Nehemiah 2:11–13:31] 106

Illustration 13: Malachi Taught at the Temple 107

92. Malachi Confronted People with God's Truth
[from Malachi 1–2] 107

93. Malachi Said God's Messenger Would Announce the Lord's Coming
[from Malachi 3–4] 108

REFLECTION 7: God's A-Team and the End of the Old Testament 109

_____

PART FIVE
The Coming of Jesus 112

94. Gabriel Told Zechariah His Son, John, Would Be the Messenger
[from Luke 1:1–25] 114

95. Gabriel Told Mary Her Son, Jesus, Would Be the Messiah
[from Luke 1:26–56] 114

Illustration 14: Gabriel Announced John the Baptist as the Messenger 115

96. An Angel Told Joseph to Marry Mary
[from Matthew 1:18–25] 116

CONNECTION 9: The Four Gospels Teach about Jesus' Life and Ministry . . 117

97. The Roman Caesar Ordered a Census
[from Luke 2:1–5] 118

Map 4: Kingdom of Herod the Great 118

98. Jesus Was Born in Bethlehem
[from Luke 2:6–20] 119

99. Wise Men Followed a Star and Searched for Jesus
[from Matthew 2:1–12] 119

100. At Age Twelve Jesus Went to Jerusalem with His Family
for Passover
[from Luke 2:41–52] 120

Illustration 15: Jesus Was Baptized in the Jordan River 121

101. John Preached Repentance and Baptized Jesus
[from Matthew 3:1–17] 121

PART SIX
Jesus' Earthly Ministry 122

REFLECTION 8: Jesus Implements God's Big-Picture Plan 124

102. God Was Pleased with Jesus, but Satan Wanted to Destroy Him
[from Matthew 4:1–13 and Luke 4:13] 125

103. Jesus Called Twelve of His Disciples to Be Apostles
[from Matthew 10:2–4; Luke 6:12–16; and John 1:35–51] 125

104. Jesus Went to a Wedding and Performed His First Miracle
[from John 2:1–12] 126

REFLECTION 9: Christian Marriage and Family Celebration 127

105. A Religious Leader Sought Out Jesus and Learned
about New Birth
[from John 3:1–21] 127

106. A Thirsty Samaritan Woman Learned about Living Water
[from John 4:7–42] 128

REFLECTION 10: Jesus Demolishes Barriers and Emphasizes
Humans' Worth and Dignity 129

107. A Paralyzed Man Came through the Roof
[from Mark 2:1–12] 130

108. Religious Leaders Accused Jesus and His Disciples
of Breaking the Rules
[from Mark 2:18–3:6] 130

REFLECTION 11: Jesus Shows Us the Reality of Spiritual Life 131

109. Jesus Went to a Mountain and Taught Crowds
[from Matthew 5:1–7:29] 132

110. Jesus Taught about Prayer
[from Matthew 6:1–15] 133

Illustration 16: Jesus Taught at a Mountain 134

CONNECTION 10: Jesus Taught in Parables 135

**111. A Parable about Differences in People's Readiness
for God's Message**
[from Luke 8:4–15] 135

112. A Parable about Knowing and Helping Your Neighbor
[from Luke 10:25–37] 136

113. A Parable about God's Amazing Kingdom
[from Luke 13:18–21] 137

114. A Parable about Selfishness and Pride
[from Luke 15:11–32] 137

115. Jesus Calmed a Storm and a Man with Demons
[from Mark 4:35–5:20] 138

116. Jesus Healed a Woman and Gave New Life to a Young Girl
[from Luke 8:40–56] 139

117. Jesus Fed Five Thousand and Walked on Water
[from John 6:1–29] 140

118. The Disciples Acknowledged Jesus as the Son of God
[from Matthew 14:22–33; 16:13–20; and John 20:30–31] 141

119. God Acknowledged Jesus as His Son
[from Matthew 14:1–12; 17:1–13] 142

120. The Religious Leaders Regarded Jesus as Their Enemy
[from Luke 11:14–54] 142

121. The Religious Leaders Decided Jesus Must Die
[from John 11:1–57] 143

**122. The Disciples Mistakenly Thought Jesus Was Working
for Their Glory**
from Mark 10:32–45] 144

CONNECTION 11: Jesus' Last Week on Earth 145

**123. Jesus Was So Popular That the Religious Leaders Made Plans
to Kill Him**
[from Mark 11:1–18] 145

**124. The Religious Leaders Formed a Plan when Judas Was Paid
Some Money**
[from Luke 22:1–6 and John 12:4–8] 146

Illustration 17: Judas Received Money from Priests to Betray Jesus 147

**125. Jesus Revealed the New Covenant when He Ate the Passover Meal
with His Apostles**
[from Luke 22:7–20] 148

**126. Judas Left Early and Missed Learning about the
New Commandment**
[from John 13:1–36] 148

127. Judas Put Money Ahead of Love and Betrayed Jesus
[from Matthew 26:36–56] 149

128. Jesus' "Crime" Was Asserting that He Was God
[from Matthew 26:57–27:10] 150

129. At His Trial before Pilate, Jesus Testified about the Truth
[from John 18:28–19:16] 151

130. Jesus Was Crucified
[from Matthew 27:27–56 and Luke 23:39–43] 151

131. Jesus Died
[from Matthew 27:27–56; Luke 23:39–46; and John 19:25–27] 152

Illustration 18: Jesus Was Crucified 153

Illustration 19: The Empty Tomb 154

132. Jesus Was Buried but Rose from the Dead
[from Matthew 27:57–28:10] 154

133. Jesus Gave His Disciples a New Assignment and New Power
[from Matthew 28:16–20 and Acts 1:4–11] 155

134. Jesus Appeared to the Eleven Apostles and Five Hundred Other People
[from Matthew 28:1–10; Luke 24:1–53; Mark 16:14; John 21:1–14; Acts 1:3–11; and 1 Corinthians 15:6] 156

Illustration 20: Jesus' Resurrection Appearance 157

PART SEVEN
God Sent His Spirit and Established His Church 158

135. The Apostles Needed a Replacement Who Was a Witness to Jesus' Resurrection
[from Acts 1:4–26]. 160

REFLECTION 12: If You Believe in Jesus, Tell Others about His Resurrection 160

Illustration 21: The Holy Spirit Anointed for Power 161

136. The Holy Spirit Brought God's Power to His Family
[from Acts 2:1–13] 161

137. Peter Preached the First Sermons to the Church
[from Acts 2:14–3:26] 162

138. The Apostles Were Arrested for Teaching about the Living Jesus
[from Acts 4:1–31 and 5:12–42] 163

139. Stephen Was the First Christian Martyr
[from Acts 6:1–8:3] 164

140. Jesus Brought Saul into the Church
[from Acts 9:1–31] 165

Illustration 22: Paul Was Blinded by Jesus 166

141. The Holy Spirit Used Peter to Bring Gentiles into the Church
[from Acts 9:43–11:18] 167

REFLECTION 13: Five Primary Truths of Life as God's Child 168

**142. The Holy Spirit Directed the Church to Send Saul (Paul)
as a Missionary**
[from Acts 11:19–26; 13:1–9; and 16:11–40] 169

**143. A Young Boy Trusted God and Acted Courageously
to Save Paul's Life**
[from Acts 21:15–23:32] 170

144. Paul Trusted God and Was Sent to Rome as a Prisoner
[from Acts 25:1–28:31] 171

PART EIGHT
God Taught His Family How to Live 172

CONNECTION 12: Primary Themes in the Epistles—Romans through
Jude 174

145. Paul Wrote to the Church in Rome
[from Romans 1:1–17] 175

146. God's Wrath and Judgment
[from Romans 1:18–3:20] 175

147. Justification before God Is by Faith
[from Romans 3:21–31] 176

REFLECTION 14: Jesus Paid Our Debt and Satisfied God's Wrath 177

148. Confidence Comes from Being Conformed to Jesus
[from Romans 8:16–30] 178

REFLECTION 15: God's Will for Our Character 178

149. A Conformed Life Is a Sacrificed Life
[from Romans 12:1–16:27] 179

150. Life without Love Is Worthless
[from 1 Corinthians 12–14] 180

REFLECTION 16: Gospel Living Is Based on Gifts of the Spirit,
Not Material Wealth or Social Status 180

151. How We Treat Each Other Matters
[from 1 Corinthians 3:1–23; 6:1–11; and 11:17–34] 181

152. God's Spirit Enables Love for Him
[from 1 Corinthians 3:1–23; 5:1–13; 6:9–20; 9:12; and 10:1–33] 182

*Illustration 23: Love: God's Spirit Brought Together the Body
of Believers* 183

153. Faith in Jesus Gives Confidence in the Resurrection of the Dead
[from 1 Corinthians 15] 183

154. Paul Suffered and Identified with Jesus
[from 2 Corinthians 1–4] 184

155. Paul Ministered and Lived as a Reconciled Child of God
[from 2 Corinthians 5–7] 185

**156. Many Gave Financially and Honored What God Had Done
for Them**
[from 2 Corinthians 8–9] 185

157. Paul's Defense Was Spiritually Based
[from 2 Corinthians 10–13] 186

158. God Appointed Paul to Teach
[from Galatians 1:1–2:14] 187

159. How Are We Made Right with God?
[from Galatians 2:15–4:31] 188

160. False Teachers Oppose Liberty in Jesus
[from Galatians 5–6] 188

161. From Spiritual Death to Immeasurable Wealth in Jesus
[from Ephesians 1–3] 189

162. **Walk Worthily in This New Life in Jesus**
[from Ephesians 4:1–5:20] 190

163. **Live in the Power of the Holy Spirit**
[from Ephesians 1:19–23 and 5:21–6:24] 190

Illustration 24: Holy Spirit Power: The Armor of God 191

164. **Have the Mind of Jesus**
[from Philippians 1–2] 192

165. **False Teachers Promote Personal Effort, Not Gospel Living**
[from Philippians 3–4] 193

166. **False Teachers Deny Jesus as God**
[from Colossians 1–2] 193

167. **Setting Your Mind on the Things of God**
[from Colossians 3–4] 194

168. **Steadfast Faith**
[from 1 Thessalonians 1:1–3:13] 195

169. **The Return of Jesus, Part One**
[from 1 Thessalonians 4:13–5:11] 195

170. **Gospel Living in a Pagan Culture**
[from 1 Thessalonians 2:9–5:28] 196

171. **The Return of Jesus, Part Two**
[from 2 Thessalonians 2:1–12] 197

172. **Gospel Living through Jesus**
[from 2 Thessalonians 1–3] 197

CONNECTION 13: Paul Wrote Four Epistles to Three Friends 198

Illustration 25: Paul Wrote about Having the Mind of Jesus 199

173. **Wage War against False Teachers**
[from 1 Timothy 1 and 4] 200

174. **Gospel Living in Church**
[from 1 Timothy 2:1–3:16] 200

175. Gospel Living in Personal Relationships
[from 1 Timothy 5–6] 201

176. False Teachers Distort and Deceive
[from 2 Timothy 1 and 3–4] 202

177. The Holy Spirit Empowers Gospel Living
[from 2 Timothy] 202

178. Appoint Godly Leaders and Confront False Teachers
[from Titus 1] 203

179. Gospel Living as God's Family
[from Titus 2–3] 204

180. A Thieving Slave Became a Humble Servant
[from Philemon] 205

CONNECTION 14: Hebrews Connects the Old and New Covenants 205

181. Jesus Is God's Final Word
[from Hebrews 1:1–2:18] 206

182. Jesus Is Our Model for Faithfulness
[from Hebrews 3:1–4:13] 207

183. Jesus Is the Ultimate High Priest, Covenant, Sanctuary, and Sacrifice
[from Hebrews 4:14–10:18] 207

184. Be Faithful with Endurance
[from Hebrews 10:19–13:25] 208

REFLECTION 17: What We Believe Matters 210

Illustration 26: Jesus: Our Ultimate Hope and Confidence 211

CONNECTION 15: Four Leaders Wrote the Last Seven Epistles 212

185. Proof of Faith
[from James 1:1–18 and 5:7–20] 212

186. James Described the Marks of Gospel Living
[from James 1:19–4:12] 213

187. James Rebuked Worldly Living

[from James 4:1–5:6] 214

REFLECTION 18: How We Worship Matters 215

188. Genuineness of Faith

[from 1 Peter 1:1–2:12 and 4:1–11] 216

189. Faith Lived in Humility

[from 1 Peter 2:13–3:13 and 5:1–11] 217

190. Faith Purified in Suffering

[from 1 Peter 3:13–22 and 4:12–19] 217

191. Anchors for True Gospel Living

[from 2 Peter 1] 218

192. Peter Condemned False Teachers

[from 2 Peter 2:1–22 and 3:17] 219

193. Why Pursue Gospel Living?

[from 2 Peter 3] 219

REFLECTION 19: Believers in Jesus Are Spirit-Crafted and Empowered
to Love and Serve 220

194. Gospel Living as Kingdom Fellowship

[from 1 John] 221

195. True Fellowship with God

[from 1 John] 221

196. False Teachings Undermine Kingdom Fellowship

[from 1 John] 222

197. John Defended Gospel Living against False Teachers

[from 2 John] 223

198. John Explained Gospel Living

[from 3 John] 223

199. Contend for True Faith against False Teachers

[from Jude] 224

REFLECTION 20: God's Will—Walking in a Manner Worthy of Jesus . . . 225

PART NINE
Revelation Ended the Bible but Not the Story 226

CONNECTION 16: John Went to Prison and Jesus Spoke to Him 228

200. John Received a Revelation of Jesus Christ
[from Revelation 1] 228

201. John Wrote Messages to Seven Churches
[from Revelation 2–3] 229

202. John Saw Jesus and a Scroll
[from Revelation 4–5] 230

REFLECTION 21: God's Big-Picture Plan 230

203. Jesus Opened the Seven Seals of the Scroll
[from Revelation 6–11] 231

204. Jesus Won the War with Satan
[from Revelation 12–20] 232

REFLECTION 22: How We Live and What We Do Matters 233

205. The Earth Remade
[from Revelation 21–22] 234

Illustration 27: The Earth Remade as the New Jerusalem 235

CONCLUDING REFLECTION: God's Family Will Live
with Him Forever 237

APPENDIX OF TIMELINES 239

RECOMMENDED READING 245

INDEX 248

ACKNOWLEDGMENTS 252

ABOUT THE AUTHOR 253

ABOUT THE ILLUSTRATOR 254

Foreword

The Panoramic Bible is a clear and insightful gateway into knowing and understanding God's message to us in the Bible, and living the Christian life.

It has been my privilege to know Bill Hollberg for more than sixty years. We grew up together in the same small town of Griffin, Georgia, in the 1950s and early 1960s. Bill and I were on the same Little League team. He is the third-born of four brothers, whereas I am an only child. Whenever I got to spend time with the "Hollberg boys," I was in heaven. In their backyard, they had a long rope swing that hung on the big limb of a magnificent tree—climb up the ladder, grab the rope, and jump for a thrill in the air. They also had a couple of pet alligators in a cage! Going to their house was indeed a memorable experience.

In time, I became a minister, while Bill became a lawyer, seeking to help people who found themselves in trouble and in need of someone who could guide them through challenging personal situations. Despite having distinctly different career callings, we shared the same underlying mission: to carry the gospel message of God's love and forgiveness through the cross of Jesus Christ and his powerful resurrection.

Several years ago, Bill and I met for lunch. He told me about a writing project he was working on and his desire to publish what would become this book. It came as no surprise to me that he would devote time, effort, and energy to write such a book. His years as an attorney have given him the mental clarity to think through different issues carefully and summarize concepts concisely. His experience as a church elder and teacher have equipped him with the ability to put the lessons of Scripture into a format that would help people get a better understanding of the message of the Bible.

Bill and I realized that we both knew many people who admitted they had a hard time reading and understanding the Bible. A friend once said to me, "I believe everything in the Bible is true. I have never read all of it, but I believe it." Although I appreciate such childlike faith and trust in God, the Bible is meant to be read and understood as well as believed. God went to great lengths to provide us with his word because he wanted us to become his children by understanding his heart and mind through the Bible.

The Panoramic Bible is a greatly needed work. The truth of God's Word is being neglected. An easy-to-read overview of the "Good Book" will surely help remedy this neglect. This book meets that need wonderfully.

This book divides the Bible into nine major parts. Within these parts, the content of the Bible is further broken down into 205 summaries, which Bill calls "pixels." Through these small snapshots of God's Word, you will see the storyline of the Scripture, and of God's big-picture plan for humanity, emerge.

The Panoramic Bible will help you to see and understand the truths contained in the greatest book of all time, the Bible. I am confident that *The Panoramic Bible* will be of great encouragement to you and will drive you to read the Bible itself.

Robert A. Rohm, PhD

President, Personality Insights, Inc.
Atlanta, Georgia
June 2018

Introduction

The Panoramic Bible encompasses the storyline of the entire Bible. Like Google Earth, *The Panoramic Bible* helps you see the big picture as well as the zoomed-in view. Using nine major divisions for the Bible, *The Panoramic Bible* presents the Bible in historical sequence, giving the storyline of Scripture in 205 summaries ("pixels") of its major themes and events—the most critical components of that larger story. This storyline is communicated in the plainest language possible, purposely avoiding church and Christian lingo. *The Panoramic Bible* assumes no prior exposure to Christianity or the Bible, so that anyone from any background can understand the significance of the smaller stories as well as the larger themes.

Of course, *The Panoramic Bible* is no substitute for the Bible. No book can tell you everything about the Bible other than the Bible itself. But *The Panoramic Bible* will give you an idea of what is in the Bible to encourage you to read, enjoy, and become immersed in the Bible on your own.

***

Why "Pixels"?

A pixel is the basic element of a digital image. It is a point of light—a snapshot. Similarly, the summaries in *The Panoramic Bible*, as points of biblical light, reveal God's truth and light that make up a composite picture of his reality, illuminated by the Bible.

In addition to the pixels, there are Reflections, Connections, and Illustrations. *Reflections* point to the larger significance of a passage, challenge you to apply the teaching of the biblical text, and encourage your spiritual formation and maturity. *Connections* give historical links to explain how one section of the Bible transitions or relates to another, assisting you in following the continuity of the Bible. *Illustrations* of original artwork depict and interpret some biblical scenes and events.

Here is a sample of a pixel and a description of each component:

89. Ezra Became the Teacher in Jerusalem ⟵
[from Ezra 7–10]

Introductory heading in **BOLD**, *followed by the reference to the section in the Bible from which the pixel is taken*

The Jews in Babylon were saved by the courageous obedience of Esther and those who supported her in fasting. God's clear message was that he would keep and maintain his special people. The temple had been rebuilt in Jerusalem. Now the question remained: Did those who lived in Jerusalem know and understand what it meant to truly honor and worship God? In the last four chapters of the book of Ezra, God provided an answer.

Still living in Babylon, the priest Ezra had a passion to know, understand, live, and teach God's laws. The king granted Ezra's request to be given everything he needed to take a few thousand Jews back to Jerusalem. When he and his group arrived in Jerusalem, he found the same sickening spiritual dullness that had existed before the exile to Babylon. So he turned to God. He prayed, confessed, and asked for forgiveness. Then God moved in the hearts of the people, and they joined with Ezra in confessing their sins to God and asking for forgiveness. People were confronted with the truth about God and his good law. They responded by changing their lives in a spirit of revival.

The text of the pixel

"For Ezra had set his heart to study the Law of the Lord, and to do it and to teach his statutes and rules in Israel." (Ezra 7:10) ⟵

A verse in italics that helps emphasize the main topic of the pixel

What have you set in your heart to accomplish? ⟵

A question in this typeface *to help you understand and apply the pixel*

***

Timelines

The dates shown in the timelines at the beginning of each of the nine parts are approximate. As you will see for the dates of Israel's exodus from Egypt, there is scholarly debate about when exactly this event occurred. By most accounts, the dating estimates differ by about 176 years. On the timelines, the more recent dates are in parentheses. In the New Testament timelines, you will see a range of dates associated with each book—the approximate time of their writings. However, these books are presented on both the timeline and in the text in the order in which they appear in the New Testament, rather than in the order in which they were written.

***

The Bible and Its Purpose

The Bible is considered by Christians to be the written record of God speaking with his people. It is estimated that more than five billion copies of the Bible have been sold, making it the best-selling book of all time. About 100 million copies are sold each year. The Bible, or portions of it, has been translated into more than one thousand languages. From Genesis, written by Moses about fifteen hundred years before Jesus was born, to Revelation, written by John about ninety years after Christ's birth, the Bible is a collection of sixty-six smaller books written by individual people, whose writing God guided (or "breathed," as 2 Timothy 3:16 puts it). *The Panoramic Bible* summarizes these books, which are separated into two parts: the thirty-nine books of the Old Testament followed by the twenty-seven books of the New Testament. (For further information about the Bible, its history, and its application, refer to the Recommended Reading list at the end of this book.)

So, what is the main purpose of the Bible? God tells us through the Bible who he is and what his plans are. *His big-picture plan is to establish for himself a special family for his treasured possession, a kingdom of priests, and a holy nation, who desire to live with him forever and by his grace will do so.* For us to understand God's purpose, we also need to think about who he is and how he goes about helping us understand things of the spirit (that is, things beyond the material world).

God is a spirit who has always existed. There was never a time when he started, and there will never be a time when he ends. God made the universe and everything in it—the stars and planets, the earth, people, and plants and animals of all kinds. Jesus was with God when God created everything. At the time of the Creation, the Bible refers to Jesus as "the Word": "In the beginning was the Word, and the Word was with God, and the Word was God. He was in the beginning with God. All things were made through him, and without him was not any thing made that was made. In him was life, and the life was the light of men. The light shines in the darkness, and the darkness has not overcome it" (John 1:1–5).

God wants us to know him. Jesus makes it possible for us to be alive spiritually so that we can know God. The Bible describes Jesus as "the radiance of the glory of God and the exact imprint of his nature," and as the one who "upholds the universe by the word of his power" (Hebrews 1:3). We get to know Jesus by the Holy Spirit giving us a heart that wants to know him, by asking God to teach us about Jesus, by reading the Bible, and by talking with other people who know him.

***

The Purpose of *The Panoramic Bible*

The purpose of *The Panoramic Bible* is to encourage you to know, understand, and believe that God has spoken, that God is speaking, and that God will continue to speak throughout the eternal fulfillment of his purposes and plans for you and for his universe.

As you read *The Panoramic Bible* and live your life, keep in mind the words of Jesus in John 8:31–32: "If you abide in my word, you are truly my disciples, and you will know the truth, and the truth will set you free." Also, remember the words of Paul in 2 Timothy 3:15, where he referred to Scripture as "the sacred writings, which are able to make you wise for salvation through faith in Christ Jesus."

Why I Wrote
The Panoramic Bible

I wrote *The Panoramic Bible* after many years as both a practicing lawyer and a follower of Jesus. The more I followed Jesus, the more I read the Bible. The more I worked as a lawyer, the more I understood that spiritual issues were at the center of the problems people brought to me. I also saw and dealt with problems as an elder and leader at church, where spiritual issues were just as present.

Over years of helping people with troubles in their lives, and dealing with difficulties in my own life, I increasingly drew on insights from the Bible. I also came to realize that few people read the Bible for themselves; they are not sure how to approach the Bible, so they don't. They go about living without seeing and incorporating the Bible's relevance to their everyday lives. This situation puzzled me. Here were Christians, most of whom owned multiple copies of the Bible and claimed to believe what God says in the Bible, and yet many of them were largely ignorant of its contents and did not understand its big-picture perspective.

It was then that I decided to apply to the Bible my skills as a lawyer—analyzing topics one by one, then evaluating, prioritizing, and presenting explanatory summaries of those topics. That is what I have set out to do in *The Panoramic Bible*: to give the storyline of Scripture in summaries of its major themes and events. My prayer is that *The Panoramic Bible* will help break down barriers to reading the Bible on your own. Then you will more fully understand who God is, enjoy who you are as his child, and know how you can better love and serve him and others.

PART ONE

God Created the World and Began His Special People

Books of the Bible Discussed in This Part:

Genesis, Job, Exodus, Leviticus, Numbers, Deuteronomy

Creation	Noah and the Flood	Job (Approximately)	Issac as Sacrifice
Before Christ (BC)	U N D A T E D	2091	2050
		(1915)*	(1874)
	Adam and Eve	Tower of Babel	Abraham Moved to Canaan

	Jacob Moved to Egypt		Ten Commandments, Tabernacle, and Sacrifices		Moses' Death
1898	1876	1446	1445	1443	1406
(1722)	(1700)	(1270)	(1269)	(1267)	(1230)
Joseph Sold as a Slave		Moses as Leader to Canaan	40 Years in Wilderness		Israel Entered Canaan

*Some scholars hold to more recent dates for events in Genesis–Deuteronomy; these dates are shown in parentheses.

1. God Created Everything
[from Genesis 1 and 2]

When God created everything, he spoke words. He said, "Let there be." On day one he said, "Let there be light" (1:3). Light appeared and God separated it from darkness. On day two he said for the land to be separate from the heavens, and it happened. On day three he said for the waters on the earth to group together so there could be dry land with plants growing on it.

On day four he said for planets to appear, providing times of light and darkness, and times for the seasons of the year. On day five he said for all kinds of fish to be in the waters and all varieties of birds in the sky. Then, on day six he said for all sorts of animals to be on the earth. Finally, in two separate events on day six, he made humans: Adam first and later Eve. He said Adam and Eve were uniquely in his image (1:26).

These were God's six days of creation. At the end of day six, God observed his creation and knew that "everything that he had made . . . was very good" (1:31). On the seventh day, God rested, and he said this seventh day was "holy" as a day of rest (2:3).

"In the beginning, God created the heavens and the earth." (Genesis 1:1)

How did God create everything?

2. Adam and Eve Were the First People God Created
[from Genesis 1 and 2]

Before God created Adam, he made a special place for him to live—the Garden of Eden. God gave Adam important work to do; he was to take care of the garden and give names to all the animals and the birds. It was then that God observed that Adam should not be alone as a human among all the other living creatures, but that he should have "a helper fit for him" (2:18, 20). So God created Eve out of one of Adam's ribs. When Adam saw Eve, he was joyful. This was God's intended plan for a man and a woman: that they would join together as husband and wife in one new union. This relationship was to be unique, permanent, and separate from their original families.

God gave Adam and Eve his blessing. Part of the blessing was to have children, who would go into all parts of the world and be stewards of God's creation, caring for the earth and other living creatures (1:28).

"Therefore a man shall leave his father and his mother and hold fast to his wife, and they shall become one flesh." (Genesis 2:24)

What is God's plan for marriage?

3. God Wanted Adam and Eve to Remain Good and Pure

[from Genesis 2:15–17]

In the beautiful garden, Adam and Eve had more than everything they could ever want or need. They were good and pure. In this special way, they were like God. Even without clothing, they had no shame about their bodies because they did not know anything about evil—yet.

God wanted them to have the freedom to make their own decision to avoid evil and to live in ways that honored him. Even before God created Eve, he gave Adam specific instructions not to eat the fruit of one particular tree. If they ate the fruit of this tree, they would die, in the sense that they would experience evil and their goodness and purity would be destroyed.

"But of the tree of the knowledge of good and evil you shall not eat, for in the day that you eat of it you shall surely die." (Genesis 2:17)

Why did God tell Adam not to eat the fruit of the particular tree?

4. Adam and Eve Disobeyed God and Were Punished

[from Genesis 3]

What came next changed the course of history. Taking the form of a snake, Satan—God's archenemy—entered the Garden of Eden and tempted Adam and Eve. Other references in the Bible affirm that God created spiritual beings known as angels (Psalm 91:11). Some of these angels "did not stay within their own position of authority," such as Satan, an angel referred to as "the devil," who hated God and rebelled against him (Jude, verse 6; Matthew 4:1). Disguising himself "as an angel of light" Satan deceived Adam and Eve into turning away from God (2 Corinthians 11:14).

With Satan's urging, in which he caused them to doubt God's word and goodness to them, Adam and Eve disobeyed God and ate the fruit of the tree from which God had forbidden them to eat. Immediately, they knew what they had done was wrong. They

had not honored God's love and care for them. They knew they had sinned against him and were ashamed.

Because Adam and Eve did not honor God by obeying him, God punished them in the same ways they had disobeyed him. They rejected God's good food and bountiful garden, so they would have to work extremely hard for what they ate. They rejected God's plan for their fulfilling relationship as husband and wife, so they began to disagree and argue with each other. They rejected God's provision of living in the peaceful garden with him, so they would be forced out into other parts of the world.

Their lives outside of the Garden of Eden would be harder in special ways for each of them; for Adam, his work would be difficult, and for Eve, childbirth would be painful. In these two consequences, God demonstrated that their rebellion had destroyed the peaceful nature of the creation and that from then on, the elements of nature would cause trouble for people. Further, Adam and Eve and people after them would experience physical death, returning to the dust from which they were made.

God made sure they would not reenter Eden when he placed an angel with a flaming sword to guard it.

"[T]herefore, the Lord God sent him out from the garden of Eden to work the ground from which he was taken. He drove out the man, and at the east end of the garden of Eden he placed the cherubim and a flaming sword that turned every way to guard the way to the tree of life." (Genesis 3:23–24)

What did Adam and Eve do to disobey God?

5. God Made a Promise of Love to Adam and Eve

[from Genesis 3]

Adam and Eve rejected God and sinned against him when they believed the lies Satan told about God. God was angry with Adam and Eve and punished them. However, God knew that because of their sin, they were aware of their physical nakedness and were ashamed. God still loved Adam and Eve, and to comfort them, he used animal skins to make clothing to cover them.

He also made a promise: In the future, a child would be born from their family who would battle against Satan and defeat him. Then Satan would no longer be able to tell lies about God or trick people into doing things that did not honor God. God was telling

Adam and Eve that he would establish his special family, who would reject Satan and live to honor him.

"I will put enmity between you [Satan] and the woman, and between your offspring and her offspring; he shall bruise your head, and you shall bruise his heel." (Genesis 3:15)

What was the promise of love God made to Adam and Eve?

***

REFLECTION 1
God's Promise of Love Is for Us

God's promise to Adam and Eve was to show them that, in spite of their disobedience and rebellion, he still loved them and wanted them to love him. As you read, you will see the constant theme of God's love for us and our love for him.

Later, in the New Testament, you will see that the offspring promised in Genesis 3:15 is Jesus. The genealogy of Jesus is in Luke 3:23–38 (from Adam) and Matthew 1:1–17 (from Abraham). Matthew 1:18–25 says that Jesus was born under God's special care to Mary, a virgin. God planned it this way so that Jesus would be the totally unique combination of a human and God himself. Keep this staggering concept in mind as you continue reading, and pray for God's help to understand it.

Also in the New Testament, you will see how God's promise to Adam and Eve was not only for them but for you and me. Romans 16:20 promises that Satan's defeat is certain. That victory will come through Jesus (1 Corinthians 15:57). And Revelation 12:10 and 20:10 tell us that Satan is permanently defeated under God's power and the authority of Jesus.

***

6. Cain Dishonored God and Then Killed Abel
[from Genesis 4]

Adam and Eve's sons were Cain and Abel. A farmer, Cain worked with crops that grew from the ground, such as grains and fruits. Abel cared for animals, such as sheep and goats. When the time came to worship God, Cain simply brought some of his produce as an offering. In contrast, Abel offered his best animals—the ones born first. Cain's offering did not honor God, and God rejected it. But Abel's offering honored God, and God accepted it. This made Cain so mad that he killed Abel.

After that, God asked Cain about Abel. Cain lied to God and was disrespectful. He said, "I do not know; am I my brother's keeper?" (4:9b). But God knew all along what Cain had done.

God punished Cain in the same ways that he had rejected God. Abel's blood had gone into the ground—now Cain's work as a farmer would become miserable; no longer would the ground produce good crops (4:11–12a). Because Cain had murdered his brother and destroyed his own family, from then on Cain would not have a family but would wander the earth (4:12b).

Just like his parents, Cain did what he wanted to do and rejected what God wanted him to do.

"The Lord said to Cain, 'Why are you angry, and why has your face fallen? If you do well, will you not be accepted? And if you do not do well, sin is crouching at the door. Its desire is for you, but you must rule over it.'" (Genesis 4:6–7)

Why did God reject Cain's offering?

7. More People Dishonored and Rejected God
[from Genesis 6:1–7]

Even though God wanted a special people who desired and loved him, after Cain killed Abel, more and more people turned away from God and did not honor him. This made God very sad. God knew that the human heart was inclined to rebel and turn against him. Other books in the Old Testament speak of this tendency toward evil. Psalm 94:7, for example, says some wicked people assume God is blind to what they do. Jeremiah 17:9 says that the human heart is "deceitful" and "desperately sick."

God determined to start over with his plans of creating a special family of his own.

"The Lord saw that the wickedness of man was great in the earth, and that every intention of the thoughts of his heart was only evil continually. And the Lord was sorry that he had made man on the earth, and it grieved him to his heart." (Genesis 6:5–6)

What was wrong with everybody? What is wrong with you and me?

8. Noah Was True and Faithful
[from Genesis 6:8–9]

God planned to judge the wicked people by bringing a flood to destroy them.

God looked at all the people to see if there was anyone who honored him and who could be counted on to obey and follow him. Noah was the man.

God confided in Noah of his plans to destroy everyone except Noah and his family. So that Noah and his family would survive the flood, God gave Noah detailed instructions about how to build an enormous boat, called an ark.

"Noah was a righteous man, blameless in his generation. Noah walked with God." (Genesis 6:9b)

What was different about Noah? Where do you fit into this picture?

9. God's Flood Killed Wicked People, but His Love Saved Noah
[from Genesis 6:14–8:12]

God instructed Noah to stock plenty of supplies in the ark for Noah's family and for many animals. He was to take seven pairs of each of the animals God considered clean; these animals were permissible for his people to eat and offer as sacrifices in worship offerings. God also told Noah to include one pair of each of the animals God considered unclean; these animals were ones his people should not eat or offer as sacrifices. Finally, Noah was to take seven pairs of all the birds.

Noah obeyed all of God's instructions. Then Noah, his family, and the animals went into the ark, and God closed the doors on them. A few days later, the rain started. It rained and rained and rained; it did not stop raining for forty days. God also caused springs of water to burst open from the earth. When the water finally stopped pouring from the heavens and the earth, only Noah, his family, and the animals in the ark had been saved.

"[God] blotted out every living thing that was on the face of the ground, man and animals and creeping things and birds of the heavens. They were blotted out from the earth. Only Noah was left, and those who were with him in the ark." (Genesis 7:23)

How did God reward Noah's obedience?

10. God's Promise of Love to Noah Was a Covenant of Life

[from Genesis 8:13–9:17]

When the rain stopped and the water dried up, God told Noah it was time to leave the ark. So Noah, his family, and all the animals left the ark in their family groups.

To honor God for saving his family and the animals, Noah built an altar and offered sacrifices to God on it. God was pleased with this offering. He blessed Noah and his family, repeating some of the blessings he gave to Adam and Eve—they would have children who would go to all parts of the world.

God surprised them all with something beautiful in the sky—a rainbow. God gave the rainbow to Noah as a sign that he would never again destroy the earth by a flood of water. This promise was God's covenant with Noah. A covenant is a promise that can never be broken. When God told Noah that a flood would cover the earth, and instructed him to build the ark, he also said it was based on his covenant with Noah (6:18). When God saved Noah, his family, and the animals, God showed how he is faithful to his covenant promises.

God's covenant with Noah was the first of a number of covenants God made with his special family; to all of those covenants, he has remained faithful.

"I establish my covenant with you, that never again shall all flesh be cut off by the waters of the flood, and never again shall there be a flood to destroy the earth." (Genesis 9:11)

What was God's covenant with Noah?

11. After the Flood, Many Rejected God and Built the Tower of Babel
[from Genesis 11:1–9]

After the Flood, Noah lived for another 350 years. He was 950 years old when he died. His family grew and grew. Sadly, after a long time, many people again no longer worshiped God. Instead, they wanted to honor themselves. To make a name for themselves and feel important, they decided to build a large city with a tower that would reach into the heavens. Because they all spoke the same language, they could talk and work together to do just about anything they wanted to do.

Their plan was to keep from being scattered, but God's plan was that people would honor him and live in all parts of the world. To stop the building of the city and the tower, and to force people to move, he mixed up their languages. When this happened, the work on the tower stopped. Then the people moved away in groups, according to their common languages, and found new places to live. After this, the city and tower were named Babel, because it was where God confused languages and scattered people to many different places. Babel, in Hebrew, means "to confuse" or "to mix."

"Then they said, 'Come, let us build ourselves a city and a tower with its top in the heavens, and let us make a name for ourselves, lest we be dispersed over the face of the whole earth.'" (Genesis 11:4)

Why did some people want to build a big city with a tall tower?

12. One Man Who Honored God Was Job

[from Job]

Job and his wife were wealthy farmers with many children, workers, and animals. Job loved God and wanted to serve him in every way. Job treasured God's words, and made special offerings to God for sins that his children might have committed (23:12; 1:5). This strong love for God made Satan angry. Satan destroyed Job's children, his animals, and many of his workers. Satan afflicted Job with a serious and painful skin disease.

Some of Job's friends came to visit him and tried to help him understand why God would allow these terrible things to happen. Job did not understand. He thought he had lived a good life and been kind to everyone. Job wondered what it would take to be made right before God (9:2). One of his friends had an idea to pray that God would teach them what they could not see, because none of them understood why God allowed Job to have so much trouble (34:32).

Then a great whirlwind came. In it, Job and his friends could hear God speaking to them (38:1). God told them who he was, and that he was the creator of the world and everything in it. God said that if they wanted to understand anything about themselves or the world, they should first try to know and understand him. Then Job apologized to God for acting as though he could solve the big problems that had hurt him so badly. Job told God that now he understood what it meant for God to be his creator, and he realized God's plans were the most important thing in life.

"Then Job answered the Lord and said: 'I know that you can do all things, and that no purpose of yours can be thwarted.'" (Job 42:1–2)

What have you learned from your troubles?

13. God Had a Special Plan for One Part of Noah's Family

[from Genesis 11:10–12:7 and 22:17–18]

One of Noah's sons was Shem. The Jewish people originated from Shem's family, and from his name comes the word Semitic, a description for the Jewish people. One of the children born to Shem's family line was Eber. From his name comes the word *Hebrew*, another description for the Jewish people. Long after Eber lived, a man named Abram was born into this family line. God had a special plan for Abram and his wife, Sarai.

With Abram's father, Terah, Abram and Sarai had moved from Ur of the Chaldeans to the city of Haran. Now God spoke to Abram and told him to move from Haran to a land he would show him (11:31–12:5).

God promised he would make a great nation from Abram's family that would be a blessing to the rest of the world (12:3; 22:18). Even though Abram was seventy-five years old, and he and Sarai had no children, they responded in faith and obeyed God. They packed all their belongings and, with their animals, started moving. Eventually they arrived in Canaan, the special land God had planned for them. Abram was so thankful to God that he built an altar and worshiped God.

"Then the Lord appeared to Abram and said, 'To your offspring I will give this land.' So he built there an altar to the Lord, who had appeared to him." (Genesis 12:7)

Why did Abram build an altar?

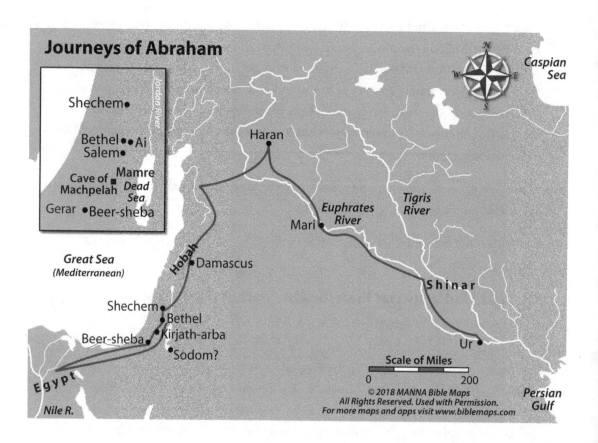

14. God's Special Plan for Abram Was a Covenant of Land and Family

[from Genesis 15–18]

This great nation would be the beginning of the people God chose to be set apart as his special family. When Abram was about eighty-five years old, God confirmed that he would give the land of Canaan to Abram for his family. This time God declared that his promise was a covenant (15:18). Abram and Sarai believed, yet they waited and waited, and still they did not have a child. They began to wonder how God would make a nation from two old, childless people.

Their personal doubt got the best of them. It was common in that time for both men and women to have slaves who were obligated to do as they were told. Sarai had a slave woman named Hagar. Sarai told Abram that it was obvious to her that she would never have a child, so Abram should take Hagar as another wife and have a child with her. They named this child Ishmael. But this was Abram and Sarai's plan, not God's.

God's plan was still at work. When Abram was ninety-nine, God appeared again to him. This time, God made another covenant with Abram. God said nations and kings would come from Abram's family (17:6). To make the covenant official, God changed their names from Abram and Sarai to Abraham and Sarah, respectively (17:5, 15). Also, as part of the covenant, God instructed that, from then on, every male in Abraham's family was to be circumcised (17:10).

"Is anything too hard for the Lord? At the appointed time I will return to you, about this time next year, and Sarah shall have a son." (Genesis 18:14)

Is it possible for God to create a great nation from one small family?

15. Abraham and Sarah Had a Son, Isaac

[from Genesis 17:9–14 and 21:1–8]

When Abraham was one hundred years old, he and Sarah finally had their first and only child. The couple was in disbelief that they had a baby in their old age. This event made them so happy that they laughed. And because of their laughter, they named the boy Isaac, which means "laughter" in Hebrew.

Sarah and Abraham, whose name means "father of many" in Hebrew, could see God's promise—that their family would become a blessing to all the nations on the earth—

was beginning to become a reality. In response to God's faithfulness to them, Abraham circumcised Isaac, just as God had instructed as a sign of God's covenant.

Abraham and Sarah loved Isaac. Sarah, whose name means "princess" in Hebrew, was proud to have a son and took great delight in him. Abraham threw a big party for Isaac when he was only a young child (21:8).

"Abraham was a hundred years old when his son Isaac was born to him. And Sarah said, 'God has made laughter for me; everyone who hears will laugh over me.'"
(Genesis 21:5–6)

Does God want us to enjoy the good things he gives us?

16. God Used Isaac to Test Abraham's Heart

[from Genesis 22:1–18]

God wanted to make sure Abraham's life did not revolve around Isaac but remained devoted to God's plan for the family. God tested Abraham by telling him to go on a three-day journey to a mountain, where Abraham was to offer Isaac as a burnt sacrifice to God. Abraham obeyed immediately. He gathered some wood, took some coals to start the fire, and set off with Isaac.

Isaac was puzzled. He asked his father about a lamb to use as the sacrifice. Abraham assured his son that God would provide the lamb. At the mountain, Abraham built the altar and arranged the wood on it. He bound up Isaac and put him on the altar to be the sacrifice. Abraham raised the knife to kill Isaac and burn him as the offering. But before Abraham's knife touched Isaac, God's angel called to Abraham and told him not to harm Isaac. The angel confirmed that Abraham had proved he loved and honored God more than Isaac. That was what God wanted to know.

Abraham looked in the bushes near the altar and saw a ram caught by its horns. Abraham helped Isaac get off the altar, and they used the ram as the sacrifice. The Bible does not discuss the personal feelings that Abraham and Isaac experienced during this event. But it does say that Abraham named the place "The Lord Will Provide" and that God reassured Abraham of his promise that his family would be a blessing to all the nations of the earth (22:14).

"After these things God tested Abraham and said to him, 'Abraham!' And he said, 'Here am I.' He said, 'Take your son, your only son Isaac, whom you love, and go to the land

of Moriah, and offer him there as a burnt offering on one of the mountains of which I shall tell you.'" (Genesis 22:1–2)

Is there something in your life that you need to give up that keeps you from loving God completely?

***

REFLECTION 2
Obedience and a Substitute Sacrifice

What was going on in Abraham's mind? And what about in Isaac's mind? God was the one who initiated the covenant with Abraham about his family becoming a great nation and a blessing to the whole world. Now it appeared God had a plan in mind that did not include Isaac.

But by this time in his life, Abraham had developed a strong trust in God's plan and goodness. The New Testament book of Hebrews says Abraham reasoned that God was able to raise Isaac from death, so he knew God's plans would be fulfilled through Isaac somehow (11:17–19). And the New Testament book of James says Abraham demonstrated his great faith by his obedience to God's commands (2:21–23).

God's testing of Abraham and Isaac holds a great lesson for all of us. God wanted to know if Abraham would put God first in his life. In the same way, God wants to know if we will put him first in our lives. When Abraham proved God was first, God provided the ram in the bushes as the substitute sacrifice for Isaac. When we desire to put God first in our lives, then God provides a substitute for us and welcomes us into his special family. That substitute is Jesus, who came to give his life for us in atonement for our sins (Mark 10:45; John 1:29; Reflection 14).

***

17. Abraham Had Confidence That God Would Fulfill His Promise
[from Genesis 24:1–10]

God blessed Abraham in every aspect of his life. But when Abraham was an old man, Sarah died. By that time, Isaac had not married. Abraham knew Isaac should have a wife from Abraham's family, rather than from the people who lived around them in Canaan.

Abraham instructed Eliezer, his trusted helper, to go back to Haran, the land from which they had moved, and find a wife for Isaac. Abraham was confident that this was part of God's plan for building his treasured family, so he assured Eliezer that God would go before him and would enable him to find a wife for Isaac.

"The Lord, the God of heaven, who took me from my father's house and from the land of my kindred, and who spoke to me and swore to me, 'To your offspring I will give this land,' he will send his angel before you, and you shall take a wife for my son from there." *(Genesis 24:7)*

Why was Abraham sure Eliezer would find a wife for Isaac?

18. Isaac Married Rebekah

[from Genesis 24:11–27:41]

After a long journey, Eliezer met Abraham's relatives in Haran. From that family, he met Rebekah, the woman he believed God intended for Isaac to marry. Eliezer told Rebekah and her family why Abraham had sent him to them. He asked Rebekah if she would go with him to be Isaac's wife. Rebekah agreed, so she and Eliezer returned to Canaan.

Isaac and Rebekah married, and after Abraham died, they had twin sons: Esau, born first, and Jacob. As the boys grew older, Jacob tricked Esau into giving him the inheritance rights Esau was supposed to have as the older son. Then, just before Isaac died, Rebekah helped Jacob trick Isaac into giving him the blessing that Isaac intended to give to Esau. In these two incidents, Jacob lived up to one meaning of his name—"he deceives"—and Esau hated Jacob for what he did, promising to kill him after Isaac died.

"Now Esau hated Jacob because of the blessing with which his father had blessed him, and Esau said to himself, 'The days of mourning for my father are approaching; then I will kill my brother Jacob.'" *(Genesis 27:41)*

Why did Esau want to kill his brother Jacob?

19. Jacob Ran Away from Esau and Met God

[from Genesis 27:41–28:22]

Rebekah realized Esau was serious about wanting to kill Jacob, so she arranged for Jacob to leave the family and live with her brother and his family in Haran. One night on this trip, while Jacob was sleeping, he had a dream about angels of God going up and down a ladder. God was at the top of the ladder and spoke to Jacob. God repeated the same promise he had made to Jacob's father, Isaac, and grandfather, Abraham. God would give Jacob and his children all the land around that area. When Jacob woke up, he realized God had used the dream to speak to him. Jacob promised to follow God if God would take care of him.

"Behold, I am with you and will keep you wherever you go, and will bring you back to this land. For I will not leave you until I have done what I have promised you."
(Genesis 28:15)

Where was the land on which Jacob understood he and his children would eventually live?

20. Jacob Married Rachel and Wrestled with God
[from Genesis 29–32]

Jacob continued on his journey. He finally reached Haran, where Rebekah's family lived. Jacob met his mother's brother, Laban, and began working for him. Before long, Jacob and one of Laban's daughters, Rachel, came to love each other and eventually were married. As sometimes happened long ago, when some men had more than one wife, Jacob ended up with four wives, although he loved Rachel the most. After a while, God told Jacob to move with his family and return to his home in Canaan (31:3). They packed up and began the long trip.

One night on this long journey, God took the form of a man and wrestled with Jacob all night. It was absolutely dark, so Jacob could not see whom he was wrestling. Before daybreak, the man dislocated Jacob's hip. Even with his hip hurting him, Jacob still clung to the man and insisted that the man bless him. The man did, and said that from then on, Jacob's name would be Israel. (In this context, the Hebrew word *Israel* likely means "he struggles with God.") By asking for the man's blessing, Jacob showed that he realized God was fulfilling his promise to take care of him and bring him back to the land God would give him and his family, God's chosen people.

"Your name shall no longer be called Jacob, but Israel, for you have striven with God and with men, and have prevailed." (Genesis 32:28)

Have you had a wrestling match with God?

21. Jacob Had Twelve Sons

[from Genesis 37]

By the time Jacob returned to Canaan, he had many children, including twelve sons. It was a big family, and God had big plans for it. But this family would have to deal with some big problems along the way. One of those problems came because Jacob did not love all of his children equally. Rachel was his favorite wife, so the sons he had with her—Joseph and Benjamin—became his favorites. In particular, Jacob favored Joseph by giving him a very special and beautiful coat. Joseph's brothers thought this special treatment was unfair, and they hated him for it.

Then Joseph's dreams began. In them, his family bowed down to him. To make matters worse, Joseph recounted these dreams to his parents and brothers. This made the other brothers so mad that some of them wanted to kill him. The oldest brother, Reuben, kept them from doing that. The fourth-oldest brother, Judah, also wanted to keep Joseph alive. Judah persuaded them to sell Joseph as a slave and then make it appear that he had been killed by wild animals.

After Joseph's brothers sold him into slavery, they took Joseph's bloodstained coat to their father. Jacob was devastated; he believed his favorite son was dead. Jacob cried and cried. The other brothers kept their secret that Joseph was still alive. They were glad Joseph was far away from them so they did not have to put up with him anymore.

"Then Judah said to his brothers, 'What profit is it if we kill our brother and conceal his blood? Come, let us sell him to the Ishmaelites, and let not our hand be upon him, for he is our brother, our own flesh.' And his brothers listened to him." (Genesis 37:26–27)

What lie did the brothers tell Jacob about Joseph?

22. Joseph Became a Slave in Egypt

[from Genesis 39–40]

The people who bought Joseph from his brothers went to Egypt and sold him to be a slave. A slave is a person who is owned by someone else and is forced to do what the owner demands. Joseph went from being his father's favorite son, with a special coat, to being a slave with shabby clothing. Instead of his family bowing down to him, as in his dream, he was a slave and had to bow down to other people. Joseph went from everything going his way to having to do things the way other people told him to. It was quite a reversal for him.

As if that were not bad enough, someone told lies about Joseph, and he was thrown into jail. While in jail, he met two men who had worked for Pharaoh, the king of Egypt. Pharaoh got mad at them and had them put in jail. While there, both men had very disturbing dreams on the same night, but no one in the jail could interpret the dreams. No one, that is, except Joseph.

Because Joseph asked God to help him, he was able to explain the dreams. Joseph told one of the men that his dream meant that the man would be released from jail and go back to work for Pharaoh. Joseph urged him to remember what Joseph had done and use his influence to get Joseph out of jail as well.

"Only remember me, when it is well with you, and please do me the kindness to mention me to Pharaoh, and so get me out of this house [jail]. For I was indeed stolen out of the land of the Hebrews, and here also I have done nothing that they should put me into the pit." (Genesis 40:14–15)

Was what happened to Joseph fair?

23. Joseph Met Pharaoh, the King

[from Genesis 41]

For two long years, Pharaoh's assistant—the one whose dream Joseph interpreted—forgot about Joseph. Joseph stayed in jail while the man enjoyed life working in the palace. Then Pharaoh had a dream that upset and troubled him. None of his advisors could tell him what the dream meant. Finally, the assistant remembered Joseph. He told Pharaoh how, years earlier, Joseph had accurately interpreted dreams.

Pharaoh immediately had Joseph brought from jail and told him about his dream. In the dream, seven poor and sickly cows ate up seven fat and healthy cows. Additionally, on a cornstalk, seven withered and thin ears of corn swallowed up seven healthy ears of corn. Joseph told Pharaoh that God would provide the interpretation of the dream. Then Joseph, with God's help, interpreted the dream for Pharaoh: There would be seven years in Egypt when there would be a great abundance of animals and crops. Those years would be followed by seven years of famine.

Joseph emphasized that this dream would begin to come true soon. He advised Pharaoh to appoint an official to gather the extra food into storage during the first seven years, so there would be enough food during the following seven years of famine. Pharaoh thought this was such a brilliant idea that he appointed Joseph to be the official in

charge. So, in the span of one day, Joseph went from being a prisoner to being the number-two official in all of Egypt—another major reversal for Joseph.

"Then Pharaoh said to Joseph, 'Since God has shown you all this, there is none so discerning and wise as you are. You shall be over my house, and all my people shall order themselves as you command. Only as regards the throne will I be greater than you.'" (Genesis 41:39–40)

Was it because Joseph was so smart that he became the second-highest-ranking official in Egypt?

24. Joseph's Brothers Went to Egypt for Food
[from Genesis 42:1–43:15]

What God showed Pharaoh in his dream came true! There were seven years of crops more abundant than ever before. Joseph had the extra food put in storage for the king. Then the seven years of famine came. There were no more crops. People in Egypt went to Joseph to buy food. People in other countries heard there was food in Egypt and went there to buy it. All the way from Canaan, Jacob sent his sons to buy food.

When they arrived, they were sent to Joseph. They had not seen him for about twenty years. With Joseph dressed as an Egyptian official, they did not recognize him. But Joseph recognized them. Without letting them know who he was, he questioned them about their family. He finally agreed to sell them food. But Joseph insisted that they come back to Egypt and bring their youngest brother, Benjamin, with them. They returned to Canaan and told all this to Jacob. Jacob was deeply troubled at the thought of Benjamin making the long trip to Egypt.

Soon all the food Joseph's brothers had bought was gone. Because of the famine, they could not grow any crops. The brothers told Jacob they should go back to Egypt to buy more food. Jacob did not want to risk Benjamin's life. Then a dramatic change happened in the leadership among the brothers. Reuben, the oldest son, promised Jacob that if anything happened to Benjamin on the journey, Jacob could put Reuben's two sons to death. Then Judah, the fourth-oldest son, promised Jacob that if anything happened to Benjamin, Jacob could hold him directly responsible. With this assurance from Judah, Jacob finally agreed for the brothers to make another trip to Egypt, taking Benjamin with them.

"And Judah said to Israel his father, 'Send the boy with me, and we will arise and go, that we may live and not die, both we and you and also our little ones. I will be a pledge of his [Benjamin's] safety. From my hand you shall require him. If I do not bring him back to you and set him before you, then let me bear the blame forever.'"
(Genesis 43:8–9)

How was the promise that Judah made to Jacob different from Reuben's promise?

25. Joseph and His Brothers Were Reunited

[from Genesis 43:16–50:21]

When the brothers went to Joseph to buy more food, Joseph saw Benjamin with them. Joseph had a great meal prepared for them and told them who he was. The brothers could not believe it. They had sold their brother as a slave and were confident they would never see him again.

Joseph told them he knew that even though they had been cruel to him, God had used everything that happened for good, and to help save many people. Joseph assured them that he forgave them for the terrible things they had done to him. Joseph urged them to go back home and get Jacob, their father, and all of their families, and come to live with him in Egypt. They would be his family in Egypt and would not have to worry about having enough to eat. He would let them have only the best.

Joseph had gone from being a prisoner in jail to the number-two official in Egypt. Now, in yet another reversal, Joseph's brothers went from having to travel all the way to Egypt to buy food, to being the family of the high-ranking official in charge of Egypt's food supply.

"But Joseph said to them, 'Do not fear, for am I in the place of God? As for you, you meant evil against me, but God meant it for good, to bring it about that many people should be kept alive, as they are today.'" (Genesis 50:19–20)

Why did Joseph forgive his brothers?

REFLECTION 3
God's Sovereignty

The story of Joseph and his brothers contains a number of reversals in fortune. One lesson from these reversals is about an attribute of God called his *sovereignty*. First, things were going one way, and suddenly they were going another way. The promise Judah made to Jacob (Pixel 24) was a reversal of the promise Reuben made to Jacob. Judah's promise is similar to God's provision of a ram in the bushes for Abraham (as the substitute for Isaac) in Genesis 22; both incidents are similar to God's later provision of a substitute sacrifice (Jesus) for the sins of his special family.

Joseph and his brothers had what they considered bad experiences, but unexpectedly, and with no apparent explanation, events turned in their favor. No explanation, that is, other than—as Joseph put it—"God meant it for good" (Genesis 50:20).

These reversals illustrate the mystery surrounding how God directs what happens in our lives and in the world. Such changes in the course of events also show us what it means to be part of the treasured family of God, who is in charge of the entire universe—from the largest aspects to the smallest details.

***

26. Jacob's Whole Family Moved to Egypt
[from Genesis 43:1–47:12]

Joseph's brothers returned to Canaan and reported to Jacob that they bought food from a high Egyptian official who turned out to be their brother. Jacob could hardly believe it! As the news sank in that Joseph was alive, Jacob's spirit was refreshed. The brothers told Jacob that Joseph wanted all of them to move to Egypt. Rather than remain in Canaan and suffer through the famine, the family could live with their brother and have plenty to eat.

Then God spoke to Jacob and told him to take the family to Egypt as Joseph had requested. Jacob was thankful and gave a worship offering of sacrifices to God. Judah, who had become the leader of the brothers, led the long journey to Egypt. When they arrived, Jacob had a wonderful reunion with Joseph. Then Joseph took Jacob to see Pharaoh, whom Jacob blessed.

"Then [God] said [to Jacob], 'I am God, the God of your father. Do not be afraid to go down to Egypt, for there I will make you into a great nation. I myself will go down with you to Egypt, and I will also bring you up again . . .'" (Genesis 46:3–4a)

How was Jacob sure that he was to take the family to Egypt?

27. Jacob's Family Stayed in Egypt after the Famine

[from Genesis 50:1–Exodus 1:14]

After the famine ended, Jacob's family stayed in Egypt. Over time, Jacob died, Joseph died, and the brothers died. But all their children, grandchildren, and great-grandchildren stayed in Egypt, and just as God had promised Abraham, Jacob's family grew and grew. The Egyptians referred to these descendants as Israelites, based on the new name God had given Jacob at the end of the all-night fight years earlier (Pixel 20).

The number of Israelites grew larger and larger—so large that a terrible thing happened. Pharaoh and many other people of Egypt started to hate the Israelites. Pharaoh worried that Israel had grown greater and stronger than Egypt. His solution was to make slaves of the Israelites. In this slave condition, the Israelites were forced to work hard for the Egyptians. The Egyptians abused the Israelites and made their lives very difficult.

"So they ruthlessly made the people of Israel work as slaves and made their lives bitter with hard service, in mortar and brick, and in all kinds of work in the field." (Exodus 1:13–14a)

Why did Pharaoh hate the Israelites?

28. Moses' Mother Saved Him from Being Killed

[from Exodus 1:15–2:25]

Pharaoh feared that the Israelites might threaten Egypt as a nation. Making them slaves was not enough. To keep the Israelites from continuing to multiply, he decided to have all the baby boys killed. He ordered the Israelite women who helped deliver babies (called midwives) to kill all baby boys when they were born.

However, because the midwives honored God and wanted to serve him, they refused to obey Pharaoh. One family in particular decided to disobey Pharaoh and save their baby boy, Moses. Moses' mother made a waterproof basket for her son and hid it in the reeds

that grew on the bank of the Nile River. Soon Pharaoh's daughter came to the river to bathe. She saw the basket and found Moses in it. She decided to keep Moses and adopt him as her son.

Although Moses was raised in the house of Pharaoh, he never forgot he was an Israelite. When he grew up, he saw an Egyptian beating an Israelite. Moses tried to stop the abuse. When he believed no one was watching, he killed the Egyptian. But someone saw the murder and told Pharaoh. Moses knew he was in trouble, so he got out of Egypt in a hurry. He went to live in the faraway country of Midian, where he became a shepherd, married, and had children.

"But the midwives feared God and did not do as the king of Egypt commanded them, but let the male children live." (Exodus 1:17)

Why did the midwives disobey Pharaoh?

29. God Called Moses to Save His People
[from Exodus 3:1–4:23]

One day when Moses was alone with the animals in Midian, a bush in front of him suddenly started burning. But the bush did not burn up; instead, it just kept burning and burning. Then he heard God speak, telling Moses that the Israelites in Egypt prayed for God to save them from their slavery and suffering. God instructed Moses to leave his work as a shepherd and go back to Egypt to help his people.

Moses could not believe it! God wanted him to go from leading a simple life, caring for animals, to being a champion for the Israelites, leading them out of slavery. Moses complained to God. He told God he was not able to speak well, and he did not think the leaders of Israel or Pharaoh would listen to him. God declared that he himself, "I AM WHO I AM," would be with Moses (3:14).

In addition, God told Moses that he was sending Aaron, Moses' brother, from Egypt to meet Moses, and that Aaron would be the one to speak to the people and Pharaoh. This response convinced Moses that when he went to tell Pharaoh to let the Israelites leave Egypt, God really would be speaking through him and his brother Aaron—and God would do the work of freeing the Israelites, through Moses. Finally, Moses obeyed.

"Go and gather the elders of Israel together and say to them, 'The Lord, the God of your fathers, the God of Abraham, of Isaac, and of Jacob, has appeared to me, saying, "I have

observed you and what has been done to you in Egypt, and I promise that I will bring you up out of the affliction of Egypt . . ."" (Exodus 3:16–17a)

What new job did God give Moses?

30. Moses Told Pharaoh to Let God's People Go
[from Exodus 4:27–10:29]

Moses walked from Midian toward Egypt. God had told his brother, Aaron, to leave Egypt and walk to meet Moses. They had not seen each other for at least forty years. Now they were together as brothers, and as a team. They would meet with the Israelites to assure them that God had heard their prayers and would free them from slavery. They would work together to give God's message to Pharaoh. God knew Pharaoh was a mean and stubborn man, and that he wanted to keep getting free work from the Israelites. Pharaoh did not believe in or honor God. God would use Moses to show Pharaoh that God is the true God, one who is to be highly respected and honored. But when Moses told this to Pharaoh and demanded that he let God's people go, Pharaoh refused.

Then God sent ten plagues on all the Egyptians to demonstrate that he is the only true God. First, God turned the Nile River and all water connected with it to blood. Second, God brought frogs to cover the land. Pharaoh changed his mind for a short time, but he still refused. Third, God allowed Moses to turn dust into gnats that were everywhere and on everyone. Pharaoh's magicians warned that the gnats were "the finger of God" at work (8:19). But Pharaoh would not let God's people go.

Fourth, God allowed flies to swarm over the land and the Egyptians. Again, Pharaoh changed his mind briefly but then refused. Fifth, God caused the animals of Egypt to get sick and die. Sixth, when Moses followed God's instructions to throw ashes into the air, they became painful boils and sores that broke out on the Egyptians and the remaining animals.

Seventh, God sent heavy and destructive hail, which crushed the crops and killed the Egyptians and animals who did not take shelter. Pharaoh again changed his mind for a short time, but then once more refused. Eighth, God sent locusts to cover Egypt and eat all the remaining plants. Pharaoh's officials asked him, "Do you not yet understand that Egypt is ruined?" (10:7). Then Pharaoh asked Moses to pray for him, but he still did not let God's people go. Ninth, God caused a thick darkness to cover Egypt. This plague was so bad that Pharaoh changed his mind again, but only for a short time before again refusing to let God's people go. At this point, Pharaoh demanded that Moses go away and never come back. Little did Egypt's ruler—who rejected God's message and Moses' warning—know that the worst was yet to come.

"Then Pharaoh said to him, 'Get away from me; take care never to see my face again, for on the day you see my face you shall die.' Moses said, 'As you say! I will not see your face again!'" (Exodus 10:28–29)

Why was Pharaoh so mad at Moses?

31. God Protected His Covenant People
[from Exodus 11:1–13:16]

God was ready to bring the tenth and final plague to Egypt. Moses instructed the people that God's angel would go through all of Egypt during the night and kill the firstborn boy in each family as well as all the firstborn male animals. There was only one way to be spared from this punishment: by putting the blood of a sacrificed lamb around their front doorposts. When the angel saw the blood, the angel would "pass over" the house, and everyone inside would be safe. In this way, God taught his people that he would recognize the blood of the lamb as a substitute for the punishment of not honoring him.

True to his promise, none of the children or animals of the Israelites were killed that night. Also true to God's promise, the firstborn male children and animals of the Egyptians died. This was a horrifying reversal of Pharaoh's earlier plot to kill the Israelite boys.

Because the pain and grief in Egypt were so great, Pharaoh called for Moses. He demanded that Moses take the Israelites and go worship God. He also demanded that Moses pray for him. So Moses and all of God's people, about two million of them, left Egypt that night. Moses assured the Israelites that they were on the way to the land God promised to give them, the same land he had promised to their ancestors Abraham, Isaac, and Jacob. When they arrived in that land, they were to celebrate Passover each year to help them remember how God had brought them out of slavery in Egypt.

"For I will pass through the land of Egypt that night, and I will strike all the firstborn in the land of Egypt, both man and beast; and on all the gods of Egypt I will execute judgments: I am the Lord." (Exodus 12:12)

Why would the angel of God pass over the houses with lamb's blood on the doorposts?

REFLECTION 4
Passover

Today, many Jewish people continue to celebrate Passover. However, Christians do not celebrate Passover as a separate holiday.

Why not? Because Christians understand that Jesus is the Lamb of God. They believe that when Jesus died and then lived again, as we will read about later in the New Testament, he took the place of the lamb sacrificed at Passover. In doing so, Jesus became the permanent substitute before God for our sin. As discussed in Pixel 125, Jesus celebrated Passover with the apostles and said the prophecy of a new covenant would be fulfilled by his blood.

***

32. God Made Dry Land in the Red Sea
[from Exodus 13:17–14:31]

When they left Egypt, God's people walked toward the Red Sea, beyond which was a vast wilderness. Meanwhile, back in Egypt, Pharaoh changed his mind *again*. His army began chasing the Israelites to capture them and take them back to Egypt as slaves. Moses was leading the people. The sea was in front of them, and Pharaoh's army was behind them. Moses challenged everyone to have confidence because God would save them from the Egyptians.

God directed Moses to lift his staff over the water. Then God brought strong winds to divide the sea to make a dry path so they could walk to the other side. When the Israelites crossed safely, Pharaoh's army assumed they could do the same thing. But then God told Moses to lift his staff again. When he did, the walls of water came crashing down on Pharaoh's army, and they all died. God had brought all his people to safety. The Israelites sang and worshiped God to thank him.

"And Moses said to the people, 'Fear not, stand firm, and see the salvation of the Lord, which he will work for you today. For the Egyptians whom you see today, you shall never see again. The Lord will fight for you, and you have only to be silent.'"
(Exodus 14:13–14)

What miracle did God use to save his people from the Egyptian army?

33. God Gave His People Food and Water in the Wilderness

[from Exodus 16:1–17:7]

Even though God had saved them from Pharaoh, the Israelites worried he would not give them all the food and water that they needed while walking through the wilderness. They had just seen God make a dry path for them in the middle of the Red Sea and bring them safely through it. But soon they grumbled against God, complaining that they did not have enough food or water (16:8).

They became so angry that Moses thought they would stone him (17:4). Moses prayed for a solution, and God answered his prayer. For food, God made something like bread appear on the ground every morning except the Sabbath. They called the bread *manna*. God also caused quail to fly into the camp every evening to provide meat for the people to eat. To provide water, God told Moses to hit a rock at Horeb, and water came out of it (17:6a).

"In the evening quail came up and covered the camp, and in the morning dew lay around the camp. And when the dew had gone up, there was on the face of the wilderness a fine, flake-like thing, fine as frost on the ground." (Exodus 16:13–14)

The Israelites said they were angry at Moses. Do you think they were angry at Moses or God?

34. God Led Israel Out of Egypt as Part of His Covenant Plan

[from Exodus 19:1–8]

God intended for his people, the Israelites, to be more than just another nation. God instructed Abraham to move his family to a land he would show him (Pixel 14). God would make a great nation from his family that would be a blessing to the rest of the world. God was still working out this plan when he allowed Abraham's grandson, Jacob, and his family to move to Egypt. About four hundred years later, God called Moses to guide them from Egypt back to Canaan, the land God originally gave Abraham.

The first step in preparing the people of Israel was for God to teach them that they were his special people. As his chosen people, they needed to understand something about God so that they could be a blessing to the rest of the world.

"Now therefore, if you will indeed obey my voice and keep my covenant, you shall be my

treasured possession among all peoples, for all the earth is mine; and you shall be to me a kingdom of priests and a holy nation." (Exodus 19:5–6a)

What did God want his special people to do?

***

REFLECTION 5

The Promise

God shows us in the lives of people from Abraham to Moses that he will be true to his promise of making a provision for us. As you keep reading, you will see that in a similar way to how God used people such as Abraham and Moses to lead his family to their homeland on earth, God uses his Son, Jesus, to lead us in a spiritual way to our eternal home with him. And just as Israel needed to prepare as a nation to be able to live in the land of Canaan, we need God to prepare us for our eternal home with him.

Keep in mind that we are much like the people of Israel; they were not perfect, just as we are not perfect, and they were prone to ungratefully grumbling against God, just as we are prone to do. Yet God's covenant faithfulness is to give us his steadfast love that never fails.

***

35. God Gave His People His Good Law in the Wilderness

[from Exodus 19:9–20:26]

God led his people to a special place in the wilderness at the base of Mount Sinai. God directed Moses to have the people wash and prepare themselves, because in three days God would come to the mountain. Then God instructed Moses to climb up the mountain alone to meet with him. The rest of the people and their animals stayed at the base of the mountain.

Moses was on the mountain for forty days. God told him about many laws the people should follow in order to honor him. God also gave Moses ten special laws, the Ten Commandments, which he wrote on stone tablets:

1. Do not have any gods other than the Lord your God.

2. Do not make idols and worship them as your gods.

3. Do not use God's name in vain (i.e., in a way that is careless, empty, or worthless).

4. Remember to keep the Sabbath day holy, to rest and not do your ordinary work on that day.

5. Honor your father and mother.

6. Do not murder.

7. Husbands and wives should remain sexually pure with each other all their lives.

8. Do not steal.

9. Do not pervert justice by telling lies.

10. Do not covet (i.e., do not let the desire to have something that belongs to another person become a driving force in your life).

"And the Lord said to Moses, 'Thus you shall say to the people of Israel: "You have seen for yourselves that I have talked with you from heaven."'" (Exodus 20:22)

Which of the ten laws do you need help obeying? Pray and ask God to help you, and ask another person to help you as well.

36. God's People Wanted a God They Could See
[from Exodus 31:18–33:17 and 34:1–28]

While Moses was on Mount Sinai listening to God tell him about his good laws, the people decided they could not trust Moses and God to lead them. Moses had been on the mountain for more than three weeks, and they worried he would not come back. So they asked Aaron, Moses' brother, to make them a god, something they could see. Sadly, Aaron did what they asked. He made a calf of gold. He announced to them the golden calf was the god who brought them out of Egypt and saved them. Then they had a big party to celebrate and worship their calf god (32:1–6).

As Moses came down the mountain with the tablets of God's laws in his arms, he heard the loud noise from the party. He became so angry and disgusted with Aaron and the

people that he threw the stone tablets to the ground, breaking them into pieces. Then he destroyed the golden calf (32:15–20). Finally, he prayed for everyone and asked God not to destroy them, even though he knew they had "sinned a great sin" and deserved punishment (32:30). God listened to Moses' plea and, in his mercy, promised to let the people live and continue to lead them to the Promised Land. God even wrote the Ten Commandments on a second set of stone tablets (34:1–28).

"Now therefore, if I [Moses] have found favor in your sight, please show me now your ways, that I may know you in order to find favor in your sight. Consider too that this nation is your people.' And [God] said, 'My presence will go with you, and I will give you rest.'" (Exodus 33:13–14)

Do you always have to see something to believe it is real?

37. The Tabernacle Was Built for Worshiping God in the Wilderness
[from Exodus 25:1–31:11 and 35:4–40:38]

While Moses was on the mountain with God, God showed him how to build a tabernacle. This moveable building would be the place Moses and the people would meet with God as he led them through the wilderness to the Promised Land.

God's plans for the tabernacle were specific and detailed. While the people were in the wilderness, the tabernacle would be something visible that reflected God's holiness and perfection. It would be worthy of God's presence among them, and help them to know God with their spirits.

Then Moses urged everyone to bring offerings and gifts so the skilled craftsmen would have the jewelry, gold, silver, fabric, and wood to make the tabernacle and all the things that would be used in it. They made the altar for burning sacrifices, and the laver, which they filled with water, for the priests to wash. They made the ark of the covenant, where Moses put the stone tablets containing the Ten Commandments, some manna, and Aaron's staff (mentioned in Hebrews 9:4). Moses also had the craftsmen make special clothing for Aaron and his sons, who would serve as priests. When they finished the work on the tabernacle, God was pleased. He confirmed his promise to be present with them and to lead them. A cloud covered the tabernacle, which was evidence of God's glory filling it. Then God led his people with a cloud during the day and in a fire during the night.

"For the cloud of the Lord was on the tabernacle by day, and fire was in it by night, in the sight of all the house of Israel throughout all their journeys." (Exodus 40:38)

Why was it important for Moses and the people to build the tabernacle exactly according to God's plans?

38. God's Priest, Aaron, Led the People in Offering Sacrifices to God

[from Leviticus 1:1–9:24 and 16:1–17:16]

In Leviticus 1:1–9:24, God instructed Moses about a variety of offerings and sacrifices for the people to make. Aaron and the priests were to lead them in these acts of worship. The grain offering was a memorial or an act of devotion to God. The peace offering was the sacrifice of an animal in worship that included giving thanks to God and being in fellowship with him. The sin offering was for unintentional sins and the failure to do something. The guilt offering was for unintentional sins and actions that harmed someone else. For these offerings, the person brought an animal to the priest for sacrifice. The priest put his hand on the animal, killed it, put some of the blood on the altar, and then burned the rest of the animal. All these sacrifices were to atone for the sins of the person making the sacrifice. In other words, the death of the animal substituted for the death of the person who had sinned.

Another type of sacrifice, the atonement, was to be made before Aaron could enter the Most Holy Place of the tabernacle (16:1–17:16). Aaron offered a bull as a sin offering for himself and the priests, a ram as a burnt offering for himself, and another ram as a burnt offering for the people. Then he took two goats. He killed one goat, put some of the blood on the altar, and then burned the remains. On the other goat, Aaron put both of his hands and confessed the sins of all the people. Then he released the goat into the wilderness as a symbol of the goat carrying those sins away.

"And Aaron shall lay both his hands on the head of the live goat, and confess over it all the iniquities of the people of Israel, and all their transgressions, all their sins. And he shall put them on the head of the goat and send it away into the wilderness . . . The goat shall bear all their iniquities on itself to a remote area . . ." (Leviticus 16:21–22)

Do you have any sins that need to be taken away?

REFLECTION 6
The Sacrifice

From these different sacrifices, we can see that God had a plan long ago to teach us what it means for someone else to be the substitute for us, taking our sin so that we do not have to be punished.

The actual sacrifices of animals were visible symbols of what God intended to do for us spiritually, in our hearts. Keep in mind this idea about a substitute for your sin as more of God's story unfolds, especially in the New Testament (Reflection 14). There we will learn about Jesus' death as a substitute for ours, and his coming back to life, which represents new spiritual life for us as children of God.

***

CONNECTION 1
Preparation to Enter the Promised Land

God's plan for the Israelites was to lead them to Canaan, the Promised Land that would be their home (Pixels 13 and 14). This was the same land to which God had called Abraham hundreds of years earlier. And it was the same land God had promised to Jacob the night he saw the vision of God at the top of the ladder (Pixel 19). The land would produce abundant crops and provide plentiful fields for the animals. More importantly, Canaan was situated at a crossroads for land travel in that part of the world. God wanted the Israelites to prosper in Canaan as his chosen people who followed and obeyed him. Then they would fulfill his promise to Abraham that he would be the father of a great nation that would be a blessing to the rest of the world.

But Canaan was the home of many different nations whose peoples did not worship or honor God; in fact, those other nations hated God and lived in ways that were opposite of what God wanted. To have the Promised Land for themselves, as God intended, the Israelites would need the strength and confidence to fight and conquer the people who lived in Canaan. To prepare for this, God wanted the Israelites to learn what it meant to trust both him and each other. He taught them this trust through his law, the tabernacle, the sacrifices, and the miracles he performed for them in the wilderness.

***

39. God Wanted His People Joined Together by Tribal Families
[from Numbers 2:1–34]

For the Israelites to learn to trust each other, God directed Moses to organize the people by the tribal families that had descended from the sons of Jacob (Pixel 21). They were to camp by these family groups in the area around the tabernacle so that they would know each other and be trained for war by their tribes.

The tribes were arranged in groups of threes. At the front of the tabernacle were the tribes of Judah, Issachar, and Zebulun. On the right side were Reuben, Simeon, and Gad. At the rear were Ephraim, Manasseh, and Benjamin. Finally, on the left side were Dan, Asher, and Naphtali. The tribal family descended from Levi camped close to the tabernacle to work there and protect it. Aaron was from Levi's family, and his descendants were to serve in the tabernacle as priests.

"The Lord spoke to Moses and Aaron, saying, 'The people of Israel shall camp each by his own standard, with the banners of their fathers' houses. They shall camp facing the tent of meeting on every side.'" (Numbers 2:1–2)

How do you think being organized by families helped the Israelites learn to trust each other?

40. God Wanted His People to See the Promised Land
[from Numbers 13:1–14:38]

God gave his laws through Moses so his special people would know how they should live with each other and reflect God's character to the world. God gave them the tabernacle so they could properly worship him. God provided for sacrifices so they could be made right with him. God organized his people by tribal families so they could know and trust each other.

They had left Egypt just over a year ago. Now they were approaching their destination and were ready to start the process of entering the Promised Land. God told Moses to choose a man from each of the twelve tribes to be a spy. These twelve spies were to go into Canaan and bring back reports about the people who lived there and the crops grown there.

When the men returned after forty days, they reported that the land and crops were wonderful. However, ten of the twelve spies complained that the people were too big and strong for the people of Israel to conquer and take the land. Only two spies, Joshua and Caleb, urged everyone to trust God to help them enter and live in the land he had promised them. The people were about to kill Joshua and Caleb when God's glory appeared. God informed Moses that, as punishment for not trusting him, the Israelites would continue walking and camping in the wilderness for forty years until everyone who had refused to believe Joshua and Caleb died. So instead of receiving the blessing God intended of going into the Promised Land, those who rejected God's promise would live in the wilderness until they died. Only their children would, eventually, enter the Promised Land.

"According to the number of days in which you spied out the land, forty days, a year for each day, you shall bear your iniquity forty years, and you shall know my displeasure." (Numbers 14:34)

When we tell God we do not believe his promises, should we be surprised when we do not receive what he has promised?

41. God Gave Phinehas a Covenant of Peace for a Perpetual Priesthood
[from Numbers 22:1–25:18]

As the forty years came to an end, Moses again led Israel toward the Promised Land. They passed through the territory of other nations, some of which worried that Israel would take over their land. The people of Moab decided to entice the people of Israel to become friendly with them and worship their god, Baal, rather than the true God. Sadly, many of the Israelites did this.

God commanded Moses to kill all the rebellious leaders of Israel who had joined with the people of Moab to worship Baal. While Moses was carrying out this order, one man of Israel took a woman from Moab into his tent right in front of Moses and the faithful leaders. Because this was such an abhorrent thing to do before God, Phinehas, Aaron's grandson, went into the tent and killed both the man and the woman (Numbers 25).

God told Moses that Phinehas showed true passion for following and honoring God, which is what a priest should do. Because Phinehas was the example for all priests of the future, God rewarded him for his zeal.

"Therefore say, 'Behold, I give to [Phinehas] my covenant of peace, and it shall be to him and to his descendants after him the covenant of a perpetual priesthood, because he was jealous for his God and made atonement for the people of Israel.'" (Numbers 25:12–13)

How do you think peace comes from something violent?

42. Moses Gave Israel a Farewell Address and a Serious Warning
[from Deuteronomy 31:1–33:29]

At the end of the forty years, God was ready to lead his set-apart people into the Promised Land. But God was not willing for Moses to continue to be the leader. One time, at a place called Meribah, the people had complained about not having any water, and Moses asked God how to get water. God had directed Moses to speak to a rock, but Moses had his own idea. Instead of speaking to the rock, he hit it with his rod. God allowed water to come out, but he declared that because Moses had not honored God in front of Israel, Moses would not be allowed to enter the Promised Land (Numbers 20:10–12).

Before Moses died, God instructed him to get everyone together and speak God's last words of advice to them. Moses reported to them what God told him, which was that in the future they would turn from God and follow other gods. When they did this, their lives would be full of problems and troubles.

"Then this people will rise and whore after the foreign gods among them in the land that they are entering, and they will forsake me and break my covenant that I have made with them. Then my anger will be kindled against them in that day, and I will forsake them and hide my face from them, and they will be devoured. And many evils and troubles will come upon them, so that they will say in that day, 'Have not these evils come upon us because our God is not among us?'" (Deuteronomy 31:16b–17)

Have you ever ignored a warning about something and did it your way instead? How did it work out for you?

PART TWO

A Homeland for God's People

Books of the Bible Discussed in This Part:

Joshua, Judges, Ruth, 1 & 2 Samuel, 1 Kings, 1 & 2 Chronicles, Psalms, Proverbs, Ecclesiastes, Song of Solomon

Israel Entered Canaan		Samuel's Birth	
1406 BC (1230)	1375	1105	1050
	Judges Ruled		Saul United the Kingdom

1 Samuel...

David Killed Goliath		Solomon as King	
1025	1010	970	959
	David as King		Solomon's Temple Completed

..............................|| 2 Samuel......................||

1 Kings...

1 Chronicles.......................|| 2 Chronicles...............................

43. God Appointed Joshua to Lead His People into the Promised Land

[from Deuteronomy 34 and Joshua 1]

Before Moses died, he appointed Joshua as the new leader of the Israelites as God had instructed. About forty years earlier, Joshua had been one of the twelve spies who inspected the new homeland. Only he and Caleb believed that God would fulfill his promise to give them victory over the people who already lived there. He and Caleb alone urged the people to trust in God and not be afraid.

Now, God spoke to Joshua to prepare him to lead the nation and people of Israel as they entered the Promised Land. In the same way Joshua had urged his fellow Israelites forty years earlier, God urged Joshua to be strong and courageous. God promised Joshua that he would overcome the difficulties they would face. Joshua had faith in God four decades earlier, and he retained his faith through all those years. But taking this new land would be neither simple nor safe.

"And Joshua the son of Nun was full of the spirit of wisdom, for Moses had laid his hands on him. So the people of Israel obeyed him and did as the Lord had commanded Moses." (Deuteronomy 34:9)

What do you know about Joshua as a leader?

44. Joshua Met God before the Battle of Jericho

[from Joshua 1:1–6:27]

The immediate obstacle Joshua and the Israelite people faced was the Jordan River: How would they cross it? The answer came in God's miracle. When the priests carrying the ark of the covenant stepped into the river, the water immediately stopped flowing. Then everyone crossed over, walking on what suddenly was a dry riverbed. But ahead of them lay another obstacle—the city of Jericho.

As the leader, Joshua scouted the area around Jericho to prepare to fight against it. While Joshua was looking for good military positions, God confronted him. God appeared in the form of a man, who declared that he was captain of the Lord's host. Joshua fell on his face in worship and asked, "What does my lord say to his servant?" (5:14). God instructed Joshua on how to attack the city. Following God's orders, Joshua led the

people in marching around the city one time each day for six days. On the seventh day, they marched around the city seven times. When they shouted and blew trumpets, the walls of the city fell down. The Israelites stormed in and captured it.

"Be strong and courageous, for you shall cause this people to inherit the land that I swore to their fathers to give them." (Joshua 1:6)

Can you name one thing God did to fulfill his promise to bring Israel into the Promised Land?

45. After Many Years and Battles, the Land Was Divided among the Tribes of Israel
[from Joshua 13:1–24:20]

While the Israelites camped in the wilderness, they arranged their tents by descent from Jacob's sons. Because God wanted the Israelites to live together in strong families, he instructed Joshua to divide the Promised Land according to those same twelve families. By this time, Joshua was old and ready to retire as the leader.

Joshua called for all of the tribes to gather together for his farewell address. Joshua challenged them to serve God and put away all foreign idols. He warned the people that God was a jealous God, who would not tolerate them worshiping another god; if they stopped following him, God would "turn and do [them] harm and consume [them]" (24:20). Everyone promised to worship and follow only God.

"'Choose this day whom you will serve . . . But as for me and my house, we will serve the Lord.' Then the people answered, '. . . we also will serve the Lord, for he is our God.'" (Joshua 24:15b–16a, 18b)

What do you think it means to serve God?

46. God Gave Israel New Leaders

[from Judges]

After Joshua's death, there was a period of time when no one specific person served as the appointed leader of all the Israelites. The Bible calls this the time of the judges. As different problems arose among the people, God appointed a person, referred to as a judge, to be the leader and respond to the situation. There were difficulties because the people did not keep the promise they had made with Joshua to follow God and serve only him. Instead, many of them refused to honor God and started worshiping other gods. Because of this, God allowed foreign nations to invade and oppress Israel (2:11–23).

One time when Israel cried out to God for help, Deborah was serving as a judge. Under her godly leadership, Israel defeated the Canaanites (4:1–5:31). But the people again turned from God, and he allowed the Midianites to rule Israel for seven years. Then God called Gideon as a judge. God allowed Gideon to have only three hundred soldiers to fight Midian. Despite having such a small army, Gideon defeated Midian, making it clear that God had accomplished the victory (6:11–8:28). But yet again, the people turned away from God. This was a terribly sad time in the history of Israel. They did not follow God as they promised, and then they did not understand why God allowed enemies to control them.

"In those days there was no king in Israel. Everyone did what was right in his own eyes." *(Judges 21:25)*

What do you think it means for people to do what is right in their own eyes?

47. Ruth Became an Adopted Daughter of Israel and Ancestor of Jesus

[from Ruth]

During the time of the judges, there was a famine in Israel. An Israelite couple, Naomi and Elimelech, had two sons. Because the famine was so bad, they moved from Israel to Moab, a nearby country. While there, Elimelech died, and Naomi's two sons married women from Moab. But then both sons died as well. Naomi was brokenhearted. She had lost her husband and children while in a foreign land. She decided to return to her people in Israel. However, she told both of her daughters-in-law to stay in Moab so they could remarry. One stayed, but the other one, Ruth, insisted on returning to Israel with Naomi.

When they arrived in Israel, Ruth was faithful to Naomi and supported her. Ruth's faithfulness to her mother-in-law attracted the attention and approval of Naomi's friends and relatives, including a man named Boaz. Naomi told Ruth that, as a close relative, Boaz had the opportunity under the law to marry Ruth and carry on the name of Ruth's deceased husband if they had a son. In this way, Boaz could redeem Ruth's original family so it would be preserved and protected.

Boaz and Ruth were indeed married. Boaz was praised by Naomi's friends because not only did his marriage to Ruth carry on the family name, but it provided a home for the widowed Naomi. In time, Boaz and Ruth had a son, Obed, who became the grandfather of David, the second king of Israel. Because Jesus ultimately was born through David's family line, Ruth is named as an ancestor of Jesus in the New Testament (Matthew 1:5).

"But Ruth said, 'Do not urge me to leave you or to return from following you. For where you go I will go, and where you lodge I will lodge. Your people shall be my people, and your God my God.'" (Ruth 1:16)

Naomi provided the way for Ruth to be adopted by Israel. What does it mean to be adopted? Do you know that Jesus makes it possible for us to be adopted and become children of God?

48. Samuel Was Israel's Last Effective Judge

[from 1 Samuel 1:1–8:9]

Also during the time of the judges, a woman named Hannah prayed earnestly to have a child. In fact, she promised God that if he enabled her to have a child, she would dedicate the child back to him. God answered her prayer, and she had a son, whom she named Samuel.

Hannah kept her promise to God. When Samuel was a young boy, she took him to Eli the priest so Samuel could serve God in the tabernacle where the ark of the covenant was kept. A few years later, while Samuel was still a young boy, God spoke to him in the middle of the night. He did not understand that the voice he heard was God's. He believed it was Eli calling for him, and he went to Eli. After the second time, Eli realized God was the one speaking to Samuel. He instructed Samuel on what to say if he heard God's voice again. When God spoke for the third time, Samuel replied, "Speak, for your servant hears" (3:10). God informed Samuel that he would remove Eli from his role as priest because his sons were not following God's laws, and because Eli did not discipline them.

Samuel became the judge of Israel after Eli. However, Samuel's sons were as bad as Eli's. The people told Samuel that they were tired of having judges. They wanted a king so they could be like the other nations. Samuel felt that the people were rejecting not only him but also God, their ultimate leader. God confirmed that he was right.

"And the Lord said to Samuel, 'Obey the voice of the people in all that they say to you, for they have not rejected you, but they have rejected me from being king over them.'" (1 Samuel 8:7)

What does it mean to reject God as the Lord?

***

CONNECTION 2
The History of Israel When Kings Ruled

The books of 1 and 2 Samuel, 1 and 2 Kings, and 1 and 2 Chronicles tell the history of the period when kings ruled Israel. First Samuel is about Samuel anointing Saul as king and the history of Saul's rule. Second Samuel tells the story of David becoming the second king and the history of his rule. First Kings picks up where 2 Samuel leaves off and is a record of the kings of Israel starting with David's son, Solomon, who was the third king. Second Kings begins with the transition of the prophetic ministry of Elijah to the ministry of Elisha. The final events in 2 Kings are the invasions of Israel by Assyria and Babylon and the beginning of what is known as the Babylonian captivity. In fact, 1 and 2 Kings were written to the Israelites while they were in captivity in Babylon, which you will read more about in Part Three.

When the captivity ended and a remnant of Israel was allowed to return to the Promised Land, the books of 1 and 2 Chronicles were written as a history of the kings of Israel to encourage those who survived the captivity. King David's history is in 1 Chronicles, while 2 Chronicles starts with King Solomon and finishes with the Babylonian captivity, adding a transitional reference to the end of the exile under Cyrus. As a result, several of these books have some overlap of events. Keep all of this in mind as you read about the history of Israel, including enemy invasions, the period of captivity, and the remnant returning to the Promised Land.

***

49. God Chose Saul as Israel's First King
[from 1 Samuel 8:22–15:35]

Samuel warned Israel that it would be best for them to honor and follow God, rather than a human being, as their leader. The prophet said a king would make them pay taxes and take some of their property and crops. The king would also take some of them and their children as servants and soldiers, and he might be cruel to them. Even with these warnings, the people of Israel insisted on having a human king.

God directed Samuel to appoint Saul as the king. Although Saul did some good things as king, he was more interested in satisfying himself than he was in honoring God. Many of the problems that Samuel had warned about came true. God knew Saul had to be replaced as king, so he instructed Samuel to start looking for someone else to be king after Saul.

"The word of the Lord came to Samuel: 'I regret that I have made Saul king, for he has turned back from following me and has not performed my commandments.' And Samuel was angry, and he cried to the Lord all night." (1 Samuel 15:10–11)

Does it surprise you that even a king can make mistakes?

50. God Told Samuel to Anoint David as Israel's New King
[from 1 Samuel 16:1–33]

God chose David to be Israel's second king after Saul. David's grandfather was Obed, the child of Ruth and Boaz. One of Obed's children was Jesse, who lived in Bethlehem. Jesse had eight sons, the youngest of whom was David. God informed Samuel that one of Jesse's sons would be the next king, and he sent Samuel to Jesse's home to anoint Saul's successor.

God did not tell Samuel in advance which son would be the next king, so when Samuel arrived at Jesse's home, he started with the oldest. But God told Samuel the oldest son was not the one. The only hint God gave Samuel was to tell him that he was looking at the heart, not the appearance. As Samuel talked with each of the next sons, God gave him the same message—*not the one*! When he finally came to David, God revealed that David was to be the next king. Then Samuel anointed David in front of his father and older brothers.

A shepherd who took care of his father's sheep, David was probably a young teenager at the time of this anointing. Being anointed did not mean David immediately took over the position of king. He would have to grow into the job, and Saul would have to be removed from it. These things would take some time and effort.

Meanwhile, Saul became more focused on himself rather than on God. He started feeling sad, and needed someone to play music for him to lift his spirits. One of the men who worked for Saul knew that David was a fine musician, so Saul brought David to the palace to play music for him. And that is how David and Saul first met each other.

"But the Lord said to Samuel, 'Do not look on his appearance or on the height of his stature, because I have rejected him. For the Lord sees not as man sees: man looks on the outward appearance, but the Lord looks on the heart.'" (1 Samuel 16:7)

What does it mean that God looks at the heart and not at our appearance?

51. Before Becoming King, David Killed Goliath

[from 1 Samuel 17:1–18:9]

Even though David had been anointed to be the future king, he still worked as a shepherd for his family and was a young musician. David was not even old enough to be in the army, but his three oldest brothers were; they served in the army with Saul, fighting the Philistines. One day, Jesse sent David to take some supplies to his brothers and bring him news about the war with the Philistines.

When David arrived at the place where the two armies were facing each other, he was in for a surprise. The Israelite army was camped in one area, while the Philistine army was camped in another area nearby. David learned that every day for the past forty days, the same thing had happened: The Philistines' giant soldier, a nine-foot-tall man named Goliath, stomped out in front of the army of Israel and challenged Israel to send one soldier to fight him to the death. The people of the winning soldier would rule over the people of the soldier who was killed.

So far, none of the soldiers of Israel were brave enough to face Goliath. David was bothered by this—that God's people were too scared to trust him to win a battle against Goliath. David told Saul that he would fight Goliath. He knew God would work through him for the victory. While tending the sheep, David had fought and killed a lion and a bear, so he would do the same thing now. Because a sling with a stone was David's weapon, he picked up five smooth stones and went out to face Goliath.

Goliath was insulted that Israel had sent a teenager—someone not even old enough to be a soldier in the army—to fight him. He laughed and laughed at David until David swung his sling around and let a rock go flying; it went straight for Goliath and struck him in the forehead. The giant fell to the ground. David then took Goliath's sword and used it to cut off Goliath's head.

The whole army of Israel was excited about this amazing victory. When the people of Israel heard about it, David became a hero. Everybody was happy about it except one person: King Saul. Saul became embarrassed that many people thought David was a better soldier than he was. So Saul decided that David had to go.

"Then David said to the Philistine, 'You come to me with a sword and with a spear and with a javelin, but I come to you in the name of the Lord of hosts, the God of the armies of Israel, whom you have defied. This day the Lord will deliver you into my hand . . . that all the earth may know that there is a God in Israel . . .'" (1 Samuel 17:45–46)

Why was David so confident that he would defeat Goliath?

52. After David Killed Goliath, Saul Tried to Kill David
[from 1 Samuel 18:10–31:13]

After killing Goliath, David became a successful military leader in the army. But just because David was to be the next king did not mean he had an easy life. Saul felt insulted and threatened by David's success and popularity. Because of his envy, Saul began thinking of ways to kill David. Saul wanted his own son, Jonathan, to be the next king.

Now, Jonathan and David had become great friends, and Jonathan knew God had chosen David to be the next king. But even Jonathan could not protect David from Saul. To keep from being killed, David fled. While those who supported Saul considered David to be an outlaw, some men who favored David joined with him. There never was an actual battle between Saul and David. Saul and his men tried many times to capture David and his followers, but they were never able to do so.

The people of Israel still needed a strong army because their enemies wanted to destroy them. The Philistines attacked Israel after David and his men left the army, and they won. In that battle, Saul and Jonathan were killed, paving the way for David to become king at last.

"For as long as the son of Jesse lives on the earth, neither you [Jonathan] nor your kingdom shall be established. Therefore send and bring [David] to me [Saul], for he shall surely die." (1 Samuel 20:31)

What happened because Saul ignored what God wanted and selfishly pushed for his own way instead?

53. David Became the King and Kept Singing

[from the Psalms]

After Saul and Jonathan were killed in battle, David became king. As a young man, David had been selected to play music for Saul. David was not only a good musician; he was also an amazing songwriter. The book of Psalms is full of prayers and praises to God. About half of these psalms or songs were written by David.

There are 150 psalms altogether. They cover a wide range of feelings, thoughts, and instructions. Psalm 23 is one well-known psalm by David. Another, Psalm 73, was written by a choir leader named Asaph, whose words provide a representative sample of the entire book of the Psalms.

"Whom have I in heaven but you?
And there is nothing on earth that I desire besides you.
My flesh and my heart may fail,
but God is the strength of my heart and my portion forever.
For, behold, those who are far from you shall perish;
you put an end to everyone who is unfaithful to you.
But for me it is good to be near God;
I have made the Lord God my refuge,
that I may tell of all your works." (Psalm 73:25–28)

Does this excerpt from Psalm 73 remind you of anything you have read so far in this book?

54. David Wanted to Build a Temple for God

[from 2 Samuel 7:1–13a and 1 Chronicles 28:1–21]

One of the main things David wanted to do as king was build a permanent place to worship God. When Moses led the Israelites in the wilderness, the moveable tabernacle was the place to worship God and where the ark of the covenant was kept (Pixel 37). Since that time, no one had built a permanent building for the place of worship and the ark.

David began gathering the materials for the temple. Through the prophet Nathan, God then told David that Solomon, David's son and the next king, should build the temple (2 Samuel 7:12–13). Although David was disappointed not to build the temple himself, he obeyed God. Before he died, David showed Solomon all the plans and materials for the temple and encouraged him to live in obedience to God (1 Chronicles 28:11–19).

"Then David said to Solomon his son, 'Be strong and courageous and do it. Do not be afraid and do not be dismayed, for the Lord God, even my God, is with you. He will not leave you or forsake you, until all the work for the service of the house of the Lord is finished.'" (1 Chronicles 28:20)

Do you remember another time when David trusted God to strengthen and encourage him?

55. God Intended to Build an Eternal Kingdom through David's Family

[from 2 Samuel 7:13b–29 and 1 Chronicles 28:4–29:20]

David's desire to honor God by building the temple pleased God. But God used David's building plans to show David, and everyone, his even bigger plans. Rather than focus on the physical structure of a building, God spoke through the prophet Nathan to reveal God's covenant plan for his eternal spiritual kingdom. Nathan declared to David that God would establish a ruler for David's throne forever (2 Samuel 7:13b).

David was overwhelmed that God had chosen his family, which descended from Judah, to lead Israel (2 Samuel 7:18–29; 1 Chronicles 28:4). The fulfillment of God's promise of an eternal ruler for Israel comes in the New Testament, when a leader from the family of Judah and the family of David—Jesus Christ—is revealed as the one to occupy this eternally established throne (Luke 1:30–33, 67–79).

"And your house and your kingdom shall be made sure before me. Your throne shall be established forever." (2 Samuel 7:16)

Have you ever realized the path you're following in life is only a small part of a bigger plan?

56. Solomon Became King and Prayed for Wisdom
[from 1 Kings 3:3–28 and 2 Chronicles 1:7–13]

Being the king of a major country is a big job. So when Solomon became the king of Israel, he went to the tabernacle to worship God and offer sacrifices. God was pleased with Solomon's worship. God appeared to Solomon and told him he could ask for anything he wanted. Rather than asking for power, prestige, or wealth, Solomon asked God for wisdom.

Solomon immediately went to work applying God's wisdom. Two women came to him, asking him to decide which one of them was the actual mother of a certain infant. The women lived in the same house and were both prostitutes. Each of them had babies about the same time. Sadly, during the night, one of the babies died. The mother of the dead baby switched her child with the baby who was still alive. The next morning, the women argued about whose baby was dead and whose was alive.

When they took this argument to Solomon, he called for a sword and said he would divide the living baby between the women. One woman screamed for him not to do that, but rather to give the child to the other woman. Solomon immediately knew that the woman who wanted the baby to live was the real mother. The child was safely returned to her. Everyone who heard of Solomon's decision knew God had given him the wisdom to rule with justice.

"Give your servant therefore an understanding mind to govern your people, that I [Solomon] may discern between good and evil, for who is able to govern this your great people?" (1 Kings 3:9)

How can Solomon be an example to us for discerning the difference between good and evil?

57. Solomon Wrote Wise Sayings Collected as Proverbs

[from Proverbs]

Just after the Psalms is the book of Proverbs. The entire book is a collection of short statements that give insight and understanding about how to live wisely. King Solomon wrote or collected most of the contents of the book, but other thoughtful people wrote or collected some of the proverbs. Summarizing the book of Proverbs is difficult because its sayings cover a wide variety of issues that come up in everyday life.

In general, four types of persons are addressed in Proverbs: the person seeking to live by God's wisdom; the foolish person seeking to live by cultural values; the confused person who cannot decide between the two; and the evil person who is intent on doing bad things.

The person seeking God's wisdom listens to the teachings of more experienced people (1:8–9), learns from personal experiences (3:7), has a proper respect for God's power and truth as the source of all knowledge, wisdom, and insight (1:7a; 9:10), and flourishes with God's blessings (24:3–6).

The foolish person who lives by the values of the culture, on the other hand, refuses to listen to or obey instruction (1:7b), will end up not having good things to enjoy, will fall into trouble (17:20), and then will blame God for it all (19:3).

The confused person cannot decide to follow wisdom, and suffers for this indecision (1:10, 15, 22, 32). The confused person is inclined to follow temptation to do evil (7:21; 25:26), envies evil people (24:1), and may or may not use good judgment in dealing with other people (26:17).

The evil person's sin is so great that it becomes a trap (5:22). Greed for money leads evil people to murder (1:15–19). They are deceitful (10:6), give bribes to pervert justice (17:23), and are always thinking up ways to cause trouble (6:14).

Here is a representative proverb, which is directed toward a young person:

"My son, do not forget my teaching, but let your heart keep my commandments, for length of days and years of life and peace they will add to you. Let not steadfast love and faithfulness forsake you; bind them around your neck; write them on the tablet of your heart. So you will find favor and good success in the sight of God and man. Trust in the Lord with all your heart, and do not lean on your own understanding. In all your ways acknowledge him, and he will make straight your paths." (Proverbs 3:1–6)

Do you see how similar the advice in Proverbs 3 is to the warnings Moses and Joshua gave to Israel (Pixels 42 and 45)?

58. Solomon Built the Temple

[from 1 Kings 9:1–9 and 2 Chronicles 2:1–3:2; 7:11–18]

The temple Solomon built was magnificent. The building symbolized the nation of Israel to all other nations. A representation of God's presence in their midst, the temple served as the focal point for all the people in Israel.

When Solomon celebrated the completion of its construction, he called everyone together for a feast of dedication. The ark of the covenant finally had a permanent home. Solomon and all of Israel worshiped God and thanked him for his provision to them. God was pleased with this worship.

"And the Lord said to [Solomon], 'I have heard your prayer and your plea, which you have made before me. I have consecrated this house that you have built, by putting my name there forever. My eyes and my heart will be there for all time.'" (1 Kings 9:3)

What symbol reminds you of God's presence?

***

CONNECTION 3

Solomon Wrote Two Unique Books— Ecclesiastes and Song of Solomon

With God's special measure of wisdom, Solomon wrote two other books in the Old Testament: Ecclesiastes and Song of Solomon.

Ecclesiastes explores the realities of human life and our search for worth, meaning, and significance. Solomon summarized human purpose in this way: We are to live according to God's plans and directions, with proper fear and reverence for him (Ecclesiastes 12:13). When "fear" is used in the Bible, the word has a broader and more comprehensive meaning than is currently used today. Fearing God begins with a respectful and reverent attitude that acknowledges his exclusive role in creating the universe and giving life to everything. This position of personal humility leads to a proper response to God, giving the honor, duty, and accountability due him. The result for us is wisdom for living, fulfilling the teaching of Psalm 111:10 and Proverbs 9:10 that "[t]he fear of the Lord is the beginning of wisdom."

Song of Solomon is also known as the Song of Songs. Envision a popular songwriter and think about that person's best song. That's what we have here—Solomon's number-one hit, and it's all about love. And as with some popular songs, the words and flow of the text are not always clear. Rather, they express the creative genius of the artist. The theme of Song of Solomon focuses on the love and marriage relationship of a country girl and a shepherd. Some Christians are content to agree that this book is a beautiful expression of the wonders of human love. Others see in it an allegory for the wonders of God's love for us—as the earthly body of Christ (his special family) being prepared as his eternal bride.

***

59. Solomon Said Life Is Vanity, but God's Plan Implements His Sovereignty

[from Ecclesiastes]

In the voice of a preacher, Solomon explored all aspects of meaning and significance of human life on earth ("under the sun," as he phrases it) in Ecclesiastes. In twelve intense chapters, Solomon set his heart to analyzing just about every facet of life, including God's big-picture plan, God's great gifts to people, and the fact that all of human life is under God's sovereign goodness. Solomon concluded by saying that all human existence is "vanity"—a vapor with no real meaning, worth, significance, or lasting value. However, he also taught that God is not lost in the universe; God has a plan, and because of his goodness, people should live by acknowledging God's sovereignty and enjoying his good gifts in life.

Solomon's first major point was that humans can't figure out anything of lasting significance because it's all hopeless and worthless. He knew from experience that life is ultimately hateful, painful, and vain. He saw evil everywhere, even in the courts. He observed that eventually everyone dies and returns to the dust.

Next, Solomon gave assurance that God has everything figured out. God's big plan is very real and very good. God gives us the circumstances we need to turn to him and fear him. God provides seasons, not only in nature but in the events of our lives. God has not left us alone in the task of living because he has put his eternal picture—and power—in our hearts.

Then Solomon enthusiastically affirmed that God gives good gifts to people. He said people should rejoice in their labors because work is a gift from God to each person. God also graciously provides food and enjoyment, which people should experience with happiness.

Finally, in view of all he observed and said, Solomon concluded that people should respond to God as the creator and sovereign Lord. Solomon had confidence that God would bring true justice at the proper time. Because God is in ultimate control of all events in life, God's truth is "the end of the matter" (12:13).

"The end of the matter; all has been heard. Fear God and keep his commandments, for this is the whole duty of man. For God will bring every deed into judgment, with every secret thing, whether good or evil." (Ecclesiastes 12:13–14)

What about your life is a vapor? What can you do to experience genuine meaning?

60. Solomon's Most Beautiful Song Teaches about Real Love

[from Song of Solomon]

As a songwriter, Solomon told the love story of a young couple. While there are numerous ways to approach the book, four main topics depict both the physical and spiritual applications of the song.

In the story, each person first sought the other as the "beloved." Physically, they wanted to be in each other's presence, and they actively looked for those opportunities. Spiritually, God wants his people to seek after him and be in his presence.

Next, the couple spoke of one another's physical beauty and their affection for each other. As God's spiritual children, he desires for his people to proclaim his wonders, the beauty of his creation, his goodness, and affection for him.

Over time, the couple's love for one another matured. Spiritual maturity is equally real, as God's people learn more about him and themselves.

Finally, the lovers gained confidence in the security of their relationship and mutual love. The spiritual parallel is that God's people grow in their knowledge of and relationship with him by seeking and experiencing his truth. They have true confidence in the security of his love.

"Set me as a seal upon your heart, as a seal upon your arm, for love is strong as death,

jealousy is fierce as the grave. Its flashes are flashes of fire, the very flame of the Lord."
(Song of Solomon 8:6)

How would you explain that jealousy in love is expressed as "flashes" from the fire of God?

61. Solomon Turned from God, and His Son Divided the Nation
[from 1 Kings 11:1–12:33]

Although Solomon prayed for and received God's wisdom, his small steps away from God to acquire wealth and pursue his own interests led him in his later years to become focused on his own glory and pleasure rather than on God's honor. He rejected the wisdom and truth God had so graciously given him. He began to rely only on himself. He took many wives from foreign nations who did not worship the true God, and with whom God had forbidden his people to marry. He followed some of these wives in worshiping false gods and idols. In so doing, Solomon continued the pattern seen so far in Israel's history, especially among its leaders—trusting and honoring God for a time, but then forgetting God and his ways, and instead going their own way.

Solomon's son Rehoboam became Israel's king after Solomon. Rehoboam immediately started going his own way and, unsurprisingly, that was a disaster. He acted so selfishly that ten of the tribal families of Israel refused to acknowledge him as their king. Instead, they made a man named Jeroboam their king. With this action, Israel was divided into two nations. Those who followed Jeroboam referred to themselves as Israel, and were also known as the Northern Kingdom. The two tribes that followed Rehoboam referred to themselves as Judah, and were also known as the Southern Kingdom. Neither Rehoboam nor Jeroboam obeyed God or followed his laws.

Jeroboam decided that in order to maintain the loyalty of the ten tribes in his kingdom, he would build altars at places other than the temple in Jerusalem. To enhance this alternative form of worship, he made two golden calves. He placed one in Bethel and the other in Dan, opposite ends of the Northern Kingdom. Then he told the people to worship the calves as their gods.

"And Jeroboam appointed a feast . . . like the feast that was in Judah, and he offered sacrifices on the altar. So he did in Bethel, sacrificing to the calves that he made."
(1 Kings 12:32)

How were Aaron and Jeroboam alike? Do you remember the party Aaron threw while Moses was on the mountain receiving the Ten Commandments (Pixel 36)?

PART THREE

God's People Rejected Him and Went into Exile

Books of the Bible Discussed in This Part:

1 & 2 Kings, Jonah, Amos, Hosea, Joel, Micah, Isaiah, Nahum, Zephaniah, Habakkuk, Obadiah, Jeremiah, Lamentations, Ezekiel, Daniel

Solomon's Temple Completed		Prophets to the Northern Kingdom (Israel)				
		Elijah	Elisha	Jonah	Amos	Hosea
959 BC	930	875			760	750
						735
				Joel		Micah, Isaiah
	Israel Divided			Prophets to the Southern		

1 Kings ....|| 2 Kings ....
2 Chronicles ....

Israel Fell to Assyria					2nd Captivity: Ezekiel to Babylon		
722				605	597		586
	660	635	625				

Nahum, Zephaniah, Habakkuk, Jeremiah   *Obadiah, Ezekial, Daniel*

Kingdom (Judah)

Judah's 1st Captivity: Daniel to Babylon

3rd Captivity: Temple Destroyed; Judah Fell to Babylon

2 Kings ....||
2 Chronicles ....||

CONNECTION 4

Divided into Two Nations,
Israel Heads toward Captivity

The division of the twelve tribal families into two nations was the beginning of the end for Israel as a nation. The ten Northern tribes took the name of Israel, while the two Southern tribes, Judah and Benjamin, took the name of Judah.

Determining the tribes counted among the ten Northern tribes and those counted in the two Southern tribes is not as clear-cut as it might first appear. This is because the identity of the tribal families of Jacob progressed from being rooted in bloodline descent (from Jacob) to being based on territory and geography. To avoid confusion, we will look at this progression now.

Jacob's twelve sons were Reuben, Simeon, Levi, Judah, Dan, Naphtali, Gad, Asher, Issachar, Zebulun, Joseph, and Benjamin. However, just before Jacob died, he "adopted" Joseph's two sons, Ephraim and Manasseh, so they and their families would be in the same position as Jacob's other sons (Genesis 48:5–6, 16). This is why Ephraim and Manasseh, rather than Joseph, are named in the arrangement of tribes around the tabernacle (Pixel 39). When the time came for Joshua to divide the land, the separate allotments to Ephraim and Manasseh were confirmed. In addition, no territory was designated to the tribe of Levi, because the Levites' inheritance was to serve and worship God as his priests (Joshua 13:14; 14:4).

In the division of the Southern land, the allocation to Simeon was totally within the area given to Judah (Joshua 19:9). By Solomon's time, Simeon's geographic identity had been lost, as it was absorbed into Judah, fulfilling Jacob's prophecy that the tribes of Simeon and Levi would be scattered (Genesis 49:7b). Even though Simeon ceased to exist as a geographically-based unit, individuals from Simeon continued to refer to themselves by their tribal identity (1 Chronicles 4:24–43; 2 Chronicles 15:9). Thus the Southern Kingdom of Judah can be numbered as two tribes, namely Judah and Benjamin, even though it also contained the *people* of a third tribe—Simeon (1 Kings 11:36; 12:21).

The calculation of ten tribes in the Northern Kingdom is equally complicated. Technically, there remained only nine tribes that received geographical allotments: Reuben, Dan, Naphtali, Gad, Asher, Issachar, Zebulun, Ephraim, and Manasseh. However, the tribe of Manasseh received very large amounts of land both west and east of the Jordan River, to the extent that the separate areas of the tribe of Manasseh became referred to as two distinct groups (Joshua 13:8; 16:1–17:18). So, practically speaking, Manasseh may be considered two tribes, giving the Northern Kingdom ten tribes.

It was in these political units that Israel and Judah, in separate ways and times, rejected God's leadership and provision, leading them to different but equally severe punishments.

Through misfortune, extremes of severe weather, the violence of war, and prophets speaking God's truth, God tried to call Israel, the Northern Kingdom, back to himself. God sent five well-known prophets to Israel over a period of about two hundred years to warn the leaders and the people. These prophets were Elijah, Elisha, Jonah, Amos, and Hosea. Even with these prophets challenging them, none of the kings of Israel followed God. Assyria conquered Israel and took many people into captivity in 722 BC.

***

Divided Kingdom c. 925 B.C.

SECTION A. ISRAEL
The Northern Kingdom
from King Jeroboam to the Assyrian Captivity

62. Elijah Called Israel to Repentance
[from 1 Kings 18:1–46 and 21:1–29]

A king of Israel after Jeroboam was Ahab. He and his wife, Jezebel, worshiped Baal (the regional god of storms) and were so evil that they killed many prophets of God. God sent the prophet Elijah to tell Ahab and Jezebel to follow God rather than Baal. Elijah prophesied that it would not rain for three years, and a severe drought occurred just as he predicted. Finally, God informed Elijah that it would rain again. But before the rain came, Elijah challenged Ahab to prove whether Baal or the Lord was the true God.

Ahab and his prophets were to meet Elijah at Mount Carmel. Elijah asked the people how long they would hesitate between serving God and Baal. They were silent. Then he and the prophets of Baal each built an altar and sacrificed an ox on it. The god who answered with fire and burned up the sacrifice would demonstrate himself to be the true god. The prophets of Baal went first. They prayed, but nothing happened. They cried out loudly and cut themselves to the point of bleeding, but still Baal was silent.

Then Elijah had his altar and sacrifice flooded with water three times. He prayed to God. Fire came from heaven and burned up the sacrifice, the altar, and all the water. Elijah called on those who believed the Lord is the true God to kill all 450 prophets of Baal, which they did. With God's victory clear to everyone, Elijah prayed for the rain to end the drought on the land, and it came. Even though many people turned to God at this time, Ahab and Jezebel sadly continued to reject God and to lead the people away from him.

"Then the fire of the Lord fell and consumed the burnt offering and the wood and the stones and the dust, and licked up the water that was in the trench. And when all the people saw it, they fell on their faces and said, 'The Lord, He is God; the Lord, He is God.'" (1 Kings 18:38–39)

Why didn't anything happen when the prophets of Baal prayed to their god?

63. Elijah Was Taken to Heaven in a Whirlwind of Fiery Chariots

[from 2 Kings 2:1–18]

After praying to God for fire to burn the altar and for rain to water the land, Elijah continued to urge the kings of Israel to follow God and not their own evil plans. After many more years, Elijah knew his life on earth was coming to an end. God appointed Elijah's helper, Elisha, to take his place as a prophet to Israel. Elisha wanted to stay with Elijah and assist him until he died, but neither one of them knew when death would come.

Elijah told Elisha to let him go on alone, but Elisha refused to leave him. Elisha even asked Elijah to give him a double portion of the Spirit of God that was on Elijah. Elijah replied that such a request was not his to grant, but that if Elisha saw him depart, then he would know God had given him the double portion for which he had asked. Just then, "chariots of fire and horses of fire" came down from heaven and took Elijah to heaven in a whirlwind. Everyone was amazed that Elijah was taken straight to heaven at the end of his life.

As Elijah went to heaven, his cloak fell to the ground. Elisha picked up and wore the garment. With the cloak, everyone knew that the Spirit of God, who had been on Elijah, had come on Elisha.

"And as they still went on and talked, behold, chariots of fire and horses of fire separated the two of them. And Elijah went up by a whirlwind into heaven." (2 Kings 2:11)

How did everyone know that God appointed Elisha to take Elijah's place as a prophet?

64. A Young Girl Knew of Elisha, Trusted God, and Acted with Courage

[from 2 Kings 5:1–3]

Naaman was the captain of the army of Syria, a country next to Israel. The two countries frequently fought each other, even when there was no major war underway. Naaman's troops raided small towns of Israel. In these raids, the Syrians would destroy a village and kill its people or take them back to Syria as slaves. A young girl of Israel, whose village had been destroyed and parents killed, was taken as a slave to work in Naaman's house. Even in these circumstances, she still believed in God and trusted in his power. When the girl learned Naaman had leprosy, she told his wife that she wished Naaman would see Elisha, the prophet in Israel, who could cure him.

Although she was a slave who had been violently separated from her family and nation, this girl still wanted the best for her master. The Bible does not give more details about her; however, from her action, she obviously grew up in a family that taught her to love and not hate. She knew that the blessing of being part of God's family was intended for others, and not just the Jewish people. Her confidence in God's power was so strong that she was willing to take the risk of urging her master to go to a prophet in a foreign country to be healed. She knew that telling him about Elisha was the right thing to do, and she did it.

"Now the Syrians on one of their raids had carried off a little girl from the land of Israel, and she worked in the service of Naaman's wife. She said to her mistress, 'Would that my lord were with the prophet who is in Samaria! He would cure him of his leprosy.'" (2 Kings 5:2–3)

Why did this young girl want to help Naaman?

65. Elisha Healed the General of Israel's Enemy from Leprosy
[from 2 Kings 5:4–19]

After he learned from the slave girl about the prophet in Samaria, Naaman acted quickly. He arranged for Syria's king to send him with a large gift to King Jehoram of Israel, along with a letter requesting that Naaman be healed. But when Naaman arrived, Jehoram thought the idea was a mean trick to start a war between the two countries. Jehoram knew he had no power to heal leprosy, and he obviously did not think to pray to God to heal Naaman.

When Elisha heard about the situation, he told Jehoram to send Naaman to see him. When Naaman arrived at Elisha's house, Elisha instructed his helper to tell Naaman to wash seven times in the Jordan River. Naaman was insulted. He was angry that Elisha did not even take the time to speak personally with as important a person as he thought he was. He was even more insulted at being told to wash in the muddy waters of the Jordan River. In a rage, he was about to leave and go home. But then his assistant encouraged him to put aside his pride and follow Elisha's simple directions. When Naaman came out of the water after the seventh washing, his skin was completely healed. Then Naaman believed in God and acknowledged him as the true God of all the earth.

Naaman returned home with perfectly healed skin and a heart full of worship. The Bible does not describe the celebration that must have happened when the slave girl and his family greeted him.

"Then [Naaman] returned to the man of God [Elisha], he and all his company, and he came and stood before him. And he said, 'Behold, I know that there is no God in all the earth but in Israel . . .'" (2 Kings 5:15a)

What do you think about a foreigner having more faith in God than the king of Israel?

66. God Sent Jonah to Tell Foreigners about God, and They Repented
[from Jonah]

A few years after God used Elisha to heal Naaman physically, God wanted some people near Israel to be healed spiritually. This place was the city of Nineveh, which was in the country of Assyria and a cruel enemy of Israel.

Jonah was a prophet in Israel when Israel took back land it had lost to enemies. When God told Jonah to go to one of these enemy territories—Nineveh—and tell the people there to repent and to worship him, Jonah could not believe it. He refused to obey God at first, because he thought the Assyrians deserved no mercy. Instead, he sailed away on a ship going in exactly the opposite direction of Nineveh. But God threatened the ship with a terrible storm.

Jonah knew God had sent the storm to discipline him. He told the ship captain to throw him into the sea and save everyone else on board. With Jonah about to drown in the ocean, the storm stopped, and the ship was saved. Then God sent an enormous fish to swallow Jonah, who stayed alive for three days inside the fish's belly. Then Jonah prayed to God to forgive him, and promised he would obey from then on. At that point, the fish spit Jonah onto the shore.

Jonah made good on his promise to God and went to Nineveh. Upon arriving, he announced to everyone that if they did not repent, in forty days God would destroy the city. To Jonah's surprise—and disappointment—the people repented, so God did not destroy Nineveh.

God had a larger purpose than Jonah realized. God intended for more than the Jewish people in Israel to know him, his mercy, and his salvation.

Later, Jesus used what happened with Jonah to teach about himself. In Matthew 12:38–41, Jesus said that Jonah being inside the fish for three days was a sign that Jesus would be dead for three days and then come to life again.

"When God saw what they did, how they turned from their evil way, God relented of the disaster that he had said he would do to them, and he did not do it." (Jonah 3:10)

When have you refused to do what you knew God wanted you to do?

67. Israel Refused to Repent When Amos Preached

[from Amos]

Amos was a farmer in Judah, but God appointed him to be a prophet to Israel. Amos declared to Israel that God was repulsed by the way they worshiped him. The people went through the motions of offering sacrifices and gathering together for religious festivals and assemblies. But when they did those activities, they were doing them for themselves and as a show to others. They did not worship God in their hearts.

Being false in their relationship with God caused them to be false in their relationships with each other. Rather than being honest and respectful of others, they became insincere, selfish, and greedy. Whenever they could take advantage of someone in business, they did so. When a poor person needed help, they were ignored and exploited for what little they had. When a decent person went to court for justice in a dispute, the judges of Israel took bribes and made decisions in favor of the bad person.

In his preaching, Amos urged the people of Israel to return to God, turn from their ways that dishonored him, and be prepared to meet him. Amos instructed everyone to hate evil, do what was good, and insist that justice be done in the courts. Amos told the people of Israel that if they did not repent and follow God, God would allow an enemy nation to invade Israel, capture them, and take them into exile as slaves.

Amos spoke to Israel, but he wrote his book for both Israel and Judah to read. Sadly, in the end, neither Israel nor Judah listened.

"But let justice roll down like waters, and righteousness like an ever-flowing stream." (Amos 5:24)

What kept the people of Israel from having justice in their courts and being right with God?

68. Hosea Was God's Last Prophet to Israel before Its Conquest by Assyria

[from Hosea]

God directed Hosea to be a living demonstration of how seriously God loved his people and wanted them to return to him. God instructed Hosea to marry a woman who refused to be loyal to him or honor him as her husband. She committed sexual adultery. Through Hosea's marriage to this adulteress, God showed Israel its spiritual adultery of rejecting him and worshiping false gods. Pointing to the example of a farmer, God told the people to break up their fallow ground—the unproductive part of their fields, which represented their insincere and unfruitful habits of pretending to worship God. When they did, they would live with each other respectfully, showing kindness and fairness.

But just as the people ignored the prophet Amos, they ignored Hosea. The people in Israel went on treating each other badly. They became more devoted to the things God allowed them to have rather than to the source of those things. The people's spirit of adultery caused them to become like the objects of their worship.

Hosea warned the people of Israel that God would punish them by allowing Assyria to invade and conquer them—and that is exactly what happened. Israel threw itself to the wind rather than to God, and it reaped a whirlwind. With the cruel violence of a conqueror, Assyria invaded Israel in 722 BC. Israel ceased to exist as a separate nation.

"Hear the word of the Lord, O children of Israel, for the Lord has a controversy with the inhabitants of the land. There is no faithfulness or steadfast love, and no knowledge of God in the land . . . My people are destroyed for lack of knowledge . . ." (Hosea 4:1, 6a)

Why is it important to have a proper knowledge of God?

***

CONNECTION 5

The Southern Portion of the Nation of Israel Became Known as Samaria

The city of Samaria was the capital of Israel. When Assyria conquered Israel, it enslaved many of the people and moved them away from the land. Meanwhile, Assyria also forced people from *other* nations that it had conquered to move to Israel. Hosea said, "Israel is swallowed up; already they are among the nations as a useless vessel. For they have gone up to Assyria . . ." (Hosea 8:8–9a).

After many years, the Jewish people who were not forcibly removed from Israel married people from other countries who had been relocated to Israel. Eventually, this group of people with mixed national and religious backgrounds came to be called the Samaritans. This primarily occurred in the southern portion of what in the past was known as the nation of Israel, and later as Samaria.

Samaria plays an important role in the New Testament. For example, Jesus referred to it when he first sent out the twelve apostles in Matthew 10:5, he talked with a Samaritan woman at a well in John 4:7–45, and he told a story about a "good Samaritan" in Luke 10:30–37.

Jesus was from Galilee, in the northern portion of the Northern Kingdom. There is scholarly debate about how this area came to have a Jewish heritage that separated it from Samaria and more closely identified it with Judea (which, in Jesus' time, was the northern portion of Judah).

***

SECTION B. JUDAH
The Southern Kingdom
from King Rehoboam to the Babylonian Captivity

***

CONNECTION 6
Judah Heads toward Exile

Judah, the Southern Kingdom, followed the same sad path as Israel, but at a slower pace. God sent eight well-known prophets to Judah over a period of about three hundred years, warning the leaders and people just as prophets did in Israel. The prophets sent to Judah were Joel, Micah, Isaiah, Nahum, Zephaniah, Habakkuk, Obadiah, and Jeremiah. During this time, eight kings of Judah followed God and, to some extent, urged the people to do the same. These kings were Asa, Jehoshaphat, Joash, Amaziah, Azariah (also referred to as Uzziah), Jotham, Hezekiah, and Josiah.

But in the end, Judah rejected God as harshly as Israel did. Babylon conquered Judah and took many of its people into captivity in three invasions—in 605 BC, 597 BC, and 586 BC. During the last invasion, the Babylonians demolished Solomon's temple, destroyed the walls of Jerusalem, and burned the city.

***

69. Joel Told Judah the Locust Plague Was Nothing Compared to the Future

[from Joel]

A black cloud of locusts swarmed over all of Judah. When the locusts left, God gave Joel a message for Judah. Joel was the first of the prophets to the Southern Kingdom, urging the leaders and people to return to and follow God. Joel said the devastation was like nothing anyone had ever seen. Joel was correct—no one then living had seen anything like this: locusts eating all the plants, and even the bark off the trees, leaving nothing growing out of the ground. Then famine came, with fires breaking out everywhere.

Joel warned Judah that the day of the Lord was coming when God would inflict his judgment on Judah—a day that would be worse than the present circumstances.

God said that if the people returned to him with sincere and genuine repentance, he would hear their prayer. They did not need to tear their garments—a reference to the custom at that time for people burdened by grief or sorrow over their sin to rip part of their clothing. Rather, in a worshipful and figurative way, the people should tear their hearts. Then, in his compassion, God would restore figuratively what the locusts had eaten. He would also pour out his Spirit on those who turned to him. But to those who did evil against his people, he would bring down on their heads the same evil they had committed.

"Return to me with all your heart, with fasting, with weeping, and with mourning; and rend your hearts and not your garments." (Joel 2:12b–13a)

Have you seen other examples of God using events in nature to point to himself?

70. Micah Was God's Prophet in Judah When Hosea Was a Prophet in Israel
[from Micah]

God called Micah to leave his small town and tell the kings, leaders, and people of Judah how much God abhorred and was disgusted by how they lived. With God's Spirit guiding him, Micah spoke the blunt truth about how horribly the leaders and priests had turned from God's ways. Micah described the situation in Israel as an incurable wound, and declared that Judah had the same injury. Rather than leaders using their positions and power to ensure that business was done honestly, they took advantage of poor people and abused them. The leaders bribed judges so they would always win in court. They twisted situations to make things work out in their favor. The priests were just as bad as the governing authorities. Rather than seek God's will and direction, the priests would take people's money and tell them what they wanted to hear.

This part of God's special people had become sick from top to bottom. Not only were the leaders and priests corrupt, but the people of Judah did not follow or honor God either. Consequently, neighbors no longer trusted each other, and members of the same household treated each other rudely and without respect. God had no choice but to punish Judah. Although it took many years before this punishment came, it finally did, and with great calamity: The nation of Babylon invaded Judah in 586 BC and took the people as captives.

God told Micah to give some encouragement along with his condemnation. Writing about seven hundred years before Jesus' birth, Micah prophesied that one day a child would be born who would be God's true ruler. This child would come from Bethlehem, King David's hometown (5:2). In his kingdom, people would no longer abuse each other, be disrespectful to each other, or go to war against each other. This true ruler would be the Messiah, and he would bring real and lasting peace for God's people.

"He has told you, O man, what is good; and what does the Lord require of you but to do justice, and to love kindness, and to walk humbly with your God?" (Micah 6:8)

When a person is in a position of leadership, how should that person treat other people?

71. Isaiah Was God's Prophet to the Leaders in Judah

[from Isaiah]

While Micah still served as a prophet in Judah, God commissioned Isaiah to be a prophet as well. Isaiah was scared, almost to death, of this role. He knew how spiritually unclean he was, and how spiritually unclean the rest of Judah was. Of course, God already knew this about Isaiah and still had a plan to use him. In a vision, an angel took a hot coal from a fire and touched Isaiah's lips with it. The angel said the burning coal showed that God had forgiven the sins that kept Isaiah from being God's prophet (6:1–13).

Whereas Micah was from a small town, Isaiah was from a leading family in Judah—probably in the city of Jerusalem. He was well educated. Both Micah and Isaiah told the leaders and the people the same thing: God recoiled at the mean way those in power treated the poor and needy, he was saddened by the way people had turned away from him, and he detested the insincere sacrifices and offerings during their worship rituals. Isaiah warned that if Judah did not turn to God to honor and obey him, a violent enemy would invade and conquer the kingdom (5:13; 39:6–7).

"Then one of the seraphim flew to me, having in his hand a burning coal that he had taken with tongs from the altar. And he touched my mouth and said: 'Behold, this has touched your lips; your guilt is taken away, and your sin atoned for.'" (Isaiah 6:6–7)

Why do you think Isaiah needed to know he was forgiven before he served God as a prophet?

72. Isaiah Said God's Messiah Would Come as the True Ruler

[from Isaiah]

Isaiah told Judah that God had a unique future for his special people. He declared that at the right time, God would remember them and fulfill his covenant promises to make a treasured family for himself (42:6).

God had promised he would make a great nation from Abraham's family that would be a blessing to all the nations of the world (Pixel 13). Isaiah prophesied that God would fulfill his promises through a child from King David's family, who would be born to a virgin woman (11:1–10; 7:14).

"For to us a child is born, to us a son is given; and the government shall be upon his shoulder, and his name shall be called Wonderful Counselor, Mighty God, Everlasting Father, Prince of Peace." (Isaiah 9:6)

Isaiah made his prophecies about seven hundred years before Jesus was born. Do you believe they came true?

73. Nahum Told Judah That Assyria Would Soon Be Conquered

[from Nahum]

Hosea's prophecy that Assyria would take the people of Israel into captivity came true! About one hundred years after Hosea's prophecy, Nahum told Judah that because Assyria had been so cruel and violent, God would allow another nation to conquer it. After destroying Israel, Assyria had attacked Judah but had not been able to defeat it. Nahum assured Judah that there was no longer anything to worry about from Assyria. The people of Judah could enjoy their lives because the cruel Assyrians would never attack them again. Judah, as part of God's special people, would have restored splendor as a nation.

Nahum focused on the fact that Assyria had rejected God so completely that God would bring that nation to an end. Historically, Assyria's fall began in 612 BC, when the Babylonians invaded the capital city, Nineveh, and completely destroyed it. The Babylonians finished the job in 605 BC, when they defeated the combined forces of the Egyptians and the remaining Assyrians in the Battle of Carchemish.

"There is no easing [Assyria's] hurt; your wound is grievous. All who hear the news about you clap their hands over you. For upon whom has not come your unceasing evil?" (Nahum 3:19)

Why should the words of a prophet be believed?

74. Zephaniah Told Judah to Prepare for God's Judgment Day
[from Zephaniah]

Nahum made clear that Assyria would not invade or conquer Judah. A few years later, the prophet Zephaniah was equally clear that if Judah did not repent and honor God, another enemy nation would invade and conquer it. Zephaniah's great-great-grandfather was Hezekiah, one of the good kings of Judah. Zephaniah knew the people in Judah had turned from God, and he warned that the day of the Lord was near.

Jerusalem had become a city of tyranny, much as it had been under the judges when, as Pixel 46 explained, "everyone did what was right in his own eyes" (Judges 21:25). The leaders acted like mean lions, the judges acted like hungry wolves, the prophets made reckless statements, and the priests dishonored God. Because of their disobedience, God said he would severely punish Judah. And that punishment would be terrifying.

God also promised that after the punishment, he would continue to be faithful to the covenant he had made with his people. He would restore the humble and those who sought and honored him. But until then, he would devour and destroy.

"At that time I will search Jerusalem with lamps, and I will punish the men who are complacent, those who say in their hearts, 'The Lord will not do good, nor will he do ill.'" (Zephaniah 1:12)

Does it surprise you that the people of Judah kept making the same mistakes?

75. Habakkuk Couldn't Believe God Would Use the Evil Babylonians to Punish Judah
[from Habakkuk]

After Zephaniah spoke to Judah, Habakkuk the prophet cried out to God. He was bewildered that some people in Judah had no respect for God's laws, and abused and mistreated others. It appeared that God paid no attention to these injustices. Then Habakkuk got some shocking news: God told him he would use the Babylonians to punish Judah! Habakkuk was in disbelief. The Babylonians were so evil that they had no respect for any other people or laws. Again, Habakkuk cried out to God. This time, his cry was with the pain of a member of God's family who knew harsh punishment was about to come.

God assured Habakkuk that Babylon would be punished in due time, but until then, he would use Babylon to punish Judah. The victory of Babylon over the Egyptians and Assyrians sealed its position as a dominant power (Pixel 73). When Babylon invaded Judah in 605 BC, it took some of the leaders into captivity. In 597 BC, Babylon invaded again and took more people captive, and in 586 BC, the Babylonians burned Jerusalem and took most of the survivors into exile.

Besides warning Judah of God's coming punishment through Babylon, Habakkuk also prepared the people of Judah to have confidence in God. He prophesied that after the time of punishment, God would remember his covenant with them, and they would be restored—a very similar message to Zephaniah's. But in order to live through the coming terrible times, Habakkuk told them, the righteous should live by their faith (2:4). He also said that loving, following, and honoring God was far superior to enjoying the material things they had and thought they needed.

"Though the fig tree should not blossom, nor fruit be on the vines, the produce of the olive fail and the fields yield no food, the flock be cut off from the fold and there be no herd in the stalls, yet I will rejoice in the Lord; I will take joy in the God of my salvation. God, the Lord, is my strength; he makes my feet like the deer's; he makes me tread on my high places." (Habakkuk 3:17–19)

Think back to the life of Job (Pixel 12). What did Job say he learned during his trials that is similar to what Habakkuk told Judah?

76. Obadiah Spoke to Edom and Judah about What It Means to Be Family

[from Obadiah]

Obadiah was God's prophet, who rebuked the country of Edom because it joined with another foreign nation in attacking Judah. This likely occurred just after Habakkuk's prophecy. If so, then Edom joined with Babylon to conquer Judah, rob Judah of its resources, and abuse its people. Obadiah told the people of Edom that they were deceived by their own arrogance and would be punished because of their country's violence against Judah. Edom would again be deceived, but this time by the nation with which it joined to fight Judah. So, in the end, just as Edom had betrayed its own family, it would be betrayed by its former ally. A few years after Babylon totally defeated Judah, Babylon decimated Edom.

Obadiah referred to Judah and Edom as family because these two nations came from the brothers Jacob and Esau, the twin sons of Isaac and Rebekah. As a nation, Judah had tried to be friendly with Edom, but Edom only responded to these gestures of goodwill with hatefulness.

"As you have done, it shall be done to you; your deeds shall return on your own head." (Obadiah, verse 15b)

What happens when you turn against those you are supposed to love?

77. Jeremiah Was the Last Prophet to Judah before the Babylonian Captivity

[from Jeremiah]

Jeremiah was a priest whom God appointed to tell the people of Judah that their punishment was about to happen. Jeremiah was only a young man when God called him. God promised to give Jeremiah the words to say (1:6–7). Jeremiah said that by intentionally and continuously turning away from God, the people of Judah were bringing judgment on themselves (5:3b; 2:17; 4:18).

God was appalled at how the prophets gave false prophesies, the priests ruled under their own authority, and the people loved having leaders who lied to them (5:30–31). Jerusalem had become a city known for oppression, greed, dishonest business dealings, and superficial claims of peace (6:14). Rather than being content as God's treasured people, those in Judah rejected God and worshiped idols just as their ancestors had done (11:13). God became so angry with Judah that he instructed Jeremiah not even to pray for its welfare (7:16; 11:14; 14:11).

The king and many officials hated Jeremiah so strongly for exposing their evil ways and telling them about God's judgment that they had him thrown in prison (37:15). They then had him put in the bottom of a well with no water, only mud (38:6). Had it not been for the kindness of one of the king's officials, who feared God and appealed to the king to save Jeremiah, the prophet would have died in the mud (38:8–13).

"An appalling and horrible thing has happened in the land: the prophets prophesy falsely, and the priests rule at their direction; my people love to have it so, but what will you do when the end comes?" (Jeremiah 5:30–31)

How do you think God felt when his covenant family continued to reject him?

***

CONNECTION 7

Jerusalem Was Destroyed and Judah Went into Exile in Babylon

The events happened just as Jeremiah and God's other prophets said they would. The Babylonians invaded Judah, attacked Jerusalem, and laid siege to the city for more than two years until they captured it in 586 BC. The people in Jerusalem suffered enormously during this war, and many were killed. As victors, the Babylonians demolished Jerusalem, leveled the temple, and burned what they could. We know from Jeremiah 39:11–14 that the Babylonians did not kill Jeremiah but instead gave him freedom. Many people believe this act of mercy toward Jeremiah allowed him to be the eyewitness who wrote the book of Lamentations (Pixel 78).

The Babylonians took most other survivors into captivity. Among those taken captive in earlier Babylonian invasions were Ezekiel, in 597 BC, and Daniel in 605 BC. In some of the following pixels, we will read more about these men who lived through this humiliating period.

Even with his people in exile, God continued to speak to them and love them, fulfilling his covenant promises. After the seventy years of captivity ended, God's people were allowed to return to Judah. The primary priests and prophets during the era of the return were Ezra, Haggai, Zechariah, Nehemiah, and Malachi, about whom we will also read in some of the following pixels.

***

78. All That Remained of Jerusalem Was a Lament

[from Lamentations]

The prophet Jeremiah is believed to have been the eyewitness to the destruction of Jerusalem and the survivor of the gruesome war who wrote about these events in the book of Lamentations. A series of five laments, the book is written in the form of intense and skillfully crafted poems, which express sadness and grief about this horrible loss and defeat. Lamentations gives a firsthand description of living through the terror of the war that resulted in the Babylonian conquest of Jerusalem.

During the long siege, life became miserable in Jerusalem. The city, once a jewel and the pride of Israel, became a wasteland. Judah was not only abandoned by its former allies and friends, but some of them also deceived Judah and even joined in the attack. Food and water were in short supply during the overthrow of the city. It was a brutal time. Some children died in their mothers' arms, and others died of starvation in the streets looking for food. Even worse, some parents were so antagonistic toward God that they killed their own children for food. The devastation was overwhelming. Jerusalem's political and religious leaders assumed God would protect them and the people, even though they lived in ways that dishonored God. They refused to follow his plans and instead followed their own selfish desires.

When the Babylonians arrived, they were fast, tough, and ruthless, killing young and old people alike. The Babylonians were fierce tools of God's wrath—his instrument of punishment for the sins of Jerusalem and Judah. The Babylonians went into the sanctuary of the temple—forbidden to anyone but the Jews—and completely destroyed it. They also burned what remained of the city.

Yet in the midst of reporting this horror, Jeremiah stopped. In some of the most well-known verses in the Bible, he pointed to God as the ultimate basis for hope and provision: "But this I call to mind, and therefore I have hope: The steadfast love of the Lord never ceases; his mercies never come to an end; they are new every morning; great is your faithfulness" (3:21–23). This statement of hope did not prevent any further devastation, but the words offer a realistic and God-honoring perspective on the events.

"The Lord has become like an enemy; he has swallowed up Israel; he has swallowed up all its palaces; he has laid in ruin its strongholds, and he has multiplied in the daughter of Judah mourning and lamentation." (Lamentations 2:5)

Do you think God has any reason to direct his wrath and anger toward you?

79. God Promised to Make a New Covenant with Israel and Judah

[from Jeremiah]

Jeremiah was in Jerusalem when he wrote a letter to the exiles in Babylon to assure them God had not forgotten them. He told them the punishment would last for seventy years (29:10). During their exile in Babylon, they were to carry on with their normal lives—working, raising families, and worshiping God. They were to have confidence that God had good plans for their future (29:11).

Jeremiah also assured the exiles that God would establish a new covenant with the houses of Israel and Judah. In this new covenant, God would not give his laws in written form, as he did with the Ten Commandments, but instead put them in the hearts of his special and treasured family (31:31–34). The new covenant of which Jeremiah spoke would be the fulfillment of God's original covenant with Abraham, to whom he had promised a countless number of descendants, through whom he would bless the entire world (Genesis 12:1–3). In Luke 22:19–20 in the New Testament, Jesus said he came to complete the implementation of the new covenant when he gave himself up for us— the "once-for-all" sacrifice who secured for us "an eternal redemption," as Hebrews 9:11–15 describes.

"Behold, the days are coming, declares the Lord, when I will make a new covenant with the house of Israel and the house of Judah . . . I will put my law within them, and I will write it on their hearts. And I will be their God, and they shall be my people." (Jeremiah 31:31, 33b)

Do you find it hard to wait, even when you know things will turn out well?

80. Ezekiel Was a Priest Taken Captive in Babylon

[from Ezekiel]

God's people were being punished as prisoners in Babylon. They wondered how long their captivity would last. They also wondered what would happen to them when the captivity ended.

God instructed Ezekiel to give this message to the captives in Babylon: God would fulfill his promises, given through Jeremiah, to restore them and build his covenant family. God would continue to use other nations to punish his people, but he would eventually allow his people to return to Jerusalem, rebuild the temple and the city, and ultimately be led into his new covenant.

To emphasize God's intention for his people to be restored, God gave Ezekiel a vision of a valley full of dry bones. He asked Ezekiel if the bones could ever come back to life. Ezekiel answered respectfully, saying only God knew. Then God answered that he would put his Spirit in his people and bring them back to life (37:1–14). God also said these reborn people would have new hearts—not cold, hardened hearts of stone, rebellious against him and his ways, but new hearts of warmth and life, truly living hearts that would be directed by God's Spirit (36:26–27).

"And I will put my Spirit within you, and you shall live, and I will place you in your own land. Then you shall know that I am the Lord; I have spoken, and I will do it,' declares the Lord." (Ezekiel 37:14)

Have you ever had a problem so big that you could not see how God could make anything good come from it?

81. Daniel and His Three Friends Were Captives in Babylon but Stayed Faithful to God
[from Daniel 1–2]

The Babylonians were shrewd rulers who knew they could better control their captives if they used some of them as leaders. The Babylonians also knew some of the captives might be smart enough to help the Babylonian government work better.

Daniel was a teenager when taken to Babylon as a prisoner of war in 605 BC. He and three of his friends were required to go into service for the Babylonian government as high-level officials. But in their new roles, they refused to worship the gods of Babylon. They remained devoted to the one true God and made up their minds to follow him. God answered their prayers and gave them intelligence and wisdom. In particular, God gave Daniel the ability to understand and interpret dreams and visions.

Daniel interpreted a dream for Nebuchadnezzar, an extremely prideful king of Babylon. The king's dream was about four different kingdoms that would govern that part of the world. The first was Nebuchadnezzar's government, which would be followed by the three others. The last kingdom would be destroyed by a rock that increased in size and covered the entire earth (2:34–35). When Daniel finished interpreting the dream, Nebuchadnezzar praised and worshiped Daniel's God as the greatest of all gods

(2:46–47). Recognizing Daniel's great insight and abilities, King Nebuchadnezzar then made Daniel an administrator over the entire nation, as well as chief of all his wise counselors. He also made Daniel's three friends administrators over Babylon.

"[Nebuchadnezzar] answered and said to Daniel, 'Truly your God is God of gods and Lord of kings, and a revealer of mysteries, for you have been able to reveal this mystery." (Daniel 2:47)

What kind of religious training do you think Daniel and his three friends had as young men in Judah?

82. Daniel's Three Friends Served the King, but Other Officials Hated Them

[from Daniel 3]

Turning from his previous acknowledgment of God's supremacy, King Nebuchadnezzar made an enormous image of gold; he ordered everyone to worship it, or else they would be burned to death in a large furnace.

Some of the officials hated Daniel's three friends, who served with him in the king's administration. These officials reported to Nebuchadnezzar that Daniel's friends did not worship the golden idol. The king was so furious that he had the furnace heated extra hot before they were thrown in. After sending them into the furnace, the king looked in and saw the three men still alive; he also saw a fourth man in the furnace with them. God performed a miracle, sending his angel to protect Daniel's friends so that they emerged unharmed. In fact, they did not even smell like the burning of a fire!

"If this be so, our God whom we serve is able to deliver us from the burning fiery furnace, and he will deliver us out of your hand, O king. But if not, be it known to you, O king, that we will not serve your gods or worship the golden image that you have set up." (Daniel 3:17–18)

Do you expect that other people will always understand you when you live in a way that honors God first?

83. Daniel Served the King, but Other Officials Hated Him

[from Daniel 5:31–6:28]

During the Jewish people's exile in Babylon, the combined forces of the Medes and the Persians conquered the nation of Babylon. The leader of the newly-installed government was Cyrus. Many understand him to be the same person referenced as "Darius" in Daniel 5:31 and 11:1. He was also the leader prophesied by Isaiah 150 years earlier to overthrow the Babylonians (Isaiah 41:25; 44:28-45:4; 46:11; 48:15).

When Cyrus first started to rule, he was so impressed with Daniel's work that he intended to make Daniel the chief administrator over the entire nation of Babylon. The other administrators resented Daniel and tried to keep him out of the top job. They knew that Daniel, in his work as an official, was totally honest and did superior work. These administrators realized the only way to discredit him would be by his worship of God.

They conspired to get Cyrus to make a law that required everyone to worship Cyrus. If anyone refused, that person would be thrown into a den of hungry lions. Of course, Daniel did not obey this new law but instead kept worshiping God. The conspirators reported his disloyalty to the king. Daniel was thrown to the lions, but another miracle happened. God sent an angel to calm the lions, so Daniel was not hurt at all during the night he spent with them. The next morning, the king had Daniel brought out of the lions' den, safe and unharmed. The king punished the conspirators for their hateful trickery by throwing *them* to the lions. The lions killed these officials before they even landed at the bottom of the pit.

"Then the king commanded, and Daniel was brought and cast into the den of lions. The king declared to Daniel, 'May your God, whom you serve continually, deliver you!'" (Daniel 6:16)

Can you trust God's presence with you when something really bad happens?

PART FOUR

God Restored His People to the Homeland

Books of the Bible Discussed in This Part:

Daniel, Ezra, Haggai, Zechariah, Esther, Nehemiah, Malachi

3rd Captivity: Temple Destroyed; Judah Fell to Babylon		Cyrus' Decree for Jews to Return to Judah		Temple Construction Stopped		
Daniel					*Haggai*	*Zechariah*
586 BC	539	538	536	530		520
	Babylon Fell to Cyrus		Second Temple's Construction Began			Temple Construction Continued

Temple Completed		Ezra to Jerusalem		Jerusalem's Walls Rebuilt	
	Esther	*Ezra*	*Nehemiah*		*Malachi*
516	479	458	445	444	430
	Esther as Queen of Babylon		Nehemiah to Jersualem		Malachi as Prophet

CONNECTION 8

A Remnant of God's People
Returned to Jerusalem after Exile

The time for the punishment of God's people was completed. God would fulfill the promise given through Jeremiah. As discussed in Pixel 83, the Medes and the Persians conquered Babylon. Then God moved the hearts of the new rulers to let the captives go back to Judah. What do you think God had to do with the rulers' decisions? Read carefully to explore the answer to this question.

Much of what we know about God's people leaving Babylon after seventy years comes from some of the shortest books in the Bible. These books are in different parts of the Bible rather than side by side. However, we will follow them—as we have done with the rest of the Old Testament—in the order in which their events happened. Daniel provides the transition to the first six chapters of Ezra; from there, we will move to Haggai, Zechariah, and Esther, before returning to the last four chapters of Ezra, which discuss the time Ezra actually was in Jerusalem. Then we will go to Nehemiah, and finally to Malachi, the last book in the Old Testament.

Because not every person taken captive from Israel and Judah returned from Babylon, we often speak of those who did return as the "remnant" of God's people. Also, as we discussed earlier, the Northern Kingdom was originally called Israel, but after the Assyrians invaded and mixed up the population, the southern portion of it was called Samaria. As the Babylonian captivity ended, the people who returned went primarily to the northern portion of Judah (the Southern Kingdom), an area within modern-day Israel.

***

84. Ezra and Daniel Wrote about the First Group to Return to Judah

[from Ezra 1–2 and Daniel 5:31–11:1]

Ezra, a priest, wrote that in the first year of the reign of King Cyrus, 538 BC, God "stirred up the spirit of Cyrus" to issue the order for Jews to return to Jerusalem and rebuild the temple (Ezra 1:1–4). This group was led by men named Sheshbazzar and Zerubbabel. The king gave these returning exiles some of the elegant utensils and dishes that were taken from the temple during the earlier invasions so they could use them in the new temple. About fifty thousand people made this trip from Babylon to Jerusalem. This means two million to three million Jewish exiles remained in Babylon and its provinces.

Other interesting events happened during the first year of Cyrus' rule. That was the year Cyrus threw Daniel into the lions' den, confident that Daniel's God would save him, as he did. When Daniel came out alive, Cyrus acknowledged the power of Daniel's God. That was the year Daniel said he knew from Jeremiah's letter that the captivity would last for seventy years. After reading the prophet's words, Daniel said, "Then I turned my face to the Lord God, seeking him by prayer and pleas for mercy with fasting and sackcloth and ashes" (Daniel 9:3). That was the year an angel said to Daniel in a vision, "I stood up to confirm and strengthen" Cyrus (Daniel 11:1b).

"Thus says Cyrus king of Persia: The Lord, the God of heaven, has given me all the kingdoms of the earth, and he has charged me to build him a house at Jerusalem, which is in Judah." (Ezra 1:2)

Daniel was faithful to God and served Cyrus with respect and diligence. Do you think this had anything to do with Cyrus deciding it was time for God to be worshiped again in his temple in Jerusalem?

85. Zerubbabel Led in Building the Temple's Foundation, but Then Work Stopped
[from Ezra 3–6]

Zerubbabel, who was in King David's family line, led the people in rebuilding the temple in Jerusalem. First, they built an altar for the new temple. An altar was the priority because it was necessary for properly offering sacrifices in worship. God gave Moses extremely detailed instructions about offerings and sacrifices (Pixel 38), which required an altar. Zerubbabel—living about eight hundred years after those instructions were given—knew this; therefore, the altar was the place to start when rebuilding the temple.

Some of the non-Israelite people who had moved to Jerusalem and the surrounding area during the Babylonian captivity knew that once the altar was built, the reconstruction of the entire temple was imminent. These people feared that the Israelites' return to Jerusalem and reestablishment of the place to worship God meant trouble for them. So as Zerubbabel and the Israelites finished the altar and then set to work on the foundation of the new temple, their enemies tried to stop them. These enemies went so far as to write to the Babylonian king Artaxerxes, who came after Cyrus, making false accusations against Zerubbabel and his workers. The king agreed with the enemies of Israel. Thus, soon after the foundation was completed, the king ordered the work on the new temple to stop.

"And I made a decree, and search has been made, and it has been found that this city from of old has risen against kings, and that rebellion and sedition have been made in it. And mighty kings have been over Jerusalem, who ruled over the whole province Beyond the River, to whom tribute, custom, and toll were paid. Therefore make a decree that these men be made to cease, and that this city be not rebuilt, until a decree is made by me." (Ezra 4:19–21)

Why do you think God allowed his enemies to halt construction of the temple?

86. Haggai Told the Israelites to Get Back to Work on the Temple
[from Haggai]

King Artaxerxes ordered the construction to stop, and Zerubbabel and the Israelites, for their part, made no effort to move ahead with it. In fact, most people used the king's order as an excuse to ignore the temple and focus on their personal finances and plans instead.

Haggai was a prophet who left Babylon with Zerubbabel to return to Judah. God appointed Haggai to declare that God wanted the people to complete the rebuild, after not working on the temple for about fourteen years. At the same time, another prophet, named Zechariah, assured the people that God expected them to go right to work and rebuild the temple (Zechariah 6:15). The people responded to the messages of Haggai and Zechariah, and the temple was completed in about three and a half years.

"You looked for much, and behold, it came to little. And when you brought it home, I blew it away. Why? declares the Lord of hosts. Because of my house that lies in ruins, while each of you busies himself with his own house. Therefore the heavens above you have withheld the dew, and the earth has withheld its produce." (Haggai 1:9–10)

Have ever known in your heart what God wanted you to do, but you first ignored him and instead did what you wanted to do?

87. Zechariah Encouraged the People to Build the Temple

[from Zechariah]

Like Haggai, Zechariah was a prophet who returned to Judah with Zerubbabel's group. God instructed Haggai to give the people a strong and sharp rebuke for putting their personal interests ahead of God's plans for the new temple. Then God directed Zechariah to give a message of hope and encouragement. Zechariah reminded the people that only through God's strength would the temple be completed: "Not by might, nor by power, but by my Spirit, says the Lord of hosts" (4:6b).

Zechariah said the temple was important for the people and their worship of God. But even more than that, the temple would represent what God planned to do throughout history. God's big plan, the one he promised Abraham, was to create a special family to be his very own for all eternity. He continued to work out this plan, year by year, generation by generation.

"Sing and rejoice, O daughter of Zion, for behold, I come and I will dwell in your midst, declares the Lord. And many nations shall join themselves to the Lord in that day, and shall be my people. And I will dwell in your midst, and you shall know that the Lord of hosts has sent me to you." (Zechariah 2:10–11)

Do you want to know more about what it means to be part of God's treasured family and live with him forever?

88. Esther Served God in Babylon and Saved God's People through Obedience

[from Esther]

Back in Babylon, life went on for the Jews as it had during the early part of the exile—that is, until an incident occurred involving the king. (God's people came to be called *Jews* during their time in Babylon, as a shortened word for Judah, the primary tribe of Israel taken into captivity and the family tribe of King David.) King Ahasuerus became furious when his wife refused to dance for him and his guests at one of his big parties. He divorced her and sent her off into seclusion. But then the king needed a new wife to be the queen.

After a long search by his assistants, the king chose a young woman named Esther to be his wife and the queen. However, no one in the king's palace knew she was Jewish. About four years after she became queen, the king's chief assistant, Haman, decided he hated the Jewish people. He was so despicable that he tricked the king into signing an order allowing the Jews to be killed. Esther's cousin, Mordecai, learned of this evil plot and reported it to Esther, urging her to appeal to the king. Esther knew that if she approached the king without his invitation, she could be killed. But she and Mordecai also knew that God wanted to preserve his people and not allow them to be destroyed. It was under the direction of Cyrus and the leadership of Zerubbabel about sixty years earlier that many Jews had returned to Jerusalem and the temple rebuilt. So Mordecai urged Esther to tell the king he had been deceived and ask him to save the Jewish people. The queen called on her family and friends to fast with her for three days before she approached the king.

When Esther asked for an audience with the king, he was pleased to see her. She told him about Haman's scheme, and he was shocked. The king issued orders permitting the Jewish people to defend and save themselves, for Haman to be killed, and for Mordecai to take Haman's position.

"For if you [Esther] keep silent at this time, relief and deliverance will rise for the Jews from another place, but you and your father's house will perish. And who knows whether you have not come to the kingdom for such a time as this?" (Esther 4:14)

Have you ever had something happen that made you so happy that you did not want to do anything to risk losing it?

89. Ezra Became the Teacher in Jerusalem
[from Ezra 7–10]

The Jews in Babylon were saved by the courageous obedience of Esther and those who supported her in fasting. God's clear message was that he would keep and maintain his special people. The temple had been rebuilt in Jerusalem. Now the question remained: Did those who lived in Jerusalem know and understand what it meant to truly honor and worship God? In the last four chapters of the book of Ezra, God provided an answer.

Still living in Babylon, the priest Ezra had a passion to know, understand, live, and teach God's laws. The king granted Ezra's request to be given everything he needed to take a few thousand Jews back to Jerusalem. When he and his group arrived in Jerusalem, he found the same sickening spiritual dullness that had existed before the exile to Babylon. So he turned to God. He prayed, confessed, and asked for forgiveness. Then God moved in the hearts of the people, and they joined with Ezra in confessing their sins to God and asking for forgiveness. People were confronted with the truth about

God and his good law. They responded by changing their lives in a spirit of revival.

"For Ezra had set his heart to study the Law of the Lord, and to do it and to teach his statutes and rules in Israel." (Ezra 7:10)

What have you set in your heart to accomplish?

90. Nehemiah Anguished over the Disgrace of God's People
[from Nehemiah 1:1–2:10]

Meanwhile, back in Babylon, a devout Jewish man named Nehemiah was the chief assistant to the king. His brother, Hanani, had been with Ezra and Zerubbabel in Jerusalem. About twelve years after Ezra confronted the people with God's command to obey and worship him, Hanani went back to Babylon. He and some others reported to Nehemiah that Jerusalem was still in terrible condition. The city walls and gates that Zerubbabel and his group started building had been destroyed by enemies under the authority of an earlier king. The people were in great distress, and the city was a disgrace. Life in Jerusalem was not safe, and the pitiful situation of the people was an embarrassment to God's honor.

This news about Jerusalem hurt Nehemiah deeply. He went off by himself for a few days and cried before God in fasting and prayer. He confessed his personal sins and those of God's people. He prayed for God's hand to direct him in the proper response. Later, when Nehemiah was back at work, the king asked him why he had such sadness in his heart. In fear, Nehemiah quickly prayed for God's power. Then he told the king about the terrible condition of his homeland and the people there. The king immediately offered to help. Nehemiah asked for permission to take a group to Jerusalem to rebuild the city walls and restore Jerusalem to a place of honor for God's people. The king agreed, and sent Nehemiah to be the governor of Judah. With him, he sent supplies and the authority to use timber from the king's forest.

"And I said 'O Lord God of heaven, the great and awesome God who keeps covenant and steadfast love with those who love him and keep his commandments, let your ear be attentive and your eyes open, to hear the prayer of your servant that I now pray before you day and night for the people of Israel your servants, confessing the sins of the people of Israel, which we have sinned against you. Even I and my father's house have sinned.'" (Nehemiah 1:5–6)

Why did Nehemiah feel so bad, and what did he do about it?

91. God Used Nehemiah to Rebuild Jerusalem's Walls

[from Nehemiah 2:11–13:31]

When Nehemiah arrived in Jerusalem, he conducted himself with the same attitude he had in Babylon. He respected others, lived in a way that was above reproach, and exercised incredibly effective leadership. He called together the leaders in Jerusalem and encouraged them to work on rebuilding the walls. He assured them that God would grant success. When some people used the wall-building project to make money, he confronted them; they repented and began using their energy to build the wall for God's honor. When enemies threatened to attack and destroy the wall, the people took turns working while others stood guard to protect their work. Some people even did their jobs with one hand while holding a weapon in the other.

But many people became so afraid of an attack by enemies that Nehemiah feared the work would stop again. Nehemiah convinced them to keep working by reminding them of God's promise. God wanted the walls rebuilt, and he intended for Judah's respectability as a nation to be restored. The protective walls around Jerusalem that had been in ruins for almost 150 years were rebuilt in fifty-two days in 444 BC. When the work on the walls was finished, everyone rejoiced. They gathered in a large assembly to hear Ezra read from the books of God's law. People responded with sincere confession and true worship of God.

Nehemiah served as governor of Judah for a few more years, until the king called him back to serve him in Babylon. During Nehemiah's absence, many people turned away from honoring God. God appointed Malachi as a prophet to once again challenge the people to seek him.

"And I looked and arose and said to the nobles and to the officials and to the rest of the people, 'Do not be afraid of them. Remember the Lord, who is great and awesome, and fight for your brothers, your sons, your daughters, your wives and your homes.'"
(Nehemiah 4:14)

Does anything in this pixel remind you of these words from Psalm 23:4 "Even though I walk through the valley of the shadow of death, I will fear no evil, for you are with me; your rod and your staff, they comfort me"?

92. Malachi Confronted People with God's Truth

[from Malachi 1–2]

Without Nehemiah's positive leadership, many people returned to some of the same self-centered patterns of living that Haggai, Zechariah, Ezra, and Nehemiah had confronted earlier. Even though these people suffered many years of captivity in Babylon as exiles, they repeated the same cycle of following God, then rejecting him, following, rejecting—and on and on.

God appointed Malachi as a prophet to rebuke the priests and the people about their unfaithfulness. Instead of offering healthy animals as sacrifices, they offered sick animals. They complained about how much trouble it was to worship God. The priests turned away from God and set bad examples. People dealt treacherously with each other, so that no one could trust anyone else. People cheated each other in business.

Sadly, many men abandoned their wives and destroyed God's covenant families. Divorce in the human family showed disrespect for the covenant faithfulness God showed his people. Malachi told them that God in fact *hates* divorce—strong but fitting words for the destruction of a relationship intended to reflect his own relationship with his people (2:16).

"You have wearied the Lord with your words. But you say, 'How have we wearied him?' By saying, 'Everyone who does evil is good in the sight of the Lord, and he delights in them.' Or by asking, 'Where is the God of justice?'" (Malachi 2:17)

Why do you think it is so difficult to live in a way that honors God?

93. Malachi Said God's Messenger Would Announce the Lord's Coming
[from Malachi 3–4]

Malachi ended the Old Testament with a clear prophecy about God's plans for the future. Malachi warned that judgment would come promptly and strongly on those who continued to reject God's good life for them. Many people failed to honor God with proper offerings. Many people abused their workers by not paying them honest wages, and many were deceitful in their relationships. Many people were arrogant, thinking that they, instead of God, were in control of their own lives and property. In these and more ways, the people failed to fulfill God's covenant plan to be a blessing to the nations.

Malachi said God would send his messenger to prepare the way for God's coming (3:1). Malachi asked who would be able to stand before the Lord on that day. It certainly would not be those who rejected him. Rather, it would be those whom the Lord calls "mine," and those whom he has prepared for his own possession.

"They shall be mine, says the Lord of hosts, in the day when I make up my treasured possession, and I will spare them as a man spares his son who serves him. Then once more you shall see the distinction between the righteous and the wicked, between one who serves God and one who does not serve him." (Malachi 3:17–18)

Does it seem that God has a permanent remedy to the historical problem of his people never following him completely?

REFLECTION 7
God's A-Team and the End of the Old Testament

As the last book of the Old Testament, Malachi brings to a climax all that we have read about so far.

God's A-Team of Leaders and Prophets

The groups that returned to Jerusalem to rebuild the temple and the walls of the city had not only the king's blessing, but God's A-Team of leaders and prophets. Zerubbabel, Ezra, and Nehemiah encouraged and led the rebuilding of the temple and walls. Back in Babylon, Daniel and Esther were Jews who held some of the highest positions of leadership. The prophets Haggai, Zechariah, and Malachi pointed people away from their selfish desires to the wonders of God's love and provision. Yet people acted just as their ancestors had done for centuries. Wasn't God's A-team enough to lead people back to him and help them maintain their relationship with him, living lives that fully honored him?

Is Continuous Faithfulness to God Even Possible?

Is God powerful enough to call and set apart his own people, and then keep them on the right track? Or is human nature so strongly inclined to turn from God that even he cannot overcome it?

After Malachi, there were no more prophets for about four hundred years. God was silent. His people continued to reject him, and as a nation, they fell under the political control of one foreign government after the other, until finally they were subjects of Rome.

Out with the Heart of Stone, In with the Heart of Flesh

What possibly could or would God do to remedy this continuous downward human spiral? Read carefully as we move into the New Testament. Listen to the message of Jesus there, and consider how it fits with this message from Ezekiel:

"And I will give them one heart, and a new spirit I will put within them. I will remove the heart of stone from their flesh and give them a heart of flesh, that they may walk in my statutes and keep my rules and obey them. And they shall be my people, and I will be their God." (Ezekiel 11:19–20)

It's a Person and Nothing Else!

So after all, does knowing, following, and honoring God happen because we have a special place to worship, live, or work? We will see in the New Testament that what really makes the difference is not a place, but a person.

Malachi said God would send his messenger. And then John the Baptist came. Was he the messenger of whom Malachi spoke? But wait—if John the Baptist was the messenger, then what, or who, was the message?

Jesus is the message! And now, as we enter the New Testament, you will read about him and how he makes it possible for us to have a new heart.

PART FIVE

The Coming of Jesus

Books of the Bible Discussed in This Part:

Luke, Matthew

Malachi as
Prophet

430 BC		6/5

John the
Baptist's
Birth

Jesus' Birth			Jesus' Baptism
5/4 BC	Anno Domino (AD; in the year of our Lord)	7/8	27/30
		Jesus Age 12 at the Temple	

94. Gabriel Told Zechariah His Son, John, Would Be the Messenger

[from Luke 1:1–25]

Malachi prophesied four hundred years earlier that a messenger would come to prepare the way for the Messiah. No one knew when or where this would happen. But one of God's priests, Zechariah, and his wife, Elizabeth, knew that they would love to have a child. Even though they were elderly, they prayed that God would do this for them. Regardless of how God answered their prayer, and the deep yearning of their hearts, both of them were faithful to God and followed the requirements of the law.

One day, while Zechariah was doing his most special duties as a priest, the angel Gabriel came and spoke to him. Gabriel declared to Zechariah that God would answer his prayer for a child and that Elizabeth would have a son. This son, to be named John, would not be an ordinary child or person; John would be the messenger of whom Malachi the prophet spoke. Elizabeth was so excited when she became pregnant that she stayed in seclusion for the first five months of her pregnancy.

"And he will turn many of the children of Israel to the Lord their God, and he will go before him in the spirit and power of Elijah, to turn the hearts of the fathers to the children, and the disobedient to the wisdom of the just, to make ready for the Lord a people prepared." (Luke 1:16–17)

How did God use the faithful prayers of Zechariah and Elizabeth for a child of their own to fulfill his plans?

95. Gabriel Told Mary Her Son, Jesus, Would Be the Messiah

[from Luke 1:26–56]

Besides the Malachi prophecy discussed in Pixel 94, devout Jews knew of many prophecies stating that God would send the Messiah. King David was told there would be a ruler on his throne forever. Micah said that God's true ruler would be born in Bethlehem. Isaiah wrote that the Messiah would come from David's family and be born to a virgin.

Mary was not married, but she was engaged to Joseph. They lived in Nazareth. Both of their families traced their ancestry back to King David. One day, when nothing else special was happening, the angel Gabriel spoke to Mary. He assured her that she had

found favor with God and would have a son, who would be called the "Son of the Most High" (1:32). This son, to be named Jesus, would have a kingdom that would never end. Mary was very puzzled about how she could have a child while she was still a virgin and before she and Joseph were married. Gabriel said that the Holy Spirit would come to her in a special way, in the power of the Most High, so that her child would be holy and called the Son of God.

Elizabeth and Mary were cousins. After hearing Gabriel's message, Mary went to stay with Elizabeth and Zechariah for a few months. When Mary arrived, Elizabeth's developing child moved in her womb. Elizabeth exclaimed about how wonderfully Mary had been blessed. Then Mary sang a song of praise to God, telling of her trust in him and how she rejoiced in him. Mary's song is known as the *Magnificat* because she began with praising God for how magnificent he is.

"And the angel said to her, 'Do not be afraid, Mary, for you have found favor with God. And behold, you will conceive in your womb and bear a son, and you shall call his name Jesus.'" (Luke 1:30–31)

Why do you think Mary found favor with God? Does anything about her remind you of Job (Pixel 12) and Noah (Pixel 8)?

96. An Angel Told Joseph to Marry Mary

[from Matthew 1:18–25]

During their engagement, Joseph realized that Mary was pregnant. He knew he was not the father of the child. Because Joseph lived in a way that honored God and his principles, Joseph decided to cancel the engagement secretly so that Mary would not be disgraced.

As Joseph was thinking about how to get out of his engagement with Mary, an angel of God came to him in a dream. The angel confirmed that Joseph should not be afraid to marry Mary, because her child had been conceived by the Holy Spirit (1:20). The angel instructed Joseph to name the child Jesus, and told him that Jesus would save God's people from their sins (1:21). Joseph obeyed the angel. He married Mary but kept her a virgin until after Jesus was born.

"But as he considered these things, behold, an angel of the Lord appeared to him in a dream, saying, 'Joseph, son of David, do not fear to take Mary as your wife, for that

which is conceived in her is from the Holy Spirit. She will bear a son, and you shall call his name Jesus, for he will save his people from their sins.'" (Matthew 1:20–21)

Why did angels tell both Mary and Joseph to name the boy Jesus?

***

CONNECTION 9

The Four Gospels Teach about Jesus' Life and Ministry

The first four books of the New Testament—Matthew, Mark, Luke, and John—together are known as the Gospels. All four Gospels tell us about Jesus. While there is some overlap of information, each book reported about Jesus from a different perspective, with a somewhat different audience in mind.

Matthew gave an eyewitness account as one of the twelve apostles, the group Jesus chose to train as his closest associates, who would continue his work after his death. Matthew's primary audience was the Jews. His writing assumed familiarity with Jewish laws, traditions, worship practices, and the Old Testament, particularly the parts telling about the Messiah. Matthew wanted his readers to understand that Jesus was the long-expected Messiah.

Mark was not an eyewitness to Jesus' life, but he was a close assistant to and associate of Peter, who was, like Matthew, one of the twelve apostles and among Jesus' three best friends, along with James and John. Mark wrote primarily to people in Rome to give them succinct, action-packed insights into Jesus' life and ministry.

Luke, like Mark, was not an eyewitness to the life and resurrection of Jesus, but he traveled with and assisted Paul, who was God's chosen Apostle to the Gentiles (non-Jewish people). As a medical doctor, Luke applied his skills (e.g., being very methodical and meticulous) toward writing a carefully researched book that would appeal to Gentile readers. The Gospel of Luke gives a detailed account of Jesus' life. Luke also wrote the book of Acts, which follows John's Gospel. The quality of his writing is superb.

John was an eyewitness to Jesus' life and resurrection, one of the twelve apostles, and an especially close friend to Jesus. His Gospel strongly focused on affirming the divinity of Jesus—the true Messiah, sent from God, who *was* and *is* God. John's main audience included both Jews and Gentiles who did not live in Israel.

Pixels 97–134 are taken from all four Gospels in historical sequence of the events' occurrence.

***

97. The Roman Caesar Ordered a Census

[from Luke 2:1–5]

The nation of Israel and its Jewish inhabitants were ruled by Rome. The head of the Roman government was known as Caesar. The Caesar at this time was Augustus, and he wanted to know how many people were under his control. Tabulating this number required that everyone under Roman rule go to the town of their original family and be counted by government officials. This counting process was known as the census.

Because both Mary and Joseph were from King David's family, they had to travel from their home in Nazareth to Bethlehem. It didn't matter that the journey would be hard for Mary, who was pregnant with Jesus; they had to obey the orders of the Roman government.

"And Joseph also went up from Galilee, from the town of Nazareth, to Judea, to the city of David, which is called Bethlehem, because he was of the house and lineage of David, to be registered with Mary, his betrothed, who was with child." (Luke 2:4–5)

How did God use the selfish plans of Caesar to fulfill the prophecy we read about in Micah (Pixel 70) for Jesus to be born in Bethlehem?

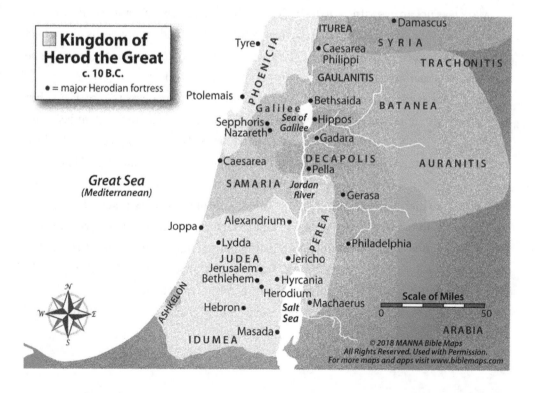

98. Jesus Was Born in Bethlehem

[from Luke 2:6–20]

When Joseph and Mary arrived in Bethlehem, there was no place for them to rent a room because so many other people were there for the census. However, someone offered to let them stay in a stable that was normally for the animals. When Jesus was born, Mary let him sleep in the manger—the trough for the animals' dry food.

Soon after Jesus was born, an angel appeared to shepherds in a nearby field as they were tending a flock of sheep. The angel assured the shepherds they should not be afraid. Rather, the angel told them, they should be excited, because the Savior, Jesus, had just been born in Bethlehem. Then the sky filled with a great number of angels, who sang praises to God. When all the angels left, the shepherds went immediately to Bethlehem to see the baby Jesus. They found him in the manger and repeated what the angel told them. Then the shepherds went back to their fields and their sheep. Mary pondered carefully what the shepherds had said.

"When the angels went away from them into heaven, the shepherds said to one another, 'Let us go over to Bethlehem and see this thing that has happened, which the Lord has made known to us.' And they went with haste and found Mary and Joseph, and the baby lying in a manger." (Luke 2:15–16)

Why do you think God allowed his own Son to be born in such humble circumstances?

99. Wise Men Followed a Star and Searched for Jesus

[from Matthew 2:1–12]

Herod was appointed by the Roman government to rule over Israel as its king. Some important travelers described as *magi*, or wise men, from a distant country in the East went to Herod's palace. They reported that they had been following an unusual star from their country that would lead them to the King of the Jews. They asked King Herod for directions to this newborn king so they could go and worship him.

Herod was troubled by the magi's questions, so he asked the religious leaders for help. The religious leaders explained to Herod that one of their prophets had said the Messiah would be born in Bethlehem. King Herod shared this information with the travelers and sent them on their way, instructing them to look for the child king and report back to him when they found him. When the magi arrived in Bethlehem, the star stopped moving, and they found Jesus with his parents living in a house. The visitors fell to the ground and worshiped the child, and then gave him unique and special gifts of gold, frankincense, and myrrh.

"Now after Jesus was born in Bethlehem of Judea in the days of Herod the king, behold, wise men from the east came to Jerusalem, saying, 'Where is he who has been born king of the Jews? For we saw his star when it rose and have come to worship him.'" (Matthew 2:1–2)

The religious leaders knew from the prophet Micah that the Messiah was to be born in Bethlehem. Why do you think they did not go with the travelers to find the Messiah and worship him?

100. At Age Twelve Jesus Went to Jerusalem with His Family for Passover
[from Luke 2:41–52]

An important part of being a faithful Jew was to travel from one's home to Jerusalem every year to celebrate the Feast of the Passover. When Jesus was twelve years old, he went with his parents from Nazareth to Jerusalem for Passover. At the end of the feast, his parents left Jerusalem with the group from Nazareth.

They assumed Jesus was also with the departing crowd. After traveling for a day, however, they did not find him with their friends. So Joseph and Mary hurried back to Jerusalem to look for Jesus. Three long and extremely anxious days later, they found him in the temple. He was sitting with the religious teachers, "listening to them and asking them questions . . . [a]nd all who heard him were amazed at his understanding and his answers" (2:46b–47). Mary scolded Jesus for being rude to her and Joseph and causing them to worry about him. But Jesus was surprised that she did not know he needed to be at the temple. Jesus, without intending any disrespect to his father Joseph, referred to the temple as his "Father's house." Even at this early age, Jesus was aware of his deity and his special relationship to God the Father.

"And he said to them, 'Why were you looking for me? Did you not know that I must be in my Father's house?'" (Luke 2:49)

What did Jesus mean by saying he had to be in his Father's house?

101. John Preached Repentance and Baptized Jesus

[from Matthew 3:1–17]

When Jesus became an adult, he visited John, his cousin and the child of Zechariah and Elizabeth. The Bible does not give us any details about the relationship of Jesus and John as children growing up. But when John became an adult, he became the messenger who proclaimed that the Messiah was coming (3:2–3). John told the people of Israel to turn from their sins and live in a way that showed their repentance was sincere. As a sign of repentance after confession of sin, John baptized those who repented by immersing them in the Jordan River. John came to be known as John the Baptist.

Jesus asked John to baptize him. At first, John refused. John knew Jesus was the Messiah and did not have any sin, so he had no need to repent. However, Jesus insisted on being baptized. Jesus knew that being baptized would fulfill prophecies, and it would also show people that he identified with them. When Jesus came out of the water after his baptism, God appeared as a dove and spoke.

"And when Jesus was baptized, immediately he went up from the water, and behold, the heavens were opened to him, and he saw the Spirit of God descending like a dove and coming to rest on him; and behold, a voice from heaven said, 'This is my beloved Son, with whom I am well pleased.'" (Matthew 3:16–17)

What does repenting of sin mean to you?

PART SIX

Jesus' Earthly Ministry

Books of the Bible Discussed in This Part:

Matthew, Mark, Luke, John

Jesus' Baptism		Jesus Chose 12 Apostles
27/30 AD	27/30	28/31
	Jesus Began His Ministry	

Jesus Was Crucified and
Raised, Then Appeared
and Ascended

29/32	30/33

Jesus Fed
5,000

REFLECTION 8

Jesus Implements God's Big-Picture Plan

In God's big-picture plan, his family—his treasured possession—will live with him forever. In Part Six we will look at two major components of what Jesus did in moving human history toward this divine objective: defeating Satan, and bringing God's kingdom to earth to establish his family.

God promised Adam and Eve that a child born from their family would have victory over Satan (Genesis 3:15). The apostle Paul said this promised victory came through Jesus, while the apostle John confirmed that, through Jesus, Satan's defeat would be permanent (1 Corinthians 15:57; Revelation 12:10; 20:10).

So how did God bring his kingdom to earth? Foremost, he sent Jesus, who was God in human form: "And the Word [Jesus] became flesh and dwelt among us, and we have seen his glory, glory as of the only Son from the Father, full of grace and truth" (John 1:14). Moreover, John said that all who receive Jesus and believe in his name become the children of God (John 1:12–13).

There are four main ways Jesus, while on earth, carried out this plan of ushering in God's kingdom and redeeming people.

First, Jesus trained a few special leaders. He chose only twelve of his followers to be his closest associates and apostles, who sometimes in the Gospels are called the twelve disciples (Luke 6:13).

Second, Jesus spent a lot of time teaching and performing miracles. These miracles were signs of God's power and authority over all of creation, from the weather to our personal injuries and diseases (Hebrews 2:3–4). The miracles demonstrated that Jesus was the Messiah, both fully human and divine, with authority as God; ultimately, they were performed for our salvation, to encourage our belief in him (John 20:30–31).

Third, at his last Passover meal with his twelve apostles, Jesus declared that with his death he established and confirmed the new covenant (Luke 22:20). There he also gave them a new commandment, or mandate, that they love one another as he loved them (John13:34).

Fourth, after his resurrection, Jesus gave his followers a new assignment to accomplish through the power of his Spirit, whom God sent after Jesus was taken up into heaven (Matthew 28:19–20; Acts 1:8).

***

102. God Was Pleased with Jesus, but Satan Wanted to Destroy Him

[from Matthew 4:1–13 and Luke 4:13]

After Jesus was baptized, the Holy Spirit led him to the wilderness. There, Jesus was alone as he prepared for his ministry. However, Satan tried to tempt Jesus away from his mission as the Messiah. Satan attempted to persuade Jesus that it would be better for him to devote his life to pleasing himself with good food, extraordinary powers, and political authority. Satan offered Jesus magical powers over the physical world and political power over people and nations.

In response to each lie that Satan told, Jesus responded with a quote from God's word that refuted the lie. Jesus said that life exists "by every word that comes from the mouth of God," people must not put the Lord God "to the test," and people should worship the Lord as God and only serve him (Matthew 4:4, 7, 10). Jesus used Scripture to overpower Satan, who finally left him alone—for the time being (Luke 4:13). Then God sent angels to minister to Jesus.

"Then Jesus was led up by the Spirit into the wilderness to be tempted by the devil." (Matthew 4:1)

How can you know the difference between something that appears to be true and what is really true?

103. Jesus Called Twelve of His Disciples to Be Apostles

[from Matthew 10:2–4; Luke 6:12–16; and John 1:35–51]

After John baptized Jesus, John told two of his own followers that Jesus was the "Lamb of God" (John 1:36). They started following Jesus, as did many others. Jesus wanted a few of these followers to be his special students and friends. He knew the men he chose would represent him for the rest of his life and theirs. Before he decided who his closest associates would be, Jesus spent an entire night praying to God for wisdom and discernment.

Then Jesus chose twelve men, whom he also named as apostles, to be with him during the next three years of his ministry: Simon (whom Jesus renamed Peter), Andrew (Peter's brother), James and John (sons of Zebedee), Philip, Bartholomew, Matthew,

Thomas, James (son of Alphaeus), Simon (nicknamed "the Zealot"), Judas (also known as Jude or Judas Thaddaeus), and Judas Iscariot.

"And when day came, he called his disciples and chose from them twelve, whom he named apostles" (Luke 6:13)

What did Jesus do before he made the important decision about whom he would choose to be his twelve apostles?

104. Jesus Went to a Wedding and Performed His First Miracle
[from John 2:1–12]

A few days later, Jesus went to a wedding in the town of Cana with some of his friends and family. In Jesus' time, a wedding celebration included a feast that could go on for a few days. Unexpectedly, there was not enough wine at the wedding he attended—a major embarrassment for the hosts:

> When the wine ran out, the mother of Jesus said to him, "They have no wine." And Jesus said to her, "Woman, what does this have to do with me? My hour has not yet come." His mother said to the servants, "Do whatever he tells you." (2:3–5)

Speaking only to the servants, Jesus told them to fill six large jars with water. Then he told them to take some liquid from one of the jars and give it to the master of the feast, who was amazed at the quality of the wine. This was the first sign of Jesus' glory and authority over nature—the world he created. It convinced the disciples to believe in Jesus.

"Everyone serves the good wine first, and when people have drunk freely, then the poor wine. But you have kept the good wine until now." (John 2:10, quoting the master of the feast)

What would it take for you to believe that Jesus is the Messiah, the Son of the Living God?

REFLECTION 9

Christian Marriage and Family Celebration

In Jesus' time, as for many people today, a wedding was not only a celebration of the joining of a man and a woman in marriage, but a source of pride for their parents— the hosts of the wedding events. Jesus kept the wedding in Cana from becoming a humiliating beginning to a beautiful marriage. A marriage of a man and a woman, celebrated by the families with their friends and the community, reflects God's covenant relationship with us, his beloved. In his covenant with us, God demonstrates his loyalty, fidelity, love, and selflessness.

The human marriage covenant is intended to mirror this divine relationship. Family members and others can also point to God's sacred covenant with his people by promoting and celebrating marriages that honor his unique and specific intention in this arena of human relationships. God's desire for marriages shines through in Jesus' actions at the wedding in Cana, and is as relevant for single people as for married ones; he is the best and he provides the best. Even when we think we know what is best for us based on our human expectations, Jesus exceeds whatever our imaginations could lead us to believe or hope for.

***

105. A Religious Leader Sought Out Jesus and Learned about New Birth

[from John 3:1–21]

Later, when Jesus was in Jerusalem, a man named Nicodemus heard Jesus teach and saw some of the miracles he performed. Nicodemus was curious about who Jesus was. He went alone to see Jesus one night for a private conversation. Nicodemus was one of the Pharisees, a group of religious leaders in Israel who strictly followed the law of Moses. They even expanded the laws according to what they thought people should do. Nicodemus told Jesus that he knew Jesus came from God, because that was the only explanation for the authority with which Jesus taught and the amazing miracles he did.

Jesus answered and said that "unless one is born again he cannot see the kingdom of God" (3:3). Nicodemus did not understand how a person could reenter his mother and have a second birth. Jesus told him that as a religious leader, Nicodemus had a disappointingly limited understanding of spiritual matters. Jesus was not talking about the rebirth of a person's physical body but the rebirth of a person's spirit. Jesus told Nicodemus about God's plan for people to have eternal life: "For God so loved the world, that he gave his only Son, that whoever believes in him should not perish but have eternal life" (3:16).

Jesus ended his conversation with Nicodemus by telling him that people who practiced God's truth would live in God's light; their behavior would make it obvious to others that God was living in and working through them (3:21).

"Jesus answered, 'Truly, truly, I say to you, unless one is born of water and the Spirit, he cannot enter the kingdom of God. That which is born of the flesh is flesh, and that which is born of the Spirit is spirit.'" (John 3:5–6)

Nicodemus shows us that God is pleased when we come to him with questions. Do you have any questions for God, especially about what it means for your spirit to be reborn?

106. A Thirsty Samaritan Woman Learned about Living Water
[from John 4:7–42]

One day, Jesus and his friends were traveling from Jerusalem to Galilee. On the way, they went through the region of Samaria. Jesus rested at a well there while his disciples went into the nearby village to buy food. When a woman came to the well to draw water, Jesus asked her to give him a drink. She recognized him as a Jew. She asked why he would talk with her, a woman and a Samaritan.

As discussed in Connection 5, people in Samaria were no longer full-blooded Jews. Years before, Assyria conquered Samaria and foreign people moved there. After a few hundred years, the people of Samaria were of mixed ethnicities. The true Jews of Judea and Galilee considered these mixed-race Samaritans "unclean" and thus avoided contact with them—hence the Samaritan woman's surprise that Jesus would speak to her.

Jesus replied to the woman that whoever drank from this well would thirst again; however, anyone who drank the water he gave them would never be thirsty again. He said his water would become a spring inside a person, welling up to eternal life (4:13–14). Perhaps trying to change the subject, she asked about the different places of worship used by the Samaritans and the Jews. Jesus answered that he was the Messiah and that God did not want to be worshiped in a place but in the heart of a person worshiping him in spirit and in truth (4:23).

When the disciples returned to the well, they were surprised to find Jesus talking with a woman he did not know.

"The woman said to him, 'I know that Messiah is coming (he who is called Christ). When he comes, he will tell us all things.' Jesus said to her, 'I who speak to you am he.'" (John 4:25–26)

Have you ever let a disagreement about the form of worship distract you from worshiping the true Messiah?

***

REFLECTION 10
Jesus Demolishes Barriers and Emphasizes Human Worth and Dignity

The account in John of Jesus asking the Samaritan woman for a drink of water made no sense from the standpoint of proper Jewish social behavior. But Jesus knew this woman's life was a mess, with five wrecked marriages and a current extramarital sexual relationship, and that while she certainly needed actual water to drink, more importantly she needed the life-giving spiritual water only he could offer her.

Jesus set aside social etiquette rules in order to bring his water of eternal life to a socially-rejected woman from a second-class culture. He was more concerned about her as a person—her heart and her eternal spiritual state—than his own reputation.

Jesus also attacked the prejudice against Samaritans in the popular parable of the good Samaritan (Pixel 112). Jesus shamed the Jewish religious leaders through this story, in which two of them, a priest and a Levite, neglected to care for an injured Jewish person, while a Samaritan stopped to help and sacrifice for the neglected victim. The Samaritan, he was pointing out, was the true neighbor and friend, fulfilling the commandment to love one's neighbor as oneself.

In addition to transcending ethnic barriers, God transcended sexism when he later sent an angel to the women who came to anoint Jesus' body in the tomb. The angel gave the women a message for the disciples (Pixel 132). Cultural rules of that time did not respect the trustworthiness of women as witnesses. Yet God entrusted these women with the most important news of human history: Jesus had conquered death, had risen, and would soon visit his friends.

The honor and dignity God bestows on all people was summarized by Paul, who emphasized that all followers of Jesus are as one family. Although we may have different individual roles in God's family, we are to respect and honor each other without regard to social, racial, or gender differences, as brothers and sisters before him (Galatians 3:28; 1 Timothy 2:1–2).

***

107. A Paralyzed Man Came through the Roof
[from Mark 2:1–12]

Jesus was teaching in a home in the city of Capernaum. The place was so crowded with people wanting to hear what he said that no one else could get in. Four men brought their paralyzed friend on a stretcher so Jesus could heal him. They could not make their way through the crowd, so they devised a creative way for the paralyzed man to see Jesus. They went on the roof and tore it open directly above where Jesus was standing. Then they lowered their friend in front of Jesus. Jesus knew that the paralyzed man and his friends had great faith in his power to heal, and he said to the paralyzed man, "Son, your sins are forgiven" (2:5).

Jesus knew in his spirit that some in the room thought that he was blaspheming God, because only God has the power to forgive sins. Jesus looked at these people and said that he wanted them to know he had the authority to forgive sins. Then he told the paralyzed man to pick up his stretcher and go home. The man obeyed. All the people there, except some critics, were amazed, and praised God for what Jesus did.

"'But that you may know that the Son of Man has authority on earth to forgive sins'—he said to the paralytic—'I say to you, rise, pick up your bed, and go home.'" (Mark 2:10–11)

What does it mean to you that Jesus has the authority to forgive sins?

108. Religious Leaders Accused Jesus and His Disciples of Breaking the Rules
[from Mark 2:18–3:6]

God gave Moses the Ten Commandments (Pixel 35). Over the many years since then, the Pharisees had come up with new rules that they thought were necessary to keep these laws. One of these new rules was fasting, which was the practice of "doing without" something, usually food, for a period of time. When Jesus and his disciples did not fast at the set time, people asked him why. Following up on the wedding where he turned water into wine (Pixel 104), Jesus referred to himself as the bridegroom. He said that as long as the bridegroom was with his friends, they could not fast (2:19).

Another day, Jesus and his disciples were walking through a grain field and picking some of the grain to eat. There was a problem: It was the Sabbath day. The religious leaders believed picking grain for food qualified as work, which was prohibited on the Sabbath. They accused Jesus of breaking the law. Jesus responded that not even the Sabbath law should stop a person from eating. He then made a bigger point, telling them that God's people were more important than their man-made rule (2:27). Furthermore, he told them, *he* is the lord of the Sabbath (2:28).

On another Sabbath day, Jesus was in the synagogue when he saw a man with a withered hand. The religious leaders were watching to see what Jesus would do. Jesus knew these people were so hardened by keeping the rules that they did not want Jesus to heal the man. This made Jesus very angry. He told the man to stretch out his hand. When he did, it was healed. The religious leaders were so enraged that they met together to figure out a way to kill Jesus.

"And he looked around at them with anger, grieved at their hardness of heart, and said to the man, 'Stretch out your hand.' He stretched it out, and his hand was restored. The Pharisees went out and immediately held counsel with the Herodians against him, how to destroy him." (Mark 3:5–6)

Do you remember a time when you were playing a game with someone and that person wanted his or her "made-up" rules to be more important than the "real" (official) rules of the game?

***

REFLECTION 11
Jesus Shows Us the Reality of Spiritual Life

Think about these dramatic events that highlight some of what Jesus did. He used the wedding without enough wine to teach that the old forms of religion "ran dry." He explained to Nicodemus the meaning of spiritual rebirth. He surprised the woman at the well with living water. He healed the man lowered through the roof and declared his sins forgiven. And Jesus confronted the religious leaders, who could not comprehend that he came to replace the rigid rules with a person—himself.

Jesus taught that the old forms of religion were not (and are not) adequate. He emphasized that it never was the places or forms of worship that honored God. The new reality was that God came to us in the personal presence of Jesus. God used the external realities of the Old Testament for a purpose—to help people become conscious of their sin and aware of their desperate need for a Savior; but these old realities were supplanted by a new, superior reality when he came to earth in human form.

***

109. Jesus Went to a Mountain and Taught Crowds
[from Matthew 5:1–7:29]

Many people followed Jesus to hear him teach. One time, he was teaching at a mountain, so his teachings there are called the Sermon on the Mount. A part of these teachings is known as the Beatitudes. In the Beatitudes, Jesus taught that an individual is blessed for living in ways that honor God when that person is following Jesus and has submitted to the guidance of the Holy Spirit. These blessed attributes are: being poor in spirit, mourning, being gentle, hungering for righteousness, being merciful, being pure in heart, being peacemakers, and being persecuted and insulted for the sake of God's kingdom. The entire Sermon on the Mount is found in Matthew 5:1–7:29.

Jesus ended the Sermon on the Mount by saying people should listen to what he said and then live by his teachings. If they did this, they would be like the wise man who built his house on a good foundation, which stood sturdy against the storms. If they did not follow his teachings, they would be like the foolish man who built his house on the sand, which the storms knocked down.

"Everyone then who hears these words of mine and does them will be like a wise man who built his house on the rock." (Matthew 7:24)

How can you build your life on a solid foundation?

110. Jesus Taught about Prayer
[from Matthew 6:1–15]

In the middle of the Sermon on the Mount, Jesus warned about being hypocritical in worship. He said that when giving money to those in need, a person should do so in secret and not for recognition and praise from others.

Jesus also taught the people how to pray. Many religious leaders used their prayers to get the attention of other people rather than to spend time with God. Jesus said that rather than praying in public, they should pray in a quiet place at home. He also said not to pray using a lot of words in hopes that longer prayers would get God's attention. Jesus declared that God already knew their needs before praying, and God rewards sincere prayer, made to him personally. Jesus provided a model prayer, often called the Lord's Prayer.

"Pray then like this:
'Our Father in heaven,
hallowed be your name.
Your kingdom come
your will be done,
on earth as it is in heaven.
Give us this day our daily bread,
and forgive us our debts,
as we also have forgiven our debtors.
And lead us not into temptation,
but deliver us from evil.'" (Matthew 6:9–13)

What should you do for your prayer to be sincere and made to God personally?

CONNECTION 10
Jesus Taught in Parables

Jesus did not always teach in a direct way, as in the Sermon on the Mount. Sometimes he used a story or example, speaking through a *parable*. This way of teaching, he said, fulfilled a prophecy in Psalm 78:2 that wisdom would be taught by parables (Matthew 13:35).

The purpose of a parable is to teach a truth or moral lesson, usually with only one significant focus. The details of the parable are most often used to make the main point and not to present a complex problem. The puzzling nature of parables is that they make the point of Jesus' teaching clear and memorable for some people but obscure his lessons for others.

The disciples asked Jesus about the meaning of parables. In effect, Jesus said that those whom God prepared to understand the message would understand a parable, while those who hardened their hearts to the truth would not be able to understand (Matthew 13:10–17).

***

111. A Parable about Differences in People's Readiness for God's Message
[from Luke 8:4–15]

Jesus wanted his followers to understand that what he taught would be received by people in different ways, so he told a parable about a farmer who spread seed to grow crops. Some of the seed fell along the road. People walked on it and birds ate it. This seed represented Satan taking away the word from people's hearts, "so that they may not believe and be saved" (8:12).

Other seed fell on rocky ground. It started to grow, but without good roots in the soil, it died quickly. This seed represented people who allow temptations to distract them from God's message. Yet other seed fell among the thorns. The seed sprouted, and the crop started to grow, but the thorns choked it out. This seed represented people who allow worries, money, and pleasure to control their lives. Lastly, some seed fell on good ground. This seed represented people who hear what Jesus said, act on it, and honor God with their lives.

"As for that [seed] in the good soil, they are those who, hearing the word, hold it fast in an honest and good heart, and bear fruit with patience." (Luke 8:15)

Patience means to hang in there with gentleness. What do you think patience has to do with bearing fruit?

112. A Parable about Knowing and Helping Your Neighbor
[from Luke 10:25–37]

When Jesus was teaching, a lawyer wanted to test Jesus while under the guise of appearing agreeable. He asked Jesus what he should do to inherit eternal life. As Jesus often did, he put the question back to the questioner. He asked the lawyer what the law required. The lawyer repeated a familiar summary of the law: "You shall love the Lord your God with all your heart and with all your soul and with all your strength and with all your mind, and your neighbor as yourself" (10:27). Jesus told the man to do these things, and then he would live. But the lawyer, trying to conceal his true motive, asked a follow-up question: "And who is my neighbor?" (10:29). Jesus replied with a story many people know as the parable of the good Samaritan.

A Jewish man traveled on foot from Jerusalem to Jericho. Some robbers beat him, stripped his clothes, took his money, and left him half dead. A priest from the temple saw the abused man but walked on the other side of the road to avoid helping him. Next, a Levite, one of the assistants in the temple, passed by and, like the priest, neglected the man. When a man from Samaria came and saw the battered man, he stopped to help—even though, as discussed in Pixel 106, Jews were prejudiced against Samaritans. The Samaritan bandaged the man's wounds, put him on his donkey, and took him to an inn. He paid the innkeeper to take care of the man until he recovered.

When Jesus finished the parable, he asked the lawyer which of the three men proved to be a neighbor to the injured man. The lawyer answered that it was the Samaritan who showed mercy. Jesus told him to go and do the same.

"And he said to him, 'You have answered correctly; do this, and you will live.' But he, desiring to justify himself, said to Jesus, 'And who is my neighbor?'" (Luke 10:28–29)

When you see someone who needs help, do you ignore the person and pretend nothing is wrong, or do you stop to help? To whom can you be a neighbor?

113. A Parable about God's Amazing Kingdom
[from Luke 13:18–21]

Sometimes Jesus asked questions to draw people's attention to what he wanted to teach them. On one occasion, he asked what example people would give to describe God's kingdom.

Jesus answered his own question by comparing God's kingdom to a mustard seed. Although a mustard seed is quite small, after it is planted, it grows into a tree larger than all the other plants in a garden. In fact, it grows so large that birds can nest in its branches. God's kingdom is similar. God told Abraham that his family would be a blessing to all nations. Now Jesus was going to make that happen.

Jesus then used another example, saying God's kingdom was like a piece of leaven (yeast) put into three measures of flour, causing all of the flour to be leavened. With this example, Jesus taught that when God's people live his truth, no matter how small in worldly position or few in number, they have the power to influence the entire world.

"He said therefore, 'What is the kingdom of God like? And to what shall I compare it?'" *(Luke 13:18)*

Have you ever seen something small and later realized that small thing was only a part of something much bigger?

114. A Parable about Selfishness and Pride
[from Luke 15:11–32]

Jesus wanted people to know how desperately God longed for his children to come home to him. So he told a story about a father of two sons. The story began with the younger son deciding to move out of the house to be on his own. Before leaving, he asked his dad to give him his share of the inheritance. In effect, with this request the younger son was telling his dad, "You are as good as dead to me."

With sadness, the dad gave him a large amount of money. The son joyfully left home. But soon the inheritance money ran out. The son had nothing left: no family, no money, no friends, and no job. Eventually, a farmer hired him to feed his pigs, a repugnant job for a Jewish person. It was such a bad job that he did not earn enough money for his own food, so he ate the pigs' food with them.

Finally, the son came to his senses. He realized that the workers on his dad's farm had a better life than he did. So he started the long journey back home. He rehearsed over and over again how he would apologize to his dad and ask to become a worker on the farm.

The dad had gone to the road every day to watch for his younger son. Finally, one day, Dad recognized him a long way off. He ran to meet him, and brought him home. The father held a feast to celebrate. His son, who had been like a dead man, had come back to life (15:24)!

The older brother heard the celebration as he came in from working the fields. He learned it was a party for his younger brother. He became furious, insulted, and embarrassed; his pride was hurt. The older brother told his dad how unfair it was that he had stayed home and worked hard as a faithful son, yet Dad had never given a party for him. The younger son had dishonored and disgraced his dad, yet his bad behavior was rewarded with a big celebration. In reply, Dad assured the older son that he loved him and appreciated his work. He confirmed the older son's secure position in the family. But the dad said it was proper to be joyful because the younger brother, who had been lost, had come home.

"And he said to him, 'Son, you are always with me, and all that is mine is yours. It was fitting to celebrate and be glad, for this your brother was dead, and is alive; he was lost, and is found.'" (Luke 15:31–32)

Are you jealous when someone else gets what you think you deserve, even when nothing has been taken from you?

115. Jesus Calmed a Storm and a Man with Demons
[from Mark 4:35–5:20]

One day, Jesus again showed his supreme authority over his creation. He and his disciples were crossing the Sea of Galilee in a boat heading for the area of the Gerasenes. Jesus was asleep on a cushion when a fierce wind came. Waves started breaking over the boat, and the boat began to fill with water. The storm was out of control. Alarmed and worried, the disciples woke up Jesus and asked him to do something to save them. Jesus got up and commanded the wind, "Peace! Be still!" (4:39). Immediately, the storm calmed. Jesus turned to his disciples and asked them, "Why are you so afraid? Have you still no faith?" (4:40). Then they really were afraid! They were also amazed at the authority Jesus had over the wind and the storm.

When Jesus and his disciples landed on the other side of the lake, a man came to them who was out of control. No one in his town was able to manage him, even when they put him in chains. Jesus knew the man was possessed with demons. The demons told Jesus their name was "Legion" because there were many of them. Jesus ordered the demons to leave the man. The demons begged Jesus not to torment them and asked permission to go into a nearby herd of pigs. Jesus allowed this, and the demons drove the pigs off a cliff to their death in the lake.

News about what happened to both the man and the pigs reached the nearby town. This made the people who lived there so afraid that they urged Jesus to go away and leave them alone. But the man who had been healed wanted to join Jesus and his disciples. Instead, Jesus told him to go home and tell others what God had done for him. When he did that, those who heard him were amazed.

"And they came to Jesus and saw the demon-possessed man, the one who had had the legion, sitting there, clothed and in his right mind, and they were afraid." (Mark 5:15)

What is the difference between what the fearful disciples in the boat and what the fearful people from the town asked Jesus to do to take away their fears?

116. Jesus Healed a Woman and Gave New Life to a Young Girl
[from Luke 8:40–56]

In another town, a large crowd gathered around Jesus and his disciples. Jairus, an official of the synagogue, burst through the group and fell at Jesus' feet. Jairus' only daughter, about twelve years old, was at home dying of an illness. He begged Jesus to heal her.

Jesus went with Jairus. However, on the way, Jesus felt healing power go out of him when someone in the crowd touched him. He stopped and asked who had touched him. A woman came and fell at his feet. With a trembling voice, she told him she had suffered a permanent bleeding problem for the past twelve years. She said that when she touched his coat, she had been healed. Jesus told her, "Daughter, your faith has made you well; go in peace" (8:48).

Just then, someone from Jairus' home arrived to tell Jairus that his daughter had died, and there was no more need to bother Jesus. But upon hearing this news, Jesus told him not to be afraid; rather, he should believe, and the girl would be healed. Later, when Jesus arrived at Jairus' home, people laughed at him when he said the girl was only asleep. With her parents watching, Jesus took the girl's hand and said to her, "Child, arise" (8:54). The girl got up and had something to eat. Her parents could hardly believe it!

"Do not fear; only believe, and she will be well." (Luke 8:50b)

Amazing things happened, people fell at his feet, and he told them to believe and not to be afraid. What kind of man was Jesus?

117. Jesus Fed Five Thousand and Walked on Water
[from John 6:1–29]

Many people began following Jesus everywhere he went, watching him heal the sick and listening to him teach. One day, a crowd of more than five thousand people followed Jesus and his disciples. When it was mealtime, Jesus asked his disciples where they could get enough food to feed everyone. One of the disciples found a boy with five loaves of bread and two fish. The disciples said this small amount of food could not possibly feed the large crowd.

Jesus told his disciples to have everyone sit down. Then he took what the boy had, thanked God for it, and handed out the food to the disciples to give to the people. After the meal, the disciples gathered up the leftovers, which were enough to fill twelve baskets! This miracle convinced the people that Jesus was "the Prophet" about whom Moses had spoken (Deuteronomy 18:15). They determined they would take Jesus by force and make him their king. However, he prevented this from happening by going to a mountain alone.

His disciples, meanwhile, took a small boat across the Sea of Galilee to Capernaum without Jesus. After rowing the boat for a long time, a storm came and then they saw Jesus walking on the water near them. He called out to them not to be afraid, and then he got in the boat.

The next day, the crowd could not find Jesus. They knew he had not gotten in the boat to cross the sea with the disciples. Some of them found Jesus in that town and asked him how he got there. Jesus urged them not to seek him simply because he fed them a meal. Rather, they should work for the spiritual food that produces eternal life. They asked him how they could do the works of God. Jesus told them they should believe in him as the one whom God sent.

"Do not labor for the food that perishes, but for the food that endures to eternal life, which the Son of Man will give to you. For on him God the Father has set his seal." (John 6:27)

Have you ever been looking for one thing but in the process found something else that was far better?

118. The Disciples Acknowledged Jesus as the Son of God

[from Matthew 14:22–33; 16:13–20; and John 20:30–31]

When Jesus walked on water, all the disciples were in the boat and were terrified. Peter called out to Jesus for a command to allow him to walk on the water to meet Jesus. Jesus gave the word, so Peter climbed out of the boat and walked on the water toward Jesus. But the storm frightened Peter. He took his eyes off Jesus, became worried, and began to sink. He cried out to Jesus to save him. Jesus reached out, took Peter's hand, and helped him get in the boat. Immediately, the storm stopped. The disciples worshiped Jesus and said to him, "Truly you are the Son of God" (Matthew 14:33).

John emphasized in his Gospel that this is exactly why Jesus demonstrated his authority over nature, and performed miracles of healing—they were signs to those who observed and experienced them that Jesus had divine authority. John recorded some of these events as signs for people who came after, so that they would also believe Jesus is the Son of God and, by believing in him, have eternal life (John 20:30–31).

Another time, Jesus asked the disciples who other people said he was. They answered, "Some say John the Baptist, others say Elijah, and others Jeremiah or one of the prophets" (Matthew 16:14). Jesus asked them who *they* thought he was. Peter answered, "You are the Christ, the Son of the living God" (Matthew 16:16).

"And Jesus answered him, 'Blessed are you, Simon Bar-Jonah! For flesh and blood has not revealed this to you, but my Father who is in heaven.'" (Matthew 16:17)

How would you answer Jesus' question to the disciples, "Who do you say that I am?"

119. God Acknowledged Jesus as His Son

[from Matthew 14:1–12 and 17:1–13]

About a week later, Jesus took Peter, James, and John with him up on a high mountain. Suddenly, Jesus' face began to shine and his appearance changed. This miraculous event is known as the *Transfiguration* because Jesus' change in appearance clearly showed his divine nature. The disciples realized Moses and Elijah were talking with Jesus. Then, from a bright cloud over them, a voice said, "This is my beloved Son, with whom I am well pleased; listen to him" (17:5).

The three disciples were so terrified that they fell to the ground. Jesus told them to get up and not to be afraid. He also told them not to tell anyone about this event until he had risen from the dead (17:9). The disciples asked him about the prophecy that Elijah must first come before the Messiah. Jesus said Elijah had already come. They understood him to mean John the Baptist. Jesus told them he would suffer just as John the Baptist had suffered when he was killed by Herod, a Roman governor (17:10–13; 14:1–12).

"But I tell you that Elijah has already come, and they did not recognize him, but did to him whatever they pleased. So also the Son of Man will certainly suffer at their hands." (Matthew 17:12)

God told the disciples to "listen to Jesus." Are you listening to him?

120. The Religious Leaders Regarded Jesus as Their Enemy

[from Luke 11:14–54]

Jesus met a man unable to speak and possessed by a demon. Jesus sent the demon out of the man, and the man began to talk. Some of the religious leaders accused Jesus of using powers from Satan to get rid of the demon. Jesus told them it did not make good sense for a power to fight against itself—why would Satan fight against one of his own demons? Then Jesus declared the truth about his mission in the world. He said to the religious leaders, "If it is by the finger of God that I cast out demons, then the kingdom of God has come upon you" (11:20).

Another time, Jesus was having lunch with one of the religious leaders, a Pharisee. The Pharisee criticized Jesus for not performing a ritual washing before he ate. Using the example of cleaning dishes after a meal, Jesus told him the Pharisees did a good job of washing the outside of a cup while ignoring the waste and stains on the inside. Jesus explained that the Pharisees focused on trivial things and tried to turn them into requirements for honoring God. At the same time, they disregarded doing justice to others and truly loving God (11:42).

This was one of the many times the religious leaders got irritated by Jesus, prompting them to make plans against him.

"As he went away from there, the scribes and the Pharisees began to press him hard and to provoke him to speak about many things, lying in wait for him, to catch him in something he might say." (Luke 11:53–54)

Have you ever missed the main point about something important because you refused to see it from God's perspective?

121. The Religious Leaders Decided Jesus Must Die
[from John 11:1–57]

Lazarus and his sisters, Mary and Martha, were Jesus' dear friends. While Jesus was in another town teaching, Lazarus became seriously ill. His sisters sent a message to Jesus to come quickly and heal Lazarus. When Jesus finally arrived, Lazarus had been dead for four days. His body had been placed in a tomb with a stone covering the entrance.

Jesus knew Lazarus' death was an opportunity to show his divine power over nature and people. Martha and Mary each told Jesus that they knew he could have kept Lazarus from dying if he arrived sooner. At the tomb, Jesus asked some people to remove the stone that covered the opening. He prayed and then called, "Lazarus, come out" (11:43). Lazarus emerged from the tomb, wrapped in his grave clothes. The people removed the cloth wrappings. Lazarus was alive again!

Some who saw this incident went and told the religious leaders about it. These leaders met together. They decided that if Jesus were not stopped, the Roman government would "come and take away both our place and our nation" (11:48). They agreed they could not let this happen, so they began making plans to kill Jesus (11:53). But some who saw Lazarus walk out of the tomb alive came to believe in Jesus. Jesus explained to Martha that those who believed in him would never have spiritual death because he gave life that would never end.

"Jesus said to her, 'I am the resurrection and the life. Whoever believes in me, though he die, yet shall he live, and everyone who lives and believes in me shall never die. Do you believe this?'" (John 11:25–26)

Have you ever hated someone so badly that you wanted to kill the person?

122. The Disciples Mistakenly Thought Jesus Was Working for Their Glory
[from Mark 10:32–45]

Some time later, Jesus and his disciples were walking to Jerusalem. Jesus told them that in Jerusalem the religious leaders would have him arrested, abused, mocked, condemned to death, and killed. Then, three days later, he would rise from death.

Disengaged from the serious things Jesus said, James and John asked Jesus if he would give them the most important positions in his kingdom. Jesus told them they did not know what they were asking him to do. They assured Jesus that they would be able to endure whatever he suffered. The other ten disciples overheard this conversation and resented James and John for their request.

Next, Jesus gathered all the disciples around. He explained that his kingdom was different from the rest of the world. In the world, leaders served only their own interests and were arrogant toward others. But the followers of Jesus were to be just the reverse—they were to serve people. Their status in his kingdom was based on how they helped others while on earth, not on how they ordered people around or how they gained power over them. To emphasize the point, Jesus said he was a model for them and that serving others was the exact reason he came to earth.

"But it shall not be so among you. But whoever would be great among you must be your servant, and whoever would be first among you must be slave of all. For even the Son of Man came not to be served but to serve, and to give his life as a ransom for many." (Mark 10:43–45)

When something good happens to you, do you ever think about how you could use that good thing to then help others?

CONNECTION 11
Jesus' Last Week on Earth

Do you remember the most important week of your life? A short period when some of the most astounding things happened to you?

Discussion of the last seven days of Jesus' life takes up a significant portion of all four Gospels. The events of this crucial week are covered in the rest of this section. The week began with Jesus entering Jerusalem to enthusiastic crowds welcoming him.

One of the first things Jesus did was attack the businesses that were operating in the temple and making his Father's house a place of commerce (for selfish gain) instead of a place of prayer (for spiritual gain). His actions symbolized the cleansing of our sinful practices and thoughts when we receive him as the substitute for our sin and enjoy a restored relationship with the Father.

Jesus' immediate reason for coming to Jerusalem was to celebrate Passover. He met with the twelve apostles for the Passover meal Thursday evening. Moses and the Israelites in Egypt celebrated the first Passover in obedience to God's command that the angel of death would "pass over" them when it saw the blood on their front doors (Pixel 31). Now Jesus knew he would become the ultimate Passover sacrifice (Reflection 4), and he wanted to share this meal—his last—with his closest friends.

For good reason, the last week of Jesus' life is known by many Christians as Passion Week. The passion—intense emotional and physical suffering—experienced by Jesus during this week is a cause for thankful celebration because, as both God and human, Jesus took on himself the pain, suffering, and wrath that each person deserves to bear for his or her rebellion against God.

***

123. Jesus Was So Popular That the Religious Leaders Made Plans to Kill Him
[from Mark 11:1–18]

Before he and his disciples arrived in Jerusalem, Jesus told two of the disciples where they would find a colt on which no person had ever ridden. He asked them to bring the young animal to him. Jesus sat on the colt and rode it into Jerusalem. As usual, crowds of people gathered around Jesus. They honored him by spreading their coats and leafy branches on the road ahead of him. People also sang about Jesus, saying, "Hosanna in the highest!" *Hosanna* means "the greatest one who saves now" (11:9–10). This event is often referred to as the Triumphal Entry. It was the height of Jesus' popularity, and he fittingly made his way into Jerusalem in the style of a national leader.

The next day, Jesus and his disciples went to the temple in Jerusalem; he saw businesses operating there. Some were selling animals for use as sacrifices in worship, while others exchanged money from other countries to buy things in Jerusalem. Jesus attacked all of these businesses. He turned over the tables they used and stopped people from taking their merchandise through the temple.

Then he explained what he was doing. The temple, he said, was intended to be a house of prayer to God for all nations. Instead, the businesspeople had made the temple into a market, robbing people of their money and God of his honor. The religious leaders had allowed these businesses to operate in the temple. Now Jesus, with his extreme popularity, exercised authority that made these leaders look bad in public. They did not like this at all, so they redoubled their efforts to do something about Jesus, who was threatening their authority and reputation.

"And the chief priests and the scribes heard it and were seeking a way to destroy him, for they feared him, because all the crowd was astonished at his teaching." (Mark 11:18)

Have your ever been caught doing something wrong and then hated the person who exposed what you did wrong?

124. The Religious Leaders Formed a Plan When Judas Was Paid Some Money

[from Luke 22:1–6 and John 12:4–8]

The religious leaders were looking for a way to kill Jesus. They knew they needed to operate in secret because so many people liked Jesus. They got their opportunity when Satan took control of Judas, one of the Twelve.

Judas had already given into the temptation of dishonesty and stealing. He objected when Lazarus' sister Mary put expensive oil on Jesus' feet, seeing it as a waste of money. He said the oil could have been sold to help the poor, although this comment covered up his true motive—greed (John 12:6). Jesus praised Mary for using the oil as preparation for his death and later for his burial (John 12:4–8). Jesus made it clear he would not be with them much longer. But Judas did not understand the spiritual significance of what Jesus was saying. What Judas wanted was more money in the box. He was the "treasurer" in charge of the common funds used by Jesus and his disciples, and from the Gospel of John we know he was a thief, stealing some of these funds for himself (John 12:6).

Judas went to the religious leaders and offered to betray Jesus to them. They gladly accepted his offer and paid him money to help them catch Jesus away from the crowds (Luke 22:1–6). From then on, Judas started looking for the right time to tell them where Jesus was.

"And the chief priests and the scribes were seeking how to put him to death, for they feared the people. Then Satan entered into Judas called Iscariot, who was of the number of the twelve." (Luke 22:2–3)

Have you ever decided to do something that you knew in your heart was wrong?

125. Jesus Revealed the New Covenant When He Ate the Passover Meal with His Apostles

[from Luke 22:7–20]

It was the weekend of the Passover celebration. On Thursday night, Jesus and the twelve apostles gathered together to eat the Passover meal. Jesus told his dear friends how much he wanted to eat this meal with them. He told them more than they could comprehend at the time, including the fact that he would not eat the meal again with them "until it [was] fulfilled in the kingdom of God" (22:16).

Jesus took some bread, and after he said a prayer of thanks, he broke it into pieces and passed it around. He told them the bread represented his body, given as a sacrifice for them. He said they should repeat this celebration in the future to remember him. Jesus was trying to explain to them that he would soon suffer death, so they should always keep this evening in mind.

Then Jesus took a cup of wine and again gave thanks. He passed the cup around for them to share. He told them this was the new covenant in his blood. It was to fulfill what the prophet Jeremiah had written to the Jews who were in captivity in Babylon. He said that God would make with them a new covenant, which he would write on their hearts (Pixel 79; Jeremiah 31:31–34). Jesus made it clear that the death he was about to experience was the precise fulfillment of this prophecy.

"And likewise [he took] the cup after they had eaten, saying, 'This cup that is poured out for you is the new covenant in my blood.'" (Luke 22:20)

What is the difference between the old covenant God wrote on the stone tablets with Moses at Mount Sinai and the new covenant Jesus made in his blood?

126. Judas Left Early and Missed Learning about the New Commandment

[from John 13:1–36]

Before celebrating the Passover meal with the Twelve, Jesus demonstrated his deep love for them. After walking all day, everyone had dusty and dirty feet. It was a Jewish hospitality and cleansing custom for the lowest servant to wash the feet of those who came into a home. Taking a towel and a basin of water, Jesus sat in front of each of the

Twelve and washed their feet. He said this was an example of how they should love and serve each other.

Later in the evening, with the Twelve surrounding him, Jesus became troubled. He said he knew one of them would betray him—one who had rejected the spiritual cleansing he offered. They were shocked with disbelief. Jesus dipped some bread and gave it to Judas, indicating that he was the betrayer. Then Satan entered into Judas, and Jesus said to him, "What you are going to do, do quickly" (13:27). Judas took the bread from Jesus and immediately left the group. Only Jesus knew what Judas was going to do.

Jesus told the others that he would be glorified soon, and he would be with them only a little while longer. Being glorified meant that Jesus would reveal God's glory—his greatness and majesty—in himself. They could not yet follow him. Jesus tried to help his disciples understand that, after his death, he would rejoin God the Father in heaven, and they would eventually join him there for all eternity.

Then Jesus gave them a new commandment: "Just as I have loved you, you also are to love one another" (13:34). The law of Moses commanded them to love God and others, but Jesus wanted them to know that real love meant following his example in giving his very life for those he loved.

"By this all people will know that you are my disciples, if you have love for one another." *(John 13:35)*

How might Judas have acted differently if he had stayed a few minutes longer with Jesus at dinner and listened to him teach the new commandment?

127. Judas Put Money Ahead of Love and Betrayed Jesus

[from Matthew 26:36–56]

Jesus and the remaining eleven apostles left the Passover dinner and went to the Garden of Gethsemane to pray. He took Peter, James, and John farther into the garden with him. He told them, "My soul is very sorrowful, even to death; remain here, and watch with me" (26:38). He prayed to God that if the "cup" of death could pass, he would prefer that it would pass; but in any event, he wanted God's will to be done with his life (26:39). To the very end, Jesus' primary goal was to please the Father, even though his human side was troubled and in deep anguish. He was tempted to want some other, less grueling option, but he submitted to his Father's plan and desire.

By the time Jesus finished praying, the three waiting disciples had fallen asleep. Jesus woke them up and told them, "Rise, let us be going; see, my betrayer is at hand" (26:46). Then Judas arrived, leading a large group of armed soldiers and officers from the religious leaders. Judas walked out of the crowd and kissed Jesus, the signal that he was the one to be seized. Some of the disciples wanted to fight, but Jesus told the disciples that this was not the time to fight with weapons. If it were, his Father would send more than twelve legions of angels to fight for him. Rather, in order for God's word to be fulfilled, events had to happen this way (26:53–54).

All the disciples left Jesus and ran away.

"Jesus said to [Judas], 'Friend, do what you came to do.' Then they came up and laid hands on Jesus and seized him." (Matthew 26:50)

Judas focused on money. The disciples focused on putting up a fight, but then they ran away. Jesus focused on honoring God. Stop and think. Where would you place yourself in this cast of characters?

128. Jesus' "Crime" Was Asserting that He Was God
[from Matthew 26:57–27:10]

The soldiers took Jesus to the council of Jewish religious leaders. They brought in witnesses, who told lies about Jesus and what he had taught. Jesus did not reply to these false charges. Then Caiaphas, the high priest, asked Jesus a direct question: "Tell us if you are the Christ, the Son of God" (26:63). Jesus replied, "You have said so. But I tell you, from now on you will see the Son of Man seated at the right hand of Power and coming on the clouds of heaven" (26:64). Caiaphas declared Jesus' answer blasphemy against God. The whole council voted that Jesus should die. The Jewish leaders bound Jesus and took him to Pilate, the Roman governor.

When Judas learned that Jesus had been sentenced to death, he felt remorse for betraying Jesus. He returned the money to the religious leaders. He told them he had sinned because he had betrayed an innocent man. The religious leaders told Judas that was his problem. Judas threw the money on the floor of the temple. Then, rather than confess what he had done as a sin and ask God to forgive him, he went and hanged himself.

"Then the high priest tore his robes and said, '[Jesus] has uttered blasphemy. What further witnesses do we need? You have now heard his blasphemy. What is your judgment?' They

answered, 'He deserves death.'" (Matthew 26:65–66)

When something goes terribly wrong with the direction of our lives, it can often be traced to a bad decision. Where or when did Judas start going the wrong way?

129. At His Trial before Pilate, Jesus Testified about the Truth

[from John 18:28–19:16]

The Jewish leaders demanded that Jesus die. At that time, Israel was ruled by the Roman government, which forbade the Jewish people from carrying out a death sentence against a criminal. Pilate, a Roman governor, questioned Jesus and asked him if he was the King of the Jews. Jesus replied that his kingdom was not of this world; if it were, Jesus' servants would be fighting for him. Then Jesus acknowledged that he was a king. He said he had come into the world to testify to the truth, and all those "of the truth" would listen to his voice. Pilate responded with his own question: "What is truth?" (18:38).

Pilate tried to satisfy the religious leaders by ordering that Jesus be beaten, but they kept crying out for Jesus to be crucified. When they insisted that Jesus should die because "he has made himself the Son of God," Pilate became even more afraid to deal with Jesus (19:7). But he let the pressure from the religious leaders control him. Finally, Pilate turned Jesus over to be crucified. He announced to the Jews, "Behold your King!" (19:14).

"When the chief priests and the officers saw him, they cried out, 'Crucify him, crucify him!' Pilate said to them, 'Take him yourselves and crucify him, for I find no guilt in him.'" (John 19:6)

Why were the religious leaders so upset about Jesus claiming to be the Son of God?

130. Jesus Was Crucified

[from Matthew 27:27–56 and Luke 23:39–43]

The Roman soldiers were cruel to Jesus. Mocking his claims of being a king, they put a scarlet robe on him. They also twisted thorn branches to form a crown, which they forcefully pushed on his head. When Jesus became too weak to carry his own heavy wooden cross, the soldiers forced another man to do it. Crucifixion was a punishment to the death for horrible criminals. A horizontal piece of wood was attached to a vertical piece, and the criminal was nailed to this cross-shaped formation. It was a brutal way to kill a person. Crucifixions were carried out in public for all to see, both to humiliate the victim and to demonstrate the terrifying power of the Roman government (Matthew 27:27–34).

When the soldiers, with Jesus and a crowd of onlookers, reached a hill just outside Jerusalem called Golgotha, they nailed Jesus to a cross there. The soldiers put a sign above his head that read, "This is Jesus, the King of the Jews" (Matthew 27:37). Two robbers were crucified at the same time, one on each side of Jesus. Many people gathered to watch Jesus die. Some ridiculed him, jokingly saying that Jesus claimed to be the King of Israel but could not even save himself (Matthew 27:39–44).

One of the robbers realized Jesus was innocent of any crime. He acknowledged Jesus as God when he asked Jesus to accept him into God's kingdom. Jesus promised this robber that he would join Jesus that very day in heaven (Luke 23:39–43).

"And kneeling before him, [the soldiers] mocked him, saying, 'Hail, King of the Jews!' And they spit on him and took the reed and struck him on the head." (Matthew 27:29b–30)

Why do you think a loving God would allow his Son to be killed in such a horrible manner?

131. Jesus Died

[from Matthew 27:27–56; Luke 23:39–46; and John 19:25–27]

Before he died, Jesus called out to his Father, asking him why he had forsaken him. But then, just as the robber submitted to Jesus, Jesus submitted to God the Father when he cried out his last words: "Father, into your hands I commit my spirit! (Luke 23:46).

In his death, Jesus took on the punishment humans deserve for their sin, and experienced God's angry wrath. Because God cannot be in the presence of sin, in this sense, God the Father temporarily abandoned God the Son. Jesus cried out in anguish at being separated from the love of the Father and the fellowship they shared (Matthew 27:45–46). Even though Jesus was separated from the Father at his death, some of his disciples were present, as well as Mary Magdalene, the mother of James and John, other friends, and even Jesus' mother, Mary (John 19:25–27).

At the moment Jesus cried out and died, the veil of the temple that separated the people from the Holy of Holies—the most sacred room of the temple, where God's presence dwelled—was torn in two. The tear was from top to bottom, indicating that God had ripped the veil. Had a person done this, the rip would have been from the bottom upward. Rocks split apart as an earthquake shook the ground. Tombs were opened and dead saints came to life (Matthew 27:50–53). As Jesus died, the chief Roman soldier, a centurion, quit mocking.

"When the centurion and those who were with him, keeping watch over Jesus, saw the earthquake and what took place, they were filled with awe and said, 'Truly this was the Son of God!'" (Matthew 27:54)

What do you think? Is Jesus the Son of God?

132. Jesus Was Buried but Rose from the Dead

[from Matthew 27:57–28:10]

When Jesus was dead, Joseph, a wealthy disciple of Jesus' from the town of Arimathea, asked Pilate for permission to bury Jesus. Joseph wrapped the Savior's body in cloth and placed it in the new tomb he had prepared for himself, fulfilling the prophecy in Isaiah 53:9 that Jesus would be buried in the grave of a rich man. The tomb was a cave cut into rock, with the opening sealed by a large stone.

The next day was the Sabbath, so the religious leaders went to Pilate to arrange for Roman soldiers to guard the tomb. They knew Jesus had said he would rise from the dead. They wanted to make sure his friends did not steal the body and fake his resurrection.

Early on Sunday, the day after the Sabbath, there was another earthquake. An angel rolled the stone away from the tomb and sat on it. The Roman guards shook with fear and passed out. Two women, both named Mary, went to the tomb that morning. Each of them had been at the crucifixion. When they arrived at the tomb, the angel met them and told them not to be afraid—that Jesus had risen from the dead. The angel showed them the place where Jesus' body had been. Then he said that Jesus was going to Galilee, and he told the two women to tell the disciples to meet him there. The women ran away with both fear and joy to tell the disciples. On their way, Jesus met them. He encouraged them not to be afraid and confirmed what the angel had told them.

"He is not here, for he has risen, as he said. Come, see the place where he lay." (Matthew 28:6, quoting the angel)

Why do you think the two women felt fear and joy at the same time?

133. Jesus Gave His Disciples a New Assignment and New Power
[from Matthew 28:16–20 and Acts 1:4–11]

When the eleven remaining apostles went to Galilee, they met with Jesus and worshiped him, but some were perplexed and doubtful. Jesus pointedly spoke to both the worshiping and the doubting. He told them God had given him all authority in heaven and on earth (Matthew 28:16–18).

Then Jesus taught them about the kingdom of God and gave them their new assignment; in his power, they were to go and make disciples of all nations, baptizing them and teaching them to observe all his commands. He also assured them he would be with them forever (Matthew 28:19–20). He said that while John the Baptist baptized with water, he would baptize them with the Holy Spirit. He told them to stay in Jerusalem until this happened (Acts 1:4–5).

"But you will receive power when the Holy Spirit has come upon you, and you will be my witnesses in Jerusalem and in all Judea and Samaria, and to the end of the earth." (Acts 1:8)

Have you thought about the assignment you have from God and the power you have to accomplish it?

134. Jesus Appeared to the Eleven Apostles and Five Hundred Other People

[from Matthew 28:1–10; Luke 24:1–53; Mark 16:14; John 21:1–14; Acts 1:3–11; and 1 Corinthians 15:6]

After his death, Jesus appeared to his disciples and many of his friends over a period of forty days. These eyewitness accounts included the two women named Mary who were the first to see him that Sunday morning (Matthew 28:1–10). Then he joined two disciples who were walking on the road to the village of Emmaus, outside of Jerusalem. After realizing their fellow traveler was Jesus, those two walked back to Jerusalem and were with a larger group of disciples when Jesus appeared among all of them as well (Luke 24:13-48). Then Jesus appeared to the eleven apostles while they were having a meal together. Later, he met the apostles for the third time while they were fishing, and he ate fish with them (John 21:1–14). Paul reported that Jesus met with five hundred of his followers at the same time (1 Corinthians 15:6).

Finally, Jesus met with many of his disciples in Jerusalem. After the forty-day period, Jesus was lifted up while the disciples watched. He went into a cloud and out of their sight. Two angels appeared. They said Jesus would return in the same way as they had watched him go (Acts 1:9–11).

"He presented himself alive to them after his suffering by many proofs, appearing to them during forty days and speaking about the kingdom of God." (Acts 1:3)

What further proof do you need to believe that Jesus is alive today?

PART SEVEN

God Sent His Spirit and Established His Church

Book of the Bible Discussed in This Part:

Acts

Jesus Was Crucified and Raised, Then Appeared and Ascended	Holy Spirit Power Unleashed at Pentecost	Paul's Conversion
30/33 AD	30/33	34/35
	Matthias Replaced Judas as an Apostle	Stephen Killed; Paul Helped!

	Paul as a Missionary		Paul a Prisoner in Rome
37/40	46–57	57/59	60–64
Peter Baptized Cornelius		Paul a Prisoner in Caesarea	

135. The Apostles Needed a Replacement Who Was a Witness to Jesus' Resurrection

[from Acts 1:4–26]

After Jesus ascended to heaven, his disciples returned to Jerusalem, where they gathered together and devoted themselves to prayer. Jesus had instructed them to remain in Jerusalem until he baptized them with the Holy Spirit. Included in the group were Jesus' mother and some of his siblings.

Peter took the lead, reminding everyone that Psalm 109:8 taught that the vacancy left when Judas killed himself should be filled. He said it was necessary for there to be twelve apostles again so there would be sure witnesses to Jesus' resurrection. Two men were nominated to be the replacement. The group prayed and asked Jesus to direct them to choose the man God wanted for the job. God led them to select Matthias, who then became an apostle, completing the group of twelve official witnesses to Jesus' resurrection.

"One of these men must become with us a witness to his resurrection." (Acts 1:22b)

Do you know that just as Matthias was grafted into the group of apostles to be a witness to the resurrection of Jesus, you too can become a witness to the resurrection of Jesus by asking him into your life?

***

REFLECTION 12

If You Believe in Jesus, Tell Others about His Resurrection

The apostles believed God led them to replace Judas so that they, as a complete group of twelve, could be witnesses to the resurrection of Jesus. Matthias was the man they chose.

Many times, after people become Christians, they are not sure what God wants them to do. They wonder if they should go to another school or change jobs. Many people think they should be doing something different with their lives.

The experience of the apostles gives a clear idea to all of us that one thing always pleases God, regardless of our life situation: being living witnesses to Jesus' crucifixion and resurrection, and helping other people understand the truth of these events. Jesus wants us to share this good news with others—he said so in John 15:27 and Acts 1:8.

Because helping others know God is one way to love them, witnessing to them about Jesus is a way to follow what Jesus called the second of the great commandments: to love our neighbor as ourselves (Matthew 22:39). Other important verses in the book of Acts about being witnesses to Jesus' resurrection are Acts 1:22; 3:15; 17:18; and 18:5.

***

136. The Holy Spirit Brought God's Power to His Family

[from Acts 2:1–13]

Later, the disciples were together in a house on the day of Pentecost, a harvest festival held fifty days after Passover. Without any warning, a loud noise came from heaven. Like the wind of a storm, the noise filled the house. Then something like tongues of fire rested on each person. These symbols of fire were the outward signs of the Holy Spirit filling them. The Holy Spirit worked a miracle in them then so that they began speaking in the languages of the various people who were in Jerusalem for the Pentecost celebration. Their message was about the "mighty works of God" (2:11). The people who heard were puzzled about how the disciples could speak in so many different languages. It was an amazing demonstration of Jesus' promise that they would receive the power of the Holy Spirit to accomplish their new assignment.

God used different languages on this occasion to promote understanding and unity among many different people who wanted to know and serve him. This was exactly the opposite of what God did at the Tower of Babel, where people rejected God and wanted to be independent of him. In that event, God intentionally confused their languages so the proud people could no longer work together against him. Disorder resulted, as opposed to order and unity (Pixel 11).

"And they were all filled with the Holy Spirit and began to speak in other tongues as the Spirit gave them utterance." (Acts 2:4)

Have you ever tried to do a job before you really had the knowledge and tools to do it?

137. Peter Preached the First Sermons to the Church

[from Acts 2:14–3:26]

Peter and the other eleven apostles stood before the people in Jerusalem who had gathered for Pentecost. He told them that the disciples' ability to speak in other languages came from the Holy Spirit. Then he said that God had done miracles through Jesus to prove that Jesus came from God. Peter explained that, rather than believing Jesus was God's Son, the religious leaders thought Jesus was a fraud and insisted on his crucifixion. But God raised Jesus from death to live again. Peter and the other apostles witnessed that resurrection, and God had now made him Lord.

Upon hearing Peter's sermon, many people were troubled in their hearts. He told them that God had made Jesus, "whom [they] crucified," both "Lord and Christ"; they had "killed the Author of life, whom God raised from the dead" (2:36; 3:15). He said these things because many in the crowd had consented to or even clamored for Jesus' crucifixion just weeks earlier. Many were greatly affected by Peter's words and asked him what they should do (2:37). Peter challenged them to "repent and be baptized every one of you in the name of Jesus Christ for the forgiveness of your sins, and you will receive the gift of the Holy Spirit" (2:38). After Peter's first sermon, about three thousand people responded and were baptized.

After that, more people wanted to hear the apostles teach. The believers met together in fellowship and prayer, with these meetings developing into the church in Jerusalem (2:42–46). More and more people were amazed at what God was doing through the apostles. God brought many others, who also repented of their sins and were baptized.

"And day by day, attending the temple together and breaking bread in their homes, they received their food with glad and generous hearts." (Acts 2:46)

Have you ever seen God accomplish something that you never expected could happen?

138. The Apostles Were Arrested for Teaching about the Living Jesus
[from Acts 4:1–31 and 5:12–42]

Later, when Peter and John preached, more people believed the truth about Jesus' resurrection, increasing the number of men to five thousand. Infuriated by this, the religious leaders had Peter and John arrested. When the religious leaders met to examine Peter and John, the Holy Spirit spoke through Peter. He told them that God had raised Jesus from death; therefore, Jesus was the only way to salvation. The religious leaders told Peter and John to stop teaching this message. But Peter and John replied that they listened to God rather than to people, and they would speak of the things they saw with their own eyes and heard with their own ears, as God directed them.

Another time, all the apostles were at the temple teaching about Jesus and healing the sick. The religious leaders were jealous, so they arrested the apostles and put them in prison. God sent his angel in the night to unlock the prison and tell the apostles to return to the temple and continue teaching about new life in Jesus. When the religious leaders learned about this, they had the apostles brought before them again. The apostles repeated bluntly to the religious leaders that they obeyed God, not people. The religious leaders were so outraged that they wanted to kill the apostles. But one of the religious leaders, Gamaliel, cautioned the other leaders that they risked fighting God. With this caution, the religious leaders had the apostles beaten and let them go with the warning not to teach about Jesus.

After being beaten, the apostles left the religious leaders joyfully, recognizing that their faithfulness as witnesses caused them to suffer. They went right back to the temple and kept teaching that Jesus, as God's Son, rose from the dead and was the only way for people to be saved.

"But Peter and the apostles answered, 'We must obey God rather than men. The God of our fathers raised Jesus, whom you killed by hanging him on a tree. God exalted him at his right hand as Leader and Savior, to give repentance to Israel and forgiveness of sins. And we are witnesses to these things, and so is the Holy Spirit, whom God has given to those who obey him.'" (Acts 5:29–32)

Whom do you obey—your conscience before God or the popular culture?

139. Stephen Was the First Christian Martyr
[from Acts 6:1–8:3]

Stephen was a leader of the young church in Jerusalem and followed Peter and John's examples of preaching and teaching about Jesus. The Holy Spirit gave Stephen understanding, wisdom, and special power, so that when he preached, he was able to perform "great wonders and signs" (6:8). This enraged some of the religious people, who found men to lie and accuse Stephen of saying horrible things about God, Moses, and the temple.

They took Stephen and these false witnesses to the same council of Jewish religious leaders that condemned Jesus to die. When the council asked Stephen to defend himself, he told them the whole story of Jesus and how this same group had murdered him. They began grumbling against Stephen. But the Holy Spirit allowed Stephen to look into heaven and see Jesus. When he told them what he saw, they forced him out of the city and stoned him. As he was dying, he called on Jesus to receive his spirit.

One man who helped kill Stephen was Saul, later renamed Paul after his conversion. Later that day, Saul and others began attacking the church.

"And Saul approved of his execution. And there arose on that day a great persecution against the church in Jerusalem, and they were all scattered throughout the regions of Judea and Samaria, except the apostles." (Acts 8:1)

Have you ever been punished when you were doing the right thing?

140. Jesus Brought Saul into the Church

[from Acts 9:1–31]

Saul hated Jesus, his church, and his followers so much that he wanted to kill more of them. The religious leaders in Jerusalem gave him the authority to go to Damascus, the next-largest city, north of Jerusalem, and arrest all the Christians he could find. But while Saul was on the road to Damascus, he was blinded by a sudden light from heaven. He fell to the ground. Then he heard a voice—Jesus' voice—telling Saul to stop persecuting Christians, and to continue to Damascus for instructions.

In Damascus, Jesus appeared to one of his followers, Ananias. He told Ananias where to find Saul and how to help him. Ananias was afraid because he knew Saul intended to arrest Christians and have them killed. Jesus assured Ananias that, from now on, Saul would be Jesus' chosen instrument. Ananias found Saul, prayed for him, and welcomed him as a new follower of Jesus. Just then, Saul's eyesight, which had been gone since his encounter with Jesus, returned, and he was baptized. Immediately, Saul began explaining to others that Jesus is the Son of God, the Messiah spoken of by the prophets. He said Jesus was killed on a cross by the religious leaders and the Roman government.

In order to silence Saul, the religious leaders in Damascus wanted to kill him. Saul escaped to Jerusalem, but the religious leaders there wanted to kill him too! Christians in the church of Jerusalem helped Saul escape to his hometown, Tarsus, many miles away. With Saul now a believer in Jesus and no longer a threat, the Christians in Judea and Samaria could relax and worship God in peace.

"So Ananias departed and entered the house. And laying his hands on him he said, 'Brother Saul, the Lord Jesus who appeared to you on the road by which you came has sent me so that you may regain your sight and be filled with the Holy Spirit.'" (Acts 9:17)

Have you ever worried that God did not know what was best for you and for his church?

141. The Holy Spirit Used Peter to Bring Gentiles into the Church

[from Acts 9:43–11:18]

Peter traveled from Jerusalem to outlying areas to teach about Jesus. In the town of Joppa, he stayed with Simon, a tanner. One day during his visit, while Peter was praying, God gave him a vision of many kinds of animals to eat, some of which were improper food for Jews. Peter objected to eating the unclean animals; still God ordered Peter to eat. But Peter kept refusing to break his Jewish tradition. The vision was repeated three times, however, leaving Peter puzzled.

Then some men came to Simon's home looking for Peter, and the Holy Spirit told Peter to go with them. The men had a message from Cornelius, a Roman army officer from Caesarea, a town north of Joppa. The men said Cornelius feared God and that an angel had told him to send for Peter to come to his home and speak about God. As a proper Jew, it would make Peter unclean to enter the home of any non-Jewish person, much less that of a Roman soldier. He agreed to go with them only because the vision was fresh in his mind about God ordering him to eat unclean animals. Taking the message of Jesus to these non-Jews would fulfill God's promise to Abraham that his family would be a blessing to all nations (Genesis 12:3; 22:18; Pixel 13).

Cornelius had some relatives and close friends waiting with him when Peter arrived. Peter told them that God's message about Jesus was not only for the Jews, but for anyone who honored God and lived in a way that pleased him. Peter explained everything about Jesus: that he is God's Son, anointed by the Holy Spirit; while on earth, he was hated and eventually killed by the religious leaders. Peter and many others witnessed these things, for they were with Jesus both before and after he rose from the dead. While Peter was still speaking, the Holy Spirit fell on Cornelius and those with him. Peter knew this was God's way of welcoming Gentiles into his family, so he baptized them, expanding the church.

"'If then God gave the same gift to them as he gave to us when we believed in the Lord Jesus Christ, who was I that I could stand in God's way?' When they heard these things they fell silent. And they glorified God, saying, 'Then to the Gentiles also God has granted repentance that leads to life.'" (Acts 11:17–18)

Has God ever asked you to do something unexpected, either through his word or some other way?

REFLECTION 13

Five Primary Truths of Life as God's Child

This is a good time to reflect on who we are as children of God, and what that identity means for us. Understanding this identity in Christ matters very much, affecting our entire lives.

After Peter's experience with Cornelius, he was back in Jerusalem. Some church leaders criticized Peter for associating with Gentiles. They did not fully appreciate that every believer is God's child, and in Jesus we belong to him the way that human children belong to their parents. Peter explained the whole story about Cornelius, starting with the vision God gave him of eating unclean animals. After hearing Peter's explanation, the believers in Jerusalem agreed with Peter and rejoiced that God's church was open to both Jews and Gentiles.

Yet this truth—that our identity is totally in Jesus and not in following traditions— was difficult to fully understand and live by, even for Peter. Later, when he visited Antioch, Peter refused to eat with Gentile Christians because of the pressure of some Jewish Christians, who insisted that, to be a true follower of Jesus, a person must follow Jewish customs, traditions, and rituals. In effect, Peter was agreeing with those who claimed that following human rules was necessary to be properly reconciled to God (Galatians 1:1–14).

Paul rebuked Peter publicly, making it clear that the *only* requirement for a relationship with God is faith in Jesus and in what he did to satisfy God's requirements for our sin and rebellion against him (Galatians 2:11–14). Paul said that neither our performance nor our perfectionism can add to what Jesus did, in terms of either keeping the law or behaving in a particular way. If there were something a person could do to gain God's acceptance, Paul argued, there would have been no point to Jesus dying on the cross (Galatians 2:15–21). In short, when we are in Jesus, we are children of God and we belong to him; nothing can change the position or snatch us out of his hand.

Besides the truth that *our identity is in Christ alone,* four other truths permeate the remainder of the New Testament:

What we believe (*our faith*) matters (Reflection 17).

What we do (*our actions*) matters (Reflection 22).

How we treat others (*our relationships*) matters (Pixel 151).

How we come into God's presence (*our worship*) matters (Reflection 18).

***

142. The Holy Spirit Directed the Church to Send Saul (Paul) as a Missionary

[from Acts 11:19–26; 13:1–9; and 16:11–40]

From his hometown of Tarsus, Saul went to Antioch to help the church there. One day, when people in the church were together praying and fasting in worship, the Holy Spirit spoke to them. The Spirit said to send Barnabas and Saul to other towns to teach and encourage those who followed Jesus. During Saul's first trip with Barnabas, people started referring to him as Paul, a more Roman-sounding name than his Jewish one.

On another trip, Paul traveled with Silas. One place they went was the city of Philippi, where they encountered a slave girl who, through evil spirits, told fortunes to make money for her owners. This girl followed Paul and Silas, crying out that they were servants of God whose message was the way of salvation. This was so annoying to them that Paul commanded the evil spirit to leave her, in the name of Jesus. When the evil spirit left the girl, she could no longer tell fortunes! Angry that their profitable business had been destroyed, the girl's masters dragged Paul and Silas to the authorities. Paul and Silas were beaten badly. Then they were chained, imprisoned with the worst criminals, and had their feet fastened with locks.

In the middle of the night, Paul and Silas prayed and sang hymns. The entire prison echoed with their words and songs. Then the unexpected happened; an earthquake hit the prison. All the doors opened, and the chains and locks came undone. The jailer assumed all the prisoners had escaped, which he knew meant his own life was in danger. But Paul called out to assure him that all the prisoners were still there.

The jailer was shocked and amazed. He asked them what he needed to do to be saved. They told him about Jesus, and he along with his entire household believed, so all of them were baptized.

"Then [the jailer] brought [Paul and Silas] out and said, 'Sirs, what must I do to be saved?' And they said, 'Believe in the Lord Jesus, and you will be saved, you and your household.'" (Acts 16:30–31)

The jailer in Philippi wanted to know what to do to be saved; what did he do when he heard the answer?

143. A Young Boy Trusted God and Acted Courageously to Save Paul's Life

[from Acts 21:15–23:32]

A few years later, Paul went back to Jerusalem. People from some of the nearby towns where Paul had preached recognized him. Many of them hated Paul's message about Jesus, his resurrection, his appearance to Paul on the road to Damascus, and Paul's appointment as a witness for Jesus. These enemies of Paul started an uproar by dragging him out of the temple and attempting to kill him.

Just in time, Roman soldiers saved Paul from the mob, taking him to their military barracks. The next day, the commander ordered the religious leaders to meet with him and Paul so he could understand the charges against Paul. During this meeting, Paul told the religious leaders that they opposed him because he taught that their only hope for eternity was in the fact that Jesus came back to life after he had died. Some of the religious leaders became extremely angry because they opposed Paul's argument for resurrection from death. Others believed resurrection was possible. They argued amongst themselves so violently that the commander took Paul back to the barracks so he would not be hurt.

The next day, Paul's young nephew managed to get into the barracks to see his uncle. The boy had heard some of the religious leaders conspiring to set an ambush to kill Paul. He took the risk of challenging the religious leaders by reporting this conspiracy to Paul. Paul convinced the jailer to take the boy to the prison commander. The commander believed the boy, and immediately had his troops take Paul safely to Caesarea, the town where the Roman governor lived.

"The tribune took [Paul's nephew] by the hand, and going aside asked him privately, 'What is it that you have to tell me?' And he said, 'The Jews have agreed to ask you to bring Paul down to the council tomorrow, as though they were going to inquire somewhat more closely about him. But do not be persuaded by them, for more than forty of their men are lying in ambush for him, who have bound themselves by an oath neither to eat nor drink till they have killed him. And now they are ready, waiting for your consent.'" (Acts 23:19–21)

Have you ever thought you were too young, or for some reason not the right person, to take action when you knew something needed to be done?

144. Paul Trusted God and Was Sent to Rome as a Prisoner

[from Acts 25:1–28:31]

In Caesarea, Paul eventually was put on trial before the governor, Festus. The religious leaders could not prove any of the charges they made against Paul. Paul told Festus that these leaders wanted to kill him because he taught that Jesus rose from the dead, that all people should repent and turn to God, and that they should now live lives of repentance.

Festus asked Paul to go to Jerusalem for the trial to be continued. But rather than risk being killed in Jerusalem, Paul said he wanted his trial appealed to Caesar in Rome. Festus sent Paul, with soldiers to guard him, to Rome by ship. On the way, a great storm forced the ship to run aground on a reef near a small island. Even though the ship broke apart, everyone was safe, and in a few months, they took another ship to Rome.

Paul spent about two years imprisoned in Rome waiting for his trial. For some reason, the trial never happened, but while he was imprisoned, Paul took every opportunity to talk about Jesus to anyone who would listen. Many people came to see and hear Paul while he was in prison in Rome.

"From morning till evening he expounded to them, testifying to the kingdom of God and trying to convince them about Jesus both from the Law of Moses and from the Prophets. And some were convinced by what he said, but others disbelieved." (Acts 28:23b–24)

From what you know about Paul so far, what would you say is the most important thing in his life? What is the most important thing in *your* life?

PART EIGHT

God Taught His Family How to Live

Books of the Bible Discussed in This Part:

Romans, 1 & 2 Corinthians, Galatians, Ephesians, Philippians, Colossians, 1 & 2 Thessalonians, 1 & 2 Timothy, Titus, Philemon, Hebrews, James, 1 & 2 Peter, 1, 2, & 3 John, Jude

Paul a Prisoner in Rome		*1 & 2 Corinthians*		*Ephesians*		*Colossians*	
60–64 AD	55–58	53–57	48–55	60–63	55–63	60–63	49–53
	Romans		*Galatians*		*Philippians*		*1 & 2 Thessalonians*

1 & 2 Timothy		Philemon		James		1, 2, & 3 John	
62–67	62–66	60–62	64–68	45–50	62–68	85–95	63–68
	Titus		Hebrews		1 & 2 Peter		Jude

In Part Eight, the date of the written epistle refers to the approximate time of the writing of the epistle.

CONNECTION 12

Primary Themes in the Epistles—Romans through Jude

Except for Revelation, the last book in the Bible, the remaining twenty-one books of the New Testament after Acts are epistles. An epistle is a letter to a church, a group of churches, or an individual (usually with a church in mind as a broader audience). In an epistle, the writer gives instructions or advice about specific issues or problems. Thus, by nature, epistles tend to offer "life lessons" and guidance rather than discussing what happened or what someone did. Many of the new believers in Jesus needed help understanding how to live their new life in Jesus. You will see this content summarized in the pixels throughout Part Eight.

Paul wrote the first thirteen epistles: from Romans, which immediately follows the book of Acts, through Philemon, which precedes Hebrews. The author of the fourteenth epistle, Hebrews, is unknown. The last seven books—James through Jude—were written by four authors, all of whom were personally close to Jesus during his life and ministry on earth. These authors include Peter and John, who were apostles and two of Jesus' closest friends, along with James and Jude, half-brothers to Jesus.

Four big-picture themes appear throughout the epistles:

Godly teaching	False teaching
Gospel living	Worldly living

Of these themes, the first two "go together," and the second two "go together." If we follow godly teaching about who God is and his desires for us, we will lead lives that honor him and reflect the values of the gospel—what we call "gospel living." On the other hand, if we follow counterfeit teaching, which either does not promote God's truth or distorts it, we will end up living by the standards of the world. Whereas godly teaching and gospel living lead to life, false teaching and worldly living lead to death (Romans 8:5–11).

Of course, the epistles contain other themes as well, but be on the alert for these four categories, as many of the other teachings and ideas fall under one of them. For example, in many of his writings, Paul discussed the importance of financial support for Christians in hard circumstances, a subtopic under gospel living.

***

145. Paul Wrote to the Church in Rome

[from Romans 1:1–17]

Paul wrote the epistle of Romans to the church in Rome before he went there as a prisoner. His purpose in this letter was to help the Christians in Rome build their faith in Jesus and to encourage them to live God-honoring lives.

He upheld himself as an example of someone who was a servant of Jesus and God the Father. His purpose as an apostle and teacher was to help others live in obedience to God as an expression of their faith. He assured the Roman Christians that if they lived faithfully for Jesus, both they and Jesus would be encouraged.

The main theme of Romans is in 1:16–17. Paul wanted the Romans to know that the message of Jesus—his life, death, and resurrection—is one of salvation for *everyone* who believes, regardless of whether the person is a Jew or a Gentile. Then Paul wanted the Roman Christians to know that righteous living—doing the right thing before God— is only possible if God's Spirit lives in them. Finally, Paul explained that righteous living is only possible for those who have faith, which is itself a God-given gift.

"For I am not ashamed of the gospel, for it is the power of God for salvation to everyone who believes, to the Jew first and also to the Greek. For in it the righteousness of God is revealed from faith for faith, as it is written, 'The righteous shall live by faith.'" (Romans 1:16–17)

What have you done by faith?

146. God's Wrath and Judgment

[from Romans 1:18–3:20]

In sharp contrast to those who seek to live in the righteousness of God, some people reject God and refuse to acknowledge him as their creator. These people are blind to the truth that all of creation reveals the thoughtful work and design of God's personal and creative genius—his general revelation of himself (1:20). Paul's point was that a careful observation of the world should lead people to understand that they and the entire universe are part of God's intentional work. The intricacy of the created order leaves everyone without an excuse not to seek and honor God (1:18–20).

Instead of acknowledging their creator, those who reject God worship something he created. This is idolatry. God allows these people who insist on rejecting him to go their own way. Some of them end up undertaking sexual practices, such as homosexuality, that violate God's intentions for his creation. Some end up in other kinds of troubles, such as unhealthy patterns of living and bad relationships with other people.

Paul then discussed another aspect of God's general revelation: his kindness and patience with those he made. His kindness is intended to lead people to see the futility of their current attitudes toward life and turn to him (2:4). But instead of acknowledging God's kindness, those who reject him deceive themselves into thinking that God will accept their religious practices and their own personal efforts—yet another form of idolatry (3:20). God declares that no human is righteous, and without his aid, no one can properly respect or fear him (3:10, 18). In the end, whether a person is a Jew or not, God will punish anyone who rejects him. By contrast, he will accept anyone who acknowledges and honors him and his Son (2:9–11).

"Therefore God gave them up in the lusts of their hearts to impurity, to the dishonoring of their bodies among themselves, because they exchanged the truth about God for a lie and worshiped and served the creature rather than the Creator, who is blessed forever! Amen." (Romans 1:24–25)

In what ways do you worship the creation and ignore the Creator?

147. Justification before God Is by Faith

[from Romans 3:21–31]

Paul explained to the Roman Christians that every person has sinned against God. It does not matter if a person is Jewish or not; Old Testament heritage does not count for anything in God's kingdom of spiritual children. Neither does it matter if a person is a Gentile. Paul was clear; no person except God's Son is worthy to stand before God and claim to be innocent.

The only way to remedy the offense of sin against God is to be made right before him—a process called *justification*. Furthermore, the only way to be justified before God is to have faith that when Jesus died, God took the righteous life Jesus led and applied it to sinners, a process called *propitiation* (Reflection 14).

The justice of God's law is satisfied when he accepts a person's faith in Jesus.

"But now the righteousness of God has been manifested apart from the law, although the Law and the Prophets bear witness to it—the righteousness of God through faith in Jesus

Christ for all those who believe. For there is no distinction: for all have sinned and fall short of the glory of God, and are justified by his grace as a gift, through the redemption that is in Christ Jesus, whom God put forward as a propitiation by his blood, to be received by faith. This was to show God's righteousness, because in his divine forbearance he had passed over former sins. It was to show his righteousness at the present time, so that he might be just and the justifier of the one who has faith in Jesus." (Romans 3:21–26)

How can a sin against a perfect and holy God be made right?

***

REFLECTION 14
Jesus Paid Our Debt and Satisfied God's Wrath

In the Old Testament, an animal was offered as a sacrifice to atone for sin; the animal became a substitute before God for the person who sinned.

In Romans 3:23, Paul declared that "all have sinned and fall short of the glory of God." The only way we can be made right with God is to acknowledge that Jesus' death was the sole acceptable substitute for the punishment our sin deserves. In a theological sense, we say Jesus is the atonement, before God, for our sin.

Atonement has two aspects, both of which Jesus fulfilled for us. The first is redemption: Jesus took on himself the punishment for our sins; that is, he paid the debt for our sin—an accomplishment called *expiation*. Second is reconciliation with God, or *propitiation*: Jesus satisfied God's anger at us for rejecting him and rebelling against the good ways he prepares for us. Keep these ideas in mind for when we discuss the book of Hebrews later.

Are you able to look God in the face and tell him you have faith in what Jesus did for you as atonement for your sins? If so, rest assured that Jesus' atonement allows you to be at peace with God. Paul stated it succinctly when he said, "There is therefore now no condemnation for those who are in Christ Jesus" (Romans 8:1). Be confident that you are now his child, and he is your Father!

***

148. Confidence Comes from Being Conformed to Jesus
[from Romans 8:16–30]

Many people in the church in Rome were puzzled about why life as a Christian was so difficult. Paul wrote to encourage them so they could have confidence in God's plan for them. He explained that when God accepts our faith in Jesus, his Spirit will testify with our spirit to confirm that we are truly God's children (8:16–17). He assured the Roman Christians that in spite of their weakness and impending suffering for their faith, God's Spirit would teach them how to pray.

Then, in three of the most well-known passages in the Bible, he helped them see that God's faithful hand is on his children (8:28–30). God will make everything eventually work out to accomplish his good plans. And for all of his children, his plan is for their character—who they really are on the inside—to be changed from what it was when they were born to something new: the character of Jesus.

"And we know that for those who love God all things work together for good, for those who are called according to his purpose. For those whom he foreknew he also predestined to be conformed to the image of his Son, in order that he might be the firstborn among many brothers. And those whom he predestined he also called, and those whom he called he also justified, and those whom he justified he also glorified." (Romans 8:28–30)

Does it encourage you to know you are not stuck for the rest of eternity with being who you are now?

***

REFLECTION 15
God's Will for Our Character

We read about Paul's message that a Christian is a person who acknowledges Jesus as God's Son and believes his death and resurrection make it possible to know God personally. This work of God's Spirit takes place inside us. Throughout the rest of our lives, God wants us to cooperate with the Holy Spirit in our thoughts, beliefs, and actions, ultimately being transformed into people who think and act like Jesus. Because he now lives inside us spiritually, we speak of this as being conformed to the image of Jesus. Another way to say this is that our character is being changed into what God wants us to be as his children—a process called *sanctification*.

Other important verses in the Bible about the transformation of our character include 2 Corinthians 3:18, Galatians 4:19, Ephesians 4:13, and Colossians 1:27–28. Read these verses, and as you do, think about Jesus' conversation with the lawyer who wanted to justify himself (Pixel 112). Cooperating with God in our character transformation means implementing the first part of what Jesus said in that conversation: "Love the Lord your God with all your heart and with all your soul and with all your strength and with all your mind"—the "great and first" commandment (Matthew 22:36–38).

***

149. A Conformed Life Is a Sacrificed Life

[from Romans 12:1–16:27]

Paul ended his teaching to the Romans by explaining that they were to offer their lives and their bodies to God, just as Jesus did. He called this their spiritual worship. Doing this would reflect that they were being conformed to Jesus and not to the world around them (12:1–2).

The remainder of the book of Romans, chapters 13 through 16, gives examples of what it means to live sacrificially. These include things like being good citizens and obeying governing authorities.

Paul also wrote that love is the fulfillment of the law (13:10). Believers are to respect Christians whose opinions differ from theirs. They are to help and encourage those who don't have the material resources or understanding they have. Paul said that when Christians live this way, as a living sacrifice before God, they are demonstrating to others what it means to honor God as the first priority in their lives.

"I appeal to you therefore, brothers, by the mercies of God, to present your bodies as a living sacrifice, holy and acceptable to God, which is your spiritual worship. Do not be conformed to this world, but be transformed by the renewal of your mind, that by testing you may discern what is the will of God, what is good and acceptable and perfect." (Romans 12:1–2)

When Jesus sacrificed himself, he was killed. His death was brutal! Do you think being a living sacrifice will hurt you?

150. Life without Love Is Worthless

[from 1 Corinthians 12–14]

While on his missionary journeys, Paul taught that Jesus is God's Son who makes it possible to have a personal relationship with God. In the towns he visited, he encouraged people who came to faith in Jesus to know each other and meet together. These meetings for fellowship later became churches.

The church in Corinth, a city in Greece, had problems. People there were confused. They did not know how to live respectfully with each other, nor did they, as new believers in Jesus, know how to live in a culture that did not honor God. Neither did the Corinthians understand what the Resurrection meant. Paul wrote 1 Corinthians to help these believers.

Paul explained that the Holy Spirit gives every follower of Jesus the ability to accomplish what God wants that person to do. These spiritual gifts from the Holy Spirit enable each believer to have a unique role in the church and to build each other up (12:7–11, 28; 14:26).

Paul wrote that for God's people to use their gifts properly, they must understand that love is the most important principle—the regulating ideal that should govern and motivate everything they do. Love is the key that unlocks the power of all the spiritual gifts. Paul explained the quality and nature of this love in Chapter 13. He emphasized that, without love, everything else the Corinthians did amounted to nothing.

"Pursue love, and earnestly desire the spiritual gifts . . ." (1 Corinthians 14:1a)

Why is love so important?

***

REFLECTION 16

Gospel Living Is Based on Gifts of the Spirit, Not Material Wealth or Social Status

Paul wrote about gifts from the Holy Spirit in three of his epistles: Romans, 1 Corinthians, and Ephesians.

In Romans 12:6–8, Paul made the point that gifts are a matter of God's grace and empower us to fulfill his intentions for us. In 1 Corinthians, he explained that spiritual gifts give each person a unique role to fulfill. In Ephesians 4:11–13, Paul connected the proper use of these gifts to equipping "the saints for the work of ministry, for building up the body of Christ" (4:12). Paul summarized the practical purpose of spiritual gifts for believers, teaching in Ephesians 4:16 that Jesus is the head of the body "from whom the whole body, joined and held together by every joint with which it is equipped, when each part is working properly, makes the body grow so that it builds itself up in love."

The use of spiritual gifts out of love rather than for personal benefit or glory is the opposite of what we normally find in the world around us. Jesus taught this concept when, in a 180-degree reversal of usual human thinking, he declared that the last will be first and the first will be last in his kingdom (Matthew 19:30; 20:16, 27). He applied this principle to himself emphatically when he declared, "The Son of Man came not to be served but to serve, and to give his life as a ransom for many" (20:28).

When we live according to the culture around us, we are impressed with people's material wealth, accumulated possessions, and other external status symbols. But when we live according to the gospel, we appreciate and love each other based on the God-honoring role he gives each person in the body of Christ.

***

151. How We Treat Each Other Matters

[from 1 Corinthians 3:1–23; 6:1–11; and 11:17–34]

Some people in the church failed to love each other properly. They had disagreements about which missionary and teacher was the best. For the Corinthians, the debate focused on Paul, Apollos, and Peter. Paul told them that it is a sign of immaturity to argue about which human leader is best. The only foundation is the one Jesus alone already laid, Paul wrote (3:1–11).

People in the church also had legal disputes over money. To try to resolve these problems, some went to the secular courts for judges to make decisions. Paul told them that this was shameful for believers, who should be able to resolve their disputes with help from fellow believers in the church (6:5–8).

The church also had problems over how to celebrate the Lord's Supper. This meal, instituted by Jesus, was to be in remembrance of his death. However, when they met for the fellowship part of the celebration, some wealthy people in the church were selfish and did not share their generous portions with those who were poor. This humiliated the poor people (11:20–22). Paul told the Corinthians this behavior was wrong, and that they should be respectful of each other as they acknowledged what Jesus did for all of them (11:33).

"Do you not know that you are God's temple and that God's Spirit dwells in you? If anyone destroys God's temple, God will destroy him. For God's temple is holy, and you are that temple." (1 Corinthians 3:16–17)

Have you ever been disrespectful to another person when you should have loved that person?

152. God's Spirit Enables Love for Him

[from 1 Corinthians 3:1–23; 5:1–13; 6:9–20; 9:12; and 10:1–33]

The Corinthian church confused loving and living for God with loving the surrounding culture and living like everyone else.

Paul rebuked the church for allowing sexual impurity. He told them not to associate with immoral people, and to put such people out of the church (5:9, 13). He taught that "the unrighteous will not inherit the kingdom of God," and included a detailed list of the people whose conduct offends God's character (6:9–11). He instructed, "The body is not meant for sexual immorality, but for the Lord, and the Lord for the body" (6:13b). Moreover, when people become believers in Jesus, they are joined to God in spirit; therefore, sexually immoral people sin against their own body and God's Spirit (6:15–18).

Paul also rebuked the church for allowing some who participated in pagan worship to also take part in the Lord's Supper (10:14–22). He emphasized that a believer in Jesus participates in the "body of Christ" when taking the Lord's Supper (10:16b). In contrast, pagan worshipers offer sacrifices "to demons and not to God" (10:20b). Thus, it is not possible to partake both of Jesus and demons (10:20–22).

Paul gave himself as an example of a person who lived for God rather than for himself. He wrote that, as an apostle, he was in a position of authority to demand benefits for himself. Instead, he did not insist on his rights so that he would not put "an obstacle in the way of the gospel of Christ" (9:12b).

"Or do you not know that your body is a temple of the Holy Spirit within you, whom you have from God? You are not your own, for you were bought with a price. So glorify

God in your body." (1 Corinthians 6:19–20)

Is there something in your life that would be an obstacle to another person understanding the gospel of Jesus?

153. Faith in Jesus Gives Confidence in the Resurrection of the Dead

[from 1 Corinthians 15]

Some in the church said there was no resurrection of the dead. Paul pointed these people to Jesus, who was raised from the dead and appeared in bodily form to hundreds of people, and even to Paul. Paul wrote that the hope of Christians for eternal life is validated by Jesus' resurrection.

Others in the church wondered about the resurrection body. Paul again pointed to Jesus as the life-giving spirit (15:45). The natural, earthly body, he wrote, is sown "perishable," "in dishonor," and "in weakness," but the resurrection body will be "raised imperishable," "in glory," and "in power" (15:42–44). Just as believers have the earthly body and image of Adam, who died, they will have the spiritual body and image of Jesus, who died but did not stay dead.

The fundamental truth of Paul's teaching is that the reality of the empty tomb and Jesus' resurrection is the basis of the Christian faith.

"For if the dead are not raised, not even Christ has been raised. And if Christ has not been raised, your faith is futile and you are still in your sins. Then those also who have fallen asleep in Christ have perished. If in Christ we have hope in this life only, we are of all people most to be pitied." (1 Corinthians 15:16–19)

What would cause you to doubt that Christians will receive a resurrection body?

154. Paul Suffered and Identified with Jesus
[from 2 Corinthians 1–4]

After Paul sent the letter of 1 Corinthians, many in the church in Corinth were so offended by what he said that they opposed him and his authority. A year or so later, Paul wrote another letter to this church—2 Corinthians.

Paul suffered severely as a minister and missionary for Jesus. He wanted the church to know that being a follower of Jesus does not mean a life of ease. Instead, just as Jesus suffered for them to become children of God, "we share abundantly in Christ's sufferings, so through Christ we share abundantly in comfort too" (1:5). Paul said that being comforted, and comforting others, is not the only purpose of suffering. God also allows suffering so that his people will be transformed into the image of Jesus, and so the life of Jesus will be manifested in their bodies (3:18; 4:10b).

Suffering also strengthens believers spiritually, because it helps a person realize that God's invisible, spiritual provision is the ultimate provision, and it will not pass away like material provisions.

"For this light momentary affliction is preparing us for an eternal weight of glory beyond all comparison, as we look not to the things that are seen but to the things that are unseen. For the things that are seen are transient, but the things that are unseen are eternal." (2 Corinthians 4:17–18)

What have you learned from something you have suffered?

155. Paul Ministered and Lived as a Reconciled Child of God

[from 2 Corinthians 5–7]

Paul taught that when people become children of God, their old nature passes away and they become "new creations" in Jesus (5:17). God uses this new creation to minister to other people. The new person created by God's work increasingly develops a character conformed to the image of Jesus.

The ministry God gives his children is the same ministry Jesus had, which is to reconcile people to God as "ambassadors for Christ" (5:20). God's plan for his children and their ministry to others is to "become the righteousness of God" (5:21). This is only possible because Jesus, who was without any sin at all, became sin for everyone.

"Therefore, if anyone is in Christ, he is a new creation. The old has passed away; behold, the new has come. All this is from God, who through Christ reconciled us to himself and gave us the ministry of reconciliation; that is, in Christ God was reconciling the world to himself, not counting their trespasses against them, and entrusting to us the message of reconciliation. Therefore, we are ambassadors for Christ, God making his appeal through us. We implore you on behalf of Christ, be reconciled to God. For our sake he made him to be sin who knew no sin, so that in him we might become the righteousness of God." (2 Corinthians 5:17–21)

What must happen inside you before you can become an ambassador of reconciliation?

156. Many Gave Financially and Honored What God Had Done for Them

[from 2 Corinthians 8–9]

Paul told the church in Corinth that the church in Jerusalem was suffering and needed financial support. He said those in Macedonia generously "gave themselves first to the Lord" and then gave money for those in Jerusalem, and he challenged the Corinthians to do the same (8:5). Paul's focus on financial giving was based on people first becoming children of God, and then having their character conformed to the image of Jesus.

He described giving as an "act of grace" that proves love is genuine (8:7). He explained that by giving, the Corinthians would be following Jesus, who proved his love for them: "Though he was rich, yet for your sake he became poor, so that you by his poverty might become rich" (8:9).

In this teaching, Paul continued to expand on the scope of being conformed to the image of Jesus, and becoming ministers of reconciliation. As proof of this transformation in their lives, their money was to become part of that ministry of reconciliation. Just as Jesus sacrificed for them, they should desire to give, as a way of following his example (8:10–11).

"Each one must give as he has decided in his heart, not reluctantly or under compulsion, for God loves a cheerful giver. And God is able to make all grace abound to you, so that having all sufficiency in all things at all times, you may abound in every good work." (2 Corinthians 9:7–8)

Are you content with giving to others what God has given you, knowing that he will use your gift, multiplying its effects as Jesus did with the loaves and fish in his feeding of the five thousand, to accomplish his will?

157. Paul's Defense Was Spiritually Based

[from 2 Corinthians 10–13]

Some people in the church criticized Paul for not having sufficient spiritual authority to teach them. Some accused him of "walking according to the flesh" (10:2b). Paul dealt with these criticisms "by the meekness and gentleness of Christ" (10:1a). He said he would not use human weapons—only spiritual weapons—in his defense, because "the weapons of our warfare are not of the flesh but have divine power to destroy strongholds . . . and take every thought captive to obey Christ" (10:4–5). He told them his prayerful desire for them was restoration, because God gave him authority for building them up and not tearing them down (13:9b, 10b, 11a; 10:8).

Paul said he would not try to take credit for what someone else did. Rather, he would "boast only with regard to the area of influence God assigned" (10:13). Further, he made clear that humans may boast only about God's work in and through them, "for it is not the one who commends himself who is approved, but the one whom the Lord commends" (10:18).

Paul admitted that, as a human, he had personal failures, problems, and weaknesses. He asked God to overcome these failures, resolve his problems, and remedy his weaknesses. Here is God's answer to his prayer, along with Paul's response:

"But [God] said to me, 'My grace is sufficient for you, for my power is made perfect in weakness.' Therefore I will boast all the more gladly of my weaknesses, so that the power

of Christ may rest upon me. For the sake of Christ, then, I am content with weakness, insults, hardships, persecutions, and calamities. For when I am weak, then I am strong." (2 Corinthians 12:9–10)

If you were talking to someone about your faith in Jesus and that person challenged you to explain the authority behind your words, how would you reply?

158. God Appointed Paul to Teach

[from Galatians 1:1–2:14]

Paul was instrumental in establishing churches in an area known as Galatia. After he left Galatia to teach and encourage churches in other areas, some people back in Galatia began promoting ideas different from Paul's message. These false teachers claimed that, in addition to believing in Jesus as God's Son, it was necessary to follow some of the rules and laws of Jewish tradition. Paul wrote the book of Galatians to the churches this false teaching had infiltrated. He explained that his authority came from God, so he would follow God rather than other people.

Paul reminded the Galatians that Jesus himself appeared to Paul and appointed him as an apostle; this was not a position given to him by other people (1:1). By this time in his life, Paul knew God *and* human beings well enough to know that it was impossible to please both at the same time. He, along with everyone else, had to make a choice (1:10).

Paul was disturbed that many in the Galatian churches had made the wrong choice; they were following other people and traditions, not God. He was astonished at how quickly they deserted the gospel of Jesus in order to please people who taught lies as the truth (1:6–7). Paul asserted that his authority was grounded in the truth that God set him apart before birth, called him by grace, and revealed Jesus to him (1:15–16). This was what enabled him to teach and preach the real gospel of Jesus, and was the reason they should follow him rather than false teachers.

"For am I now seeking the approval of man, or of God? Or am I trying to please man? If I were still trying to please man, I would not be a servant of Christ." (Galatians 1:10)

Can you remember when wanting to please another person caused you to do or believe something that you knew was wrong?

159. How Are We Made Right with God?

[from Galatians 2:15–4:31]

Paul instructed the Galatian churches that faith based on performance is not true faith. Whether the performance is done before people to try and please them, or before God to ritualistically follow laws and traditions, it doesn't matter—either kind of performance-based religion misses the heart of God.

True faith, Paul wrote, is based on knowing, understanding, and trusting in Jesus for justification before God (2:16). This is possible only because Jesus performed all that is needed for our relationship with God to be restored and to thereby become his children (3:25–26).

Paul urged the Galatians not to be foolish by following the false teachers (3:1). Neither should they "turn back again to the weak and worthless elementary principles of the world" (4:9). Rather, they needed Christ living inside them, his character to be gradually formed in them; and Paul would be in personal anguish until that happened (4:19).

"I have been crucified with Christ. It is no longer I who live, but Christ who lives in me. And the life I now live in the flesh I live by faith in the Son of God, who loved me and gave himself for me." (Galatians 2:20)

How is Jesus able to make you right with God?

160. False Teachers Oppose Liberty in Jesus

[from Galatians 5–6]

Paul gave another reason for his friends to stop trying to please and follow the rules of false teachers: Jesus had given them a new liberty. He set them free, and they should "not submit again to a yoke of slavery" (5:1). Submitting to these false teachers would separate them from Jesus.

This liberty and freedom, Paul taught, is in Jesus, and is not "an opportunity for the flesh" but rather to "through love serve one another" (5:13). Pursuing the things of the flesh—things that do not please God—leads to corruption. Going after things of the spirit, by contrast, leads to eternal life, and reveals a spiritually mature understanding that true freedom is found in pursuing the things God desires and values (6:8).

To prevent any confusion about the difference between pursuing the things of the flesh and pursuing the things of the Spirit, Paul gave a detailed explanation:

"Now the works of the flesh are evident: sexual immorality, impurity, sensuality, idolatry, sorcery, enmity, strife, jealousy, fits of anger, rivalries, dissensions, divisions, envy, drunkenness, orgies, and things like these. I warn you, as I warned you before, that those who do such things will not inherit the kingdom of God. But the fruit of the Spirit is love, joy, peace, patience, kindness, goodness, faithfulness, gentleness, self-control; against such things there is no law." (Galatians 5:19–23)

Does having liberty and freedom make you more uncomfortable than knowing—and keeping—a set of very definite rules?

161. From Spiritual Death to Immeasurable Wealth in Jesus
[from Ephesians 1–3]

Paul wrote to the church in Ephesus to address the realities of living as spiritually renewed people with the richness of God's promises, provisions, purposes, and plans available to them. He emphasized three main points in this letter: (1) They were reconciled to God through the work of Jesus; (2) they were brought together to be in unity as the church of Jesus; and (3) they were empowered to live through the work of the Holy Spirit.

Paul explained to the Ephesians that, without Christ, all people are spiritually dead and in sin (2:1). However, they can have hope because God, in his mercy, chooses to make them spiritually alive in Jesus (1:4; 2:4). Therefore, through Jesus, they are God's adopted children, heirs to every spiritual blessing (1:3, 5, 11).

One of the benefits of being God's children is being part of God's spiritual house, with Jesus as the cornerstone (2:20). On earth, this house is the church, which reveals God's wisdom "to the rulers and authorities in the heavenly places" (1:22–23; 3:10). Paul emphasized that becoming part of God's family is not something that can be earned. It is a gift from God.

"For by grace you have been saved through faith. And this is not your own doing; it is the gift of God, not a result of works, so that no one may boast. For we are his workmanship, created in Christ Jesus for good works, which God prepared beforehand, that we should walk in them." (Ephesians 2:8–10)

How would you describe what it means for a person to be spiritually dead?

162. Walk Worthily in This New Life in Jesus

[from Ephesians 4:1–5:21]

Paul taught the Ephesians that they should be imitating Jesus in how they lived because they had become God's children (5:1).

Paul gave specific instructions about God's will for their character and lives. Being a child of God means living "in a manner worthy" of that identity, trying "to discern what is pleasing to the Lord," and renewing the character by putting off the "old self," renewing the spirit of the mind, and putting on the "new self" given by God (4:1–3; 5:9, 10; 4:22–24). With regard to how to live in the world, Paul said the Ephesians should speak "the truth in love," make the best use of their time, and "submit to one another out of reverence for Christ" (4:15, 25; 5:15–16, 21).

"I therefore, a prisoner for the Lord, urge you to walk in a manner worthy of the calling to which you have been called, with all humility and gentleness, with patience, bearing with one another in love, eager to maintain the unity of the Spirit in the bond of peace." (Ephesians 4:1–3)

What changes do you need to make in your life to better imitate God?

163. Live in the Power of the Holy Spirit

[from Ephesians 1:19–23 and 5:21–6:24]

Paul knew that imitating God and walking as his worthy child does not happen automatically or on its own. In the Holy Spirit, God gives believers the same power that raised Jesus from death—a power that flows from the source of *all* power and authority (1:19–23; 3:16).

It is this power that enables a believer to "be strong in the Lord" and "stand against the schemes of the devil," by taking up the "whole armor of God" (6:10–11).

One especially difficult area Paul addressed is the family. Specifically, how can people be properly submissive and honor God in their families (5:21)? For married people, Paul taught that the husband should "love his wife as himself" and the wife should "see that she respects her husband" (5:33). Paul instructed children to "obey [their] parents in the Lord" (6:1).

"For we do not wrestle against flesh and blood, but against the rulers, against the authorities,

against the cosmic powers over this present darkness, against the spiritual forces of evil in the heavenly places. Therefore take up the whole armor of God, that you may be able to withstand in the evil day, and having done all, to stand firm . . . having fastened on the belt of truth . . . the breastplate of righteousness . . . as shoes for your feet, having put on the readiness given by the gospel of peace . . . take up the shield of faith . . . take the helmet of salvation . . . and the sword of the Spirit . . . praying at all times in the Spirit . . ." (Ephesians 6:12–18)

What power is available to you to change your life to fight against the devil's schemes?

164. Have the Mind of Jesus

[from Philippians 1–2]

Paul told the church in Philippi that he was able to be joyful in Jesus even while in a Roman prison. He encouraged the Philippians to keep Jesus as their model in the face of their own suffering and internal problems; this is the only way to live properly in the world and mature in faith. Paul told the Philippian believers to acknowledge that Jesus is the supreme head of the church, and to not be influenced by false teachers.

Paul gave himself as an example to the Philippians. Even though he was suffering in prison, he was encouraged that his imprisonment "served to advance the gospel" (1:12). This joy was possible for him, as well as for them, in spite of difficult circumstances, because Christians have the mind of Christ Jesus (2:5). Christians also have confidence that Jesus will complete in them what he started (1:6). Furthermore, Christians will grow and mature in discernment and holiness (1:9–11).

Paul also emphasized that, with the mind of Christ, they could live in a manner worthy of Jesus, not only believing in him but suffering for him (1:27, 29). This worthy living includes living together as believers in unity and humility—a spirit that does not come naturally but through intention (2:2–4, 12–13). Then the Philippians would be able to say, with Paul, that "to live is Christ, and to die is gain" (1:21).

"Do nothing from rivalry or conceit, but in humility count others more significant than yourselves. Let each of you look not only to his own interests, but also to the interests of others. Have this mind among yourselves, which is yours in Christ Jesus." (Philippians 2:3–5)

How does knowing that you have the mind of Christ make a difference in how you see other people?

165. False Teachers Promote Personal Effort, Not Gospel Living

[from Philippians 3–4]

Paul urged the Philippians to avoid false teachers who claimed that proper worship of God is through personal efforts (3:2–3). Paul again pointed to himself as a prime example. Early in his life, Paul was enthusiastic about knowing and following all the religious rules and duties. He even persecuted Christians. But after he encountered Jesus, Paul realized all his past efforts were "rubbish" and his teachings false. All that mattered was that "[he] may gain Christ and be found in him, not having a righteousness of [his] own that comes from the law, but that which comes through faith in Christ, the righteousness from God that depends on faith" (3:8b–9).

Paul taught that maturity in the Christian faith means pressing on "toward the goal for the prize of the upward call of God in Christ Jesus" (3:14). With this in mind, Paul told the Philippians they should live in ways that honored God, and God's peace would be with them (4:4–9). He then thanked them for supporting him financially and assured them that God would supply their needs (4:14–19). Paul's confidence in God's provision and the power of Jesus within him left him content with his life and service.

"Not that I am speaking of being in need, for I have learned in whatever situation I am to be content. I know how to be brought low, and I know how to abound. In any and every circumstance, I have learned the secret of facing plenty and hunger, abundance and need. I can do all things through him who strengthens me." (Philippians 4:11–13)

Are you anxious about something you need? What can, or should, you do about your anxiety?

166. False Teachers Deny Jesus as God

[from Colossians 1–2]

The Colossian church had a problem with false teachers, but in a different way than the Philippian church. The false teachers in Colossae attempted to diminish the importance of Jesus. Their teachings attempted to delude and then control by making philosophical arguments (2:4–8). They judged others based on external behavior, such as the proper food to eat and how to celebrate holidays (2:16–18). These false teachers also tried to impose meaningless regulations that appeared smart on the surface but, in reality, were foolish (2:20–23).

Paul urged the Colossians to reject these false teachings and understand the supreme role of Jesus in faith. Paul taught that Jesus is "the image of the invisible God," in whom "all the fullness of God was pleased to dwell" (1:15, 19; 2:9). Consequently, Jesus holds everything together and reconciles everything to himself (1:17, 20; 2:19). In Jesus "are hidden all the treasures of wisdom and knowledge"; he is the "head of all rule and authority," and in his power "he disarmed the rulers and authorities" (2:2–3, 10, 15). As Paul explained to the Colossians, having this correct view of Jesus enables a believer to walk worthy of Jesus—pleasing him, bearing fruit, increasing in the knowledge of God, being strengthened, sharing in God's inheritance, and being transferred from darkness to the kingdom of Jesus (1:10–14). As a result, they are no longer alienated from God, but presented holy and blameless before him (1:21–22).

Paul spoke of the mystery that God shared even to the Gentiles: "Christ in you, the hope of glory" (1:27). In Jesus, God takes his children, as he took the Colossians, from being dead in their trespasses to being "made alive together with him" (2:13).

"[Jesus] is the image of the invisible God, the firstborn of all creation. For by him all things were created, in heaven and on earth, visible and invisible, whether thrones or dominions or rulers or authorities—all things were created through him and for him." (Colossians 1:15–16)

How is it possible that Jesus is the only person in the universe who can take you from being spiritually dead to being spiritually alive?

167. Setting Your Mind on the Things of God
[from Colossians 3–4]

Later in his letter, Paul instructed the Colossians to set their minds on heavenly things and not on earthly things, because Christ was in them (3:1–2). Paul told the Philippians something similar—to be intentional about pursuing their salvation.

Paul also urged the Colossians to focus on putting off "the old self with its practices" and instead "put on the new self, which is being renewed in knowledge after the image of its creator" (3:9–10). This is the same language Paul used in his instructions to the Ephesians.

Specifically, Paul challenged the Colossians to put to death "what is earthly in you" (3:5). Some of the character traits and practices he exhorted them to put on were compassion, forgiveness, peacefulness, thankfulness, the richness of Jesus' teaching, encouragement of others, submissiveness, prayerfulness, and graciousness in speech (3:12–4:5).

"If then you have been raised with Christ, seek the things that are above, where Christ is, seated at the right hand of God. Set your minds on things that are above, not on things that are on earth." (Colossians 3:1–2)

What circumstances in your life make it difficult for you to set your mind on the things of God?

168. Steadfast Faith

[from 1 Thessalonians 1:1–3:13]

Paul was instrumental in establishing the church in Thessalonica. But soon, he and his coworkers, Timothy and Silas, were run out of town by people who opposed their preaching.

In this first letter to the Thessalonians, Paul gave thanks to God for their diligence in the faith to which God had led them (1:2–4; 2:13; 3:6). Paul acknowledged that they had remained steadfast under persecution and affliction (1:6; 2:14–16). He even said believers in Jesus are destined for affliction and hard times (3:3). In the city of Philippi, Paul reported, he and his coworkers had "suffered and been shamefully treated" (2:2). But regardless of this experience, he came to the Thessalonian church to teach the gospel with boldness, "not to please man, but to please God who tests our hearts" (2:4).

"We give thanks to God always for all of you, constantly mentioning you in our prayers, remembering before our God and Father your work of faith and labor of love and steadfastness of hope in our Lord Jesus Christ." (1 Thessalonians 1:2–3)

Right now, are you living to please God rather than other people? If so, how? If not, what do you need to do to start living to please God?

169. The Return of Jesus, Part One

[from 1 Thessalonians 4:13–5:11]

Later in 1 Thessalonians, Paul addressed an apparent concern about what happens to believers who die before Jesus returns. Paul assured the Thessalonians that physical death before the return of Jesus will not cause those believers to be separated from God.

When Jesus returns, Paul explained, he first will call those who are already physically dead, and they will rise to meet Jesus. Then those who are alive will "be caught up with them in the clouds to meet the Lord in the air" (4:17).

"For the Lord himself will descend from heaven with a cry of command, with the voice of an archangel, and with the sound of the trumpet of God. And the dead in Christ will rise first. Then we who are alive, who are left, will be caught up together with them in the clouds to meet the Lord in the air, and so we will always be with the Lord." (1 Thessalonians 4:16–17)

Do you wonder if you will be separated from God when you die?

170. Gospel Living in a Pagan Culture
[from 1 Thessalonians 2:9–5:28]

Using himself and his coworkers as examples of people whose lives honored God, Paul acknowledged that the believers in Thessalonica had and would suffer the same hostile treatment from their neighbors (2:10). However, he encouraged them to follow his example, exhorting them to live in ways that please God (2:12; 4:1, 12).

The kind of life Paul urged the Thessalonians to live includes loving others with purity, being diligent in work, and motivating others. This pattern of gospel living means having a proper relationship with God, which results in an attitude of always rejoicing, always praying, always giving thanks, and always being alert.

Toward the end of 1 Thessalonians, Paul prayed that God would keep them "blameless at the coming" of Jesus, and he assured them that the God who called them would be faithful to accomplish what he promised (5:23, 24).

". . . and may the Lord make you increase and abound in love for one another and for all, as we do for you, so that he may establish your hearts blameless in holiness before our God and Father, at the coming of our Lord Jesus with all his saints." (1 Thessalonians 3:12–13)

How are you able to live a holy life?

171. The Return of Jesus, Part Two

[from 2 Thessalonians 2:1–12]

Even though Paul had previously given the Thessalonians instructions about Jesus' return, some in the church had been "shaken in mind or alarmed" by a false or deceitful message (2:2–3). They worried Jesus had already made his promised return to earth and the day of the Lord had come (2:3).

In his second letter to the church, Paul assured them this was not the case. Two events must happen before Jesus returns, Paul explained. The first is "the rebellion," and the second is the revealing of "the man of lawlessness," who will "[proclaim] himself to be God" (2:3–4). Paul said that this man was presently restrained, but when he comes, it will be "by the activity of Satan" (2: 6–7, 9). The man of lawlessness will deceive those who "refused to love the truth and so be saved" (2:10).

"The coming of the lawless one is by the activity of Satan with all power and false signs and wonders, and with all wicked deception for those who are perishing, because they refused to love the truth and so be saved." (2 Thessalonians 2:9–10)

How can you resist Satan's deceptive activity?

172. Gospel Living through Jesus

[from 2 Thessalonians 1–3]

Paul thanked the Thessalonians for their growth and steadfastness in Jesus even as they were undergoing persecution (1:3–4). He said that, although they suffered for their faith, those who do not know God or obey the gospel of Jesus are much worse off. These unbelievers will "suffer the punishment of eternal destruction" (1:8–9).

Paul further assured the Thessalonians of his prayers for them, and that God would make them "worthy of his calling" (1:11). He explained that Jesus (not they themselves) would be the one to accomplish all of this in them. Jesus would comfort their hearts, "establish them in every good work and word," and guard them "against the evil one" (2:17; 3:3).

At the same time, Paul admonished those in the church who thought they did not have to work, expecting instead that others would provide for them. He bluntly told these people "to earn their own living" (3:12).

Second Thessalonians ended with Paul's encouragement that they not "grow weary in doing good" (3:13).

"May the Lord direct your hearts to the love of God and to the steadfastness of Christ. Now we command you, brothers, in the name of our Lord Jesus Christ, that you keep away from any brother who is walking in idleness and not in accord with the tradition that you received from us." (2 Thessalonians 3:5–6)

If Jesus accomplishes God's work in and through us, why did Paul say not to grow weary in doing good?

***

CONNECTION 13
Paul Wrote Four Epistles to Three Friends

The next four books in the New Testament are Paul's letters to three of his friends. Rather than writing to an entire church, as in the previous nine epistles, these four epistles were sent to individuals, with the purpose of teaching and encouraging them, both personally and as leaders in their respective churches.

Paul wrote 1 and 2 Timothy to his young disciple, whom he left in Ephesus to help the church there. In the book of Titus, Paul wrote to another young disciple, whom he left in Crete to help the church there. Paul wrote the book of Philemon to his friend by the same name, whose slave, Onesimus, had stolen property from his master and run away.

***

173. Wage War against False Teachers

[from 1 Timothy 1 and 4]

After Paul left the church in Ephesus in Timothy's care, some in the church taught religious doctrines that differed from Paul's teachings about Jesus. Paul instructed Timothy to fight these false teachers.

Paul told Timothy to make sure his own motives were based on love coming from "a pure heart and a good conscience and a sincere faith" (1:5). He advised Timothy that the law is good because it helps disobedient people understand what God-honoring lives should be like (1:8–11).

Paul also said that, in later times, some will "depart from the faith" and make up rules about relationships and not eating certain food (4:1, 3). He reminded Timothy that "everything created by God is good, and nothing is to be rejected if it is received with thanksgiving, for it is made holy by the word of God and prayer" (4:4).

So that Timothy would be the leader the church in Ephesus needed, Paul admonished him to train himself, teach others, and realize he was at war with spiritual evil.

"This charge I entrust to you, Timothy, my child, in accordance with the prophecies previously made about you, that by them you may wage the good warfare, holding faith and a good conscience." (1 Timothy 1:18–19a)

How would you summarize Paul's instructions to Timothy?

174. Gospel Living in Church

[from 1 Timothy 2:1–3:16]

To help with the situation in Ephesus, Paul gave Timothy specific instructions about how the church there should operate, including the structure of leadership and the conduct of worship it should follow. Obeying Paul's instructions would enable the church to better accomplish its mission of representing Jesus to the community.

Paul also emphasized the importance of praying for government leaders so that they may have the wisdom to govern in ways that promote peaceful and dignified lives (2:1–2). The purpose of having an ordered society is to help all people come to know God's saving truth through Jesus Christ, the only mediator people have with God (2:3–4, 5–6).

Paul explained that men in particular should pray as a remedy for their anger and quarreling (2:8). Women, he said, should dress with modesty, act with self-control, and not teach or exercise authority over men in the church (2:9–12).

Paul then outlined some detailed qualifications for men who would be the teachers and leaders exercising authority in the church (3:1–13). In summary, Paul wrote so that Timothy, the Ephesians, and others who read Paul's epistle would know how to behave in the church of Jesus Christ (3:15).

"I am writing these things to you so that, if I delay, you may know how one ought to behave in the household of God, which is the church of the living God, a pillar and buttress of the truth." (1 Timothy 3:14–15)

What is the church, and what is its purpose?

175. Gospel Living in Personal Relationships
[from 1 Timothy 5–6]

Paul instructed Timothy through the steps and commitments necessary to build a church and encourage its members to model what it means to have a gospel view of life. Paul urged Timothy to be respectful, particularly to elders and widows, and to deal with younger women in purity as sisters.

In more detail, Paul added that the false teachers fail to understand that true godliness results in inner commitment and instead teach that godliness leads to financial gain. Their false faith in money leads them astray because they refuse to learn that "love of money is a root of all kinds of evil" (6:5–10). By contrast, Timothy was to focus on teaching the doctrines that Paul emphasized.

"But as for you, O man of God, flee these things. Pursue righteousness, godliness, faith, love, steadfastness, gentleness. Fight the good fight of the faith. Take hold of the eternal life to which you were called and about which you made the good confession in the presence of many witnesses." (1 Timothy 6:11–12)

How would you describe what it means to live as a follower of Jesus?

176. False Teachers Distort and Deceive

[from 2 Timothy 1 and 3–4]

Paul wrote a follow-up letter to Timothy. Paul knew that some in the Ephesian church were embarrassed that he, their respected leader, was in a Roman prison. However, he told Timothy that he was not ashamed, because in prison he was sharing in the sufferings to which Jesus called him (1:8–9). He was confident in Jesus' provision for him, even if his body was being poured out as a sacrificial offering to God (1:12–13; 4:6, 16–18).

What troubled Paul were the false teachers, who were deceiving people. In detail to Timothy, he exposed as lies the ideas the false teachers promote as godly wisdom (3:1–5). These people's teachings distort true gospel living, corrupt proper thinking, and undermine genuine faith, Paul explained (3:6–9).

Furthermore, false teachers are successful in gaining a hearing because some people prefer teachers who tell them what they want to hear rather than the truth (4:3–4).

"Therefore do not be ashamed of the testimony about our Lord, nor of me his prisoner, but share in suffering for the gospel by the power of God, who saved us and called us to a holy calling, not because of our works but because of his own purpose and grace, which he gave us in Christ Jesus before the ages began." (2 Timothy 1:8–9)

If you know something is true, would you be ashamed to share that truth with others?

177. The Holy Spirit Empowers Gospel Living

[from 2 Timothy]

In sharp contrast with the false teachers and people ashamed of Paul's suffering, Paul taught how Christians should live. Paul urged Timothy to remember that God's work in his life was his source of "power and love and self-control" (1:6–7). Timothy should rely on the Holy Spirit to guard what he had received and be strong in the grace of Jesus (1:14; 2:1). Paul directed Timothy to make sure there were faithful leaders in the church who understood these things and could teach others (2:2–14).

Regarding hardship, Paul told Timothy that suffering is normal for a follower of Jesus, so he should expect it (1:8; 3:12). Using himself as an example, Paul assured Timothy that because God's word cannot be imprisoned, Paul would "endure everything for the sake of the elect" coming to faith in Jesus (2:9–10). Timothy should take this same perspective and be diligent as God's servant, relying on the truth of the Scripture, which is "breathed out by God" (2:15; 4:5; 3:14–17). Paul said Timothy should preach, teach, rebuke, remain sober-minded, and endure suffering in his ministry (4:1–5).

Paul also emphasized the importance of Timothy's personal life as a model for pursuing holiness. Timothy should "depart from iniquity," be clean for honorable use in God's work, pursue what honors God, avoid controversies and distractions from what honors God, and conduct himself as a living witness to others (2:19–26).

Finally, recognizing that his life was about to end in prison, Paul asked Timothy to visit him as an act of hospitality, and to bring him some supplies when he came (4:9–18).

"And the Lord's servant must not be quarrelsome but kind to everyone, able to teach, patiently enduring evil, correcting his opponents with gentleness. God may perhaps grant them repentance leading to a knowledge of the truth, and they may come to their senses and escape from the snare of the devil, after being captured by him to do his will." (2 Timothy 2:24–26)

Are there changes you need to make for your life to honor God?

178. Appoint Godly Leaders and Confront False Teachers
[from Titus 1]

Paul began his practical letter of instructions to Titus with an encouraging statement about the certainty of God's promises, brought to fulfillment in Jesus (1:1–4). He then instructed Titus to appoint trustworthy and effective leaders in each church throughout Crete. Paul described the major character traits and life experiences that qualify men for these leadership positions (1:5–8). Having leaders with these strengths is critical because these men are responsible for teaching in the church and rebuking teachers of false doctrines—a pervasive problem throughout the Christian world (1:9).

Paul said the false teachers in Crete were insubordinate, needed to be silenced, had defiled minds and consciences, and denied God by their works even though they professed to know him (1:10–16). In summary, Paul dismissed the false teachers as being "unfit for any good work" (1:16).

"This is why I left you in Crete, so that you might put what remained into order, and appoint elders in every town as I directed you—if anyone is above reproach, the husband

of one wife, and his children are believers and not open to the charge of debauchery or insubordination." (Titus 1:5–6)

Why is it important for a church to have trustworthy leaders?

179. Gospel Living as God's Family
[from Titus 2–3]

Paul wanted to make sure Titus knew what it meant to live according to the gospel of Jesus and how to teach that gospel to others. Paul anchored this message to Titus in the "grace of God," which trains us in God's ways (2:11–12). Titus had to be the teacher of what "accords with sound doctrine" (2:1). The elders must be able to teach in the church, and older women must teach younger women (1:9).

Following these directions about teaching in the church will not result merely in academic achievement or intellectual satisfaction, but in changed lives. Titus was to embody this life transformation, showing himself "in all respects to be a model of good works," and teaching with "integrity, dignity, and sound speech" (2:7–8).

All people in the church are to be obedient to secular authorities, Paul emphasized. Christians are to be "ready for every good work, to speak evil of no one, to avoid quarreling, to be gentle, and to show perfect courtesy toward all people" (3:1–2, 8–10, 14).

The verses below are a good summary of what Paul wanted Titus to know, live, and teach.

"For the grace of God has appeared, bringing salvation for all people, training us to renounce ungodliness and worldly passions, and to live self-controlled, upright, and godly lives in the present age, waiting for our blessed hope, the appearing of the glory of our great God and Savior Jesus Christ, who gave himself for us to redeem us from all lawlessness and to purify for himself a people for his own possession who are zealous for good works." (Titus 2:11–14)

Why is proper training necessary in order for Christians to be "zealous for good works"?

180. A Thieving Slave Became a Humble Servant

[from Philemon]

Onesimus bolted from slavery under Philemon. On his way out, he stole from Philemon to finance his runaway trip to Rome. As a fugitive slave in Rome, he somehow met Paul, then a prisoner there. Paul led Onesimus to faith in Jesus, and Onesimus helped ease Paul's hard life in prison.

Amazingly, just a few years earlier, Paul had led another man to faith in Jesus: Philemon, Onesimus' master. In this epistle, Paul wrote about the need for Philemon and Onesimus to be reconciled as brothers in Jesus. Rather than tell Philemon what to do, Paul appealed to him in love to receive Onesimus as a new spiritual brother and not as a returned slave. In fact, Paul sent this letter with Onesimus for personal delivery to Philemon. Paul urged his friend Philemon to treat Onesimus as he would treat Paul. Paul even said that if Onesimus owed Philemon anything, Paul would repay him for it. Paul, the prisoner, ended by telling Philemon that Paul's heart needed refreshing by what he expected Philemon to do (1:20).

"For this perhaps is why he was parted from you for a while, that you might have him back forever, no longer as a slave but more than a slave, as a beloved brother—especially to me, but how much more to you, both in the flesh and in the Lord." (Philemon 1:15–16)

If you were Onesimus, would you have been afraid to hand-deliver Paul's letter to Philemon?

***

CONNECTION 14

Hebrews Connects the Old and New Covenants

Hebrews was specifically written to Jews who were familiar with the atonement offering and other ideas and symbols from the old covenant. The unknown author of Hebrews expressed deep conviction and used great care to show that Jesus accomplished what was incomplete in the old covenant (Hebrews 7:22).

Recall that under the old covenant, priests had to offer daily and yearly animal sacrifices. The Jewish people also offered animal sacrifices. But God promised he would make a new covenant—a promise he fulfilled through the life, death, and resurrection of Jesus (8:8–13). When Jesus ate the Passover meal with his apostles, he told them it was the "new covenant in [his] blood" (Pixel 125). The book of Hebrews explains how these two covenants, the old and the new, connect (9:1–28).

Jesus is the ultimate high priest because he overcame all human weakness and temptation during his life on earth. He did so not by any human accomplishment, but by God's power—"the power of an indestructible life" (7:16).

Jesus eliminated the need to worship in a specific place. As he told the Samaritan woman at the well, God wants people to worship him from their hearts, in spirit and in truth, and not in a particular place (Pixel 106).

Jesus gave himself as the ultimate sacrifice. As God's Son, he satisfied once and for all the need for a yearly blood sacrifice for our sins (7:27).

After his resurrection, Jesus rejoined the Father at his throne, where he continually prays for us (1:3). There can be no greater source of confidence than to know that Jesus appears before his Father on behalf of his children. What could be more encouraging? And what could be more important? (10:19–25).

Alongside this great encouragement, Hebrews also gives five stern warnings against rejecting Jesus. These warnings are mentioned in the next four pixels.

***

181. Jesus Is God's Final Word
[from Hebrews 1:1–2:18]

The author of Hebrews began this intense letter by assuring readers that, although God had spoken in many ways previously, he now speaks through Jesus, who is God in human form. God affirmed the superiority of Jesus over every other person and thing when he called Jesus his Son—the one who "laid the foundation of the earth" and whose throne will last forever (1:8, 10). God said his Son is also unique because he loves that which is true and hates what is evil (1:9a).

God has subjected everything to Jesus, and nothing is outside his control (2:8b). Through his death, Jesus destroyed "the one who has the power of death, that is, the devil" (2:14b). He helps "the offspring of Abraham," and as a "merciful and faithful high priest," he makes "propitiation for the sins of the people" (2:16b, 17b; Reflection 14).

The first warning in Hebrews against rejecting Jesus is this: "How shall we escape if we neglect such a great salvation?" (2:3a). The author then stated that salvation was spoken of by Jesus and confirmed by eyewitnesses, as well as by God's own actions of signs, wonders, miracles, and gifts of the Holy Spirit (2:3b–4).

"He is the radiance of the glory of God and the exact imprint of his nature, and he upholds the universe by the word of his power. After making purification for sins, he sat down at the right hand of the Majesty on high, having become as much superior to angels as the name he has inherited is more excellent than theirs." (Hebrews 1:3–4)

Who is Jesus to you?

182. Jesus Is Our Model for Faithfulness
[from Hebrews 3:1–4:13]

The author of Hebrews compared the faithfulness of Moses, as a servant, with that of Jesus as a son. The second warning is that believers should not act like the rebellious people under Moses, who hardened their hearts against God's leadership (3:7–9). Instead, they should encourage each other not to be "hardened by the deceitfulness of sin" (3:13). In this way, they will "share in Christ, if indeed they hold their original confidence firm to the end" (3:14b).

Just as Moses sought to lead the people to the Promised Land, Jesus will lead the people of God to "a Sabbath rest" (4:9). Followers of Jesus should "strive to enter that rest" and experience the truth of God's word in the process (4:11a).

"For the word of God is living and active, sharper than any two-edged sword, piercing to the division of soul and of spirit, of joints and of marrow, and discerning the thoughts and intentions of the heart. And no creature is hidden from his sight, but all are naked and exposed to the eyes of him to whom we must give account." (Hebrews 4:12–13)

Have you ever hardened your heart to God's word?

183. Jesus Is the Ultimate High Priest, Covenant, Sanctuary, and Sacrifice
[from Hebrews 4:14–10:18]

Jesus is God's final word and the reason to hold firm in the faith. Jesus is the "great high priest," who overcame all human weakness and temptation, thus allowing believers the full confidence to come before God's throne of grace (4:14–16). Jesus "learned obedience through what he suffered," which made him perfect, and he is "the source of eternal salvation to all who obey him" (5:8b, 9b). Believers develop mature "powers of discernment trained by constant practice to distinguish good from evil" (5:14).

For those who deliberately reject this path to maturity, there is a third warning: It will be impossible to restore a person to fellowship who returns to a life of "crucifying once again the Son of God to their own harm and holding him up to contempt" (6:4–6).

Jesus is superior to the old covenant priests, who had to offer sacrifices for their *own* sin in addition to the sin of the people (7:27). These priests were not permanent; they eventually died (7:23). However, because Jesus is at God's right hand, and "since he always lives," he continually intercedes with prayer for his children (1:13; 7:25). This makes Jesus the "guarantor" and "mediator" of a better and new covenant (7:22; 8:8–13; 9:15).

Jesus eliminated the need to worship God in a specific location. God once instructed Moses on the details for the tabernacle in the wilderness (9:1–10). However, when Jesus came as high priest, he used his own blood for entering God's throne room on behalf of his people; he is the new "place" for worship (9:11–12).

Jesus established his superiority over the old covenant when he made himself the only and permanent sacrifice (9:26b; 10:12). The priests made the daily sacrifices and yearly offering in the holy places, but Jesus purifies the "conscience from dead works to serve the living God" and "has perfected for all time those who are being sanctified" (10:11; 9:25; 9:13–14; 10:14).

"We have this as a sure and steadfast anchor of the soul, a hope that enters into the inner place behind the curtain, where Jesus has gone as a forerunner on our behalf, having become a high priest forever after the order of Melchizedek." (Hebrews 6:19–20)

What is the anchor of *your* soul?

184. Be Faithful with Endurance

[from Hebrews 10:19–13:25]

Hebrews 11 is a well-known chapter in the Bible, often called "the faith chapter." Faith is defined at the outset of the chapter as "the assurance of things hoped for, the conviction of things not seen" (11:1). The author highlighted many people from the Old Testament who lived out this definition of faith. He applauded these heroes of the faith and observed that, in Jesus, God provides the promise for which those heroes lived and died.

Jesus opened the curtain separating believers from the holiness of God, and gives the confidence to enter God's presence with a "true heart in full assurance of faith" (10:19–22). This confidence, in turn, enables his followers to live beyond self-interest, join together in worship with fellow believers, and encourage other believers to live lives of "love and good works" (10:24–25).

The fourth warning in Hebrews comes at the end of chapter 10, where the person living by faith is starkly contrasted with the person who, though aware of God's truth, sins deliberately, profaning "the blood of the covenant," and outraging "the Spirit of grace"; for such a person, there will be a "fearful expectation of judgment" (10:26–31).

The faithful, on the other hand, are commended; these believers have "endured a hard struggle with sufferings," but trust God will provide for them a "better" and "abiding" possession—that is, eternal life (10:32b, 34b). Jesus is the model for this type of endurance, and the "founder and perfecter of our faith"; he "endured the cross" and is now "seated at the right hand of the throne of God" (12:2).

The fifth warning comes in chapter 12. In light of the previous eleven chapters, the author warned readers to "not refuse [God] who is speaking" (12:25). Rather, believers should display gratitude to God in response to his promise of inheriting a "kingdom that cannot be shaken" (12:28).

Hebrews concludes with encouragement to lead lives consistent with a sincere faith in God, assured that God equips those whom he calls "with everything good that you may do his will" (13:21).

"Therefore, since we are surrounded by so great a cloud of witnesses, let us also lay aside every weight, and sin which clings so closely, and let us run with endurance the race that is set before us, looking to Jesus, the founder and perfecter of our faith, who for the joy that was set before him endured the cross, despising the shame, and is seated at the right hand of the throne of God." (Hebrews 12:1–2)

Have you refused Jesus' call to you, or have you responded in faith?

***

REFLECTION 17
What We Believe Matters

We understand that Jesus paid the price for our sins, and he also heals the hurt our sin causes God. Thankfully, if we respond in faith by accepting Jesus as the atonement for our sins, we can know with certainty that God is pleased with us as his children.

The book of Hebrews provides a deeper assurance of our relationship with God through Jesus. That assurance is anchored in the hope that Jesus can and does redeem our past, gives meaning to our present, and secures our future. Through him we have direct access to God our Father. We no longer need to offer a sacrifice. We no longer need to be in a particular place to worship him. We no longer need someone else to talk to God on our behalf.

Now we can come to God with proper awe and reverence, yet boldly, with confidence. Coming to him requires faith in our hearts, believing that Jesus perfectly satisfied God's wrath for our sin and completely met his requirements of justice. This is the kind of faith Hebrews 11:1–2 describes.

Yet, as Hebrews 11:3 indicates, our faith has a cosmic level in addition to a personal level. We are to acknowledge God as the unique and intentional creator of all that exists: "By faith we understand that the universe was created by the word of God, so that what is seen was not made out of things that are visible" (11:3). This means God exists outside of the material universe, and by his will, imagination, and power, he alone brought into existence everything we know, see, and touch.

God wants us to know with confidence that we exist as a beautiful and significant part of his amazing creation. Keeping these truths in mind is the only way we will live lives of faithfulness and endurance, just as the heroes of Hebrews 11:4–12:2 did.

***

CONNECTION 15

Four Leaders Wrote the Last Seven Epistles

All four of the authors of the next seven books in the New Testament were personally close to Jesus during his life on earth. James and Jude were half-brothers to Jesus, sharing Mary and Joseph as their earthly parents. Peter and John were part of the inner circle of the twelve apostles.

James served as an elder in the church in Jerusalem. His letter, which bears his name, is in the tradition of the wisdom literature of the Old Testament (e.g., Proverbs).

Peter was the informal leader of the disciples after Jesus' ascension. He wrote two letters, known as 1 Peter and 2 Peter. The first letter focused on encouraging Christians new in the faith to persevere while living in a hostile culture. The second letter instructed believers about the anchors they need for living gospel lives.

The author of 1, 2, and 3 John was the same John who wrote the fourth Gospel. After Jesus' ascension, John served as an elder, teacher, and preacher.

Jude, too, wrote an epistle that bears his name. In the letter, he urged followers of Jesus to be aware of false teachers, understand God's truth, and fight for the faith.

***

185. Proof of Faith

[from James 1:1–18 and 5:7–20]

The book of James begins and ends with a discussion of the differences between gospel living and worldly living. In effect, James gave us the markers, or tests, of these two diametrically opposed ways of living.

With many of his readers suffering under various kinds of problems, including persecution, James explained that their faith was being tested. Their first response should be to seek God's wisdom in the situation (1:5a). God's promise is to provide wisdom abundantly, so prayer should be grounded in confident faith (1:5b–6). The positive result of testing is a continually increasing "steadfastness," which God promises to reward with "the crown of life" (1:3–4; 5:11; 1:12).

James addressed the human tendency to blame God or other people for problems. He assured his readers that God does not, and never will, tempt anyone (1:13). Instead, temptation comes from within, when desires develop into sin and ultimately lead to death (1:14–15). He also reminded his readers that God is the source of everything good, in accordance with his perfect, unchanging character. God's plan is to lead them with his truth (1:16–18).

James urged believers to live with a patient heart and spirit until Jesus returns. In particular, they are not to "grumble against one another" (5:7–9). Rather, they should follow the example of the prophets who suffered with patience, yet remained steadfast (5:10–11). They should be honest and truthful, not casually using God's name in an oath (5:12). Anyone who is sick, he said, should exercise faith by asking others, especially the leaders of the local church, for prayer (5:14–18). Regarding someone who wanders from God's truth, they should actively seek to help that person to be restored to faithful gospel living (5:19–20).

"Count it all joy, my brothers, when you meet trials of various kinds, for you know that the testing of your faith produces steadfastness. And let steadfastness have its full effect, that you may be perfect and complete, lacking in nothing." (James 1:2–4)

What do you use as a test of whether or not you are living out gospel faith?

186. James Described the Marks of Gospel Living
[from James 1:19–4:12]

James focused on some of the most significant indicators of a life spent serving God over all other priorities, some of which are revealed in a person's speech, emotions, and practice of faith.

Speech is not only what is said, but also what is not said. It is a matter of controlling the tongue, which, James noted, is quite small but directs the entire body. His counsel in this letter was to be "quick to hear, slow to speak, slow to anger" (1:19). A person who cannot control his or her tongue is deceiving himself about having a meaningful life of faith (1:26).

Emotions reveal similar things about a person—an ability to exercise self-control over one's body. Human anger is inconsistent with God's righteousness and shows an inclination toward evil (1:19–21). Likewise, extreme jealously and personal ambition express the false wisdom of this world, not the truth and character of God (3:14–16).

In summary, James emphasized that a life of faith puts God's wisdom into practice, with a posture of humility before God and respectful decency toward others (3:13, 17–18).

This kind of life comes from hearing the truth of God's word and then putting it into practice with the help of his Spirit (1:22–25).

"But the wisdom from above is first pure, then peaceable, gentle, open to reason, full of mercy and good fruits, impartial and sincere. And a harvest of righteousness is sown in peace by those who make peace." (James 3:17–18)

How would you describe gospel living using your own words?

187. James Rebuked Worldly Living
[from James 4:1–5:6]

James expanded the instructions from 1:14–15, where he explained that temptation comes from unchecked desires inside a person that lead to sin and spiritual death.

He also described specific instances in which an improper self-focus results in worldly living rather than gospel living. Examples include quarrels and fighting, which come when people crave more material possessions. Prayer is ineffective when it is motivated by a desire to acquire more things, seeking to satisfy oneself rather than to honor God. Spiritual life is contaminated by adopting worldly values. Financial success is distorted in purpose as well when people rely on money for security, ignoring God as the provider of everything. And financial success is perverted when money is accumulated by taking advantage of others.

"You adulterous people! Do you not know that friendship with the world is enmity with God? Therefore whoever wishes to be a friend of the world makes himself an enemy of God." (James 4:4)

How would you know when you have enough things and money?

REFLECTION 18

How We Worship Matters

How believers in Jesus worship God when they are together matters very much to him.

James 2:1–13 rebukes those in the church who favor the rich and disregard the poor. Among James's readers, apparently some were encouraging the rich to take the best seats in the room, making themselves comfortable while the materially poor believers had to stand to the side, out of the way. The implication was that these poorer people were less significant and of lower worth. James taught that Christians violate the commandment to love one's neighbor when they treat other believers with prejudice and partiality. Instead, followers of Jesus are to acknowledge that God treats us with mercy, so we should do the same for others, regardless of their worldly position and wealth status.

Paul addressed a similar problem in the church in Corinth. The Christian Corinthians had prideful arguments about issues of faith, went to court to fight about money, and were rude to the poor people in the church (1 Corinthians 3:1–23; 6:1–11; 11:17–34; Pixel 152).

How we worship God when we gather together reflects our true motives about worshiping God. Jesus explained to the Samaritan woman at the well (Pixel 106) that the physical location of where we worship God does not matter. What matters is that in our innermost beings (our hearts), we worship God in spirit and in truth (John 4:23). If we are concerned about how other people dress, what kinds of jobs they have, or the types of cars they drive, then we will not be seeing them as God sees them. God looks at our hearts, not our appearances or material possessions (1 Samuel 16:7). And he wants us to look at other people the same way—having the same patience, kindness, and respect for others as he shows us. Then we will be able to truly worship God, rather than in arrogance and with manipulative expectations, and we will be better able to see ourselves correctly, as God sees us.

***

188. Genuineness of Faith

[from 1 Peter 1:1–2:12 and 4:1–11]

Peter got straight to the point in his first epistle. He wrote that followers of Jesus should rejoice in the midst of grieving over their troubles so that the "tested genuineness" of their faith will result in the praise, glory, and honor of Jesus (1:6–7). This faith is anchored in the living hope available through the resurrection of Jesus (1:3–5). But even though salvation through Jesus was a reality for Peter's readers, that salvation was only partially known and understood before his time, having been searched for by the prophets, and of deep interest to angels (1:10–12).

Peter said that a genuine faith leads to a life marked by holy conduct (1:15, 17a). This gospel living results from "preparing [one's mind] for action," and from living in the hope of the grace that Jesus gives (1:13). This new frame of mind is in contrast to the futile ways of one's past life, from which a follower of Jesus is ransomed (1:17–19).

By living in faithfulness to God's truth, Peter explained, believers purify their souls, which in turn allows them to love each other properly, putting away self-centered and manipulative conduct (1:22; 2:1–2). As Jesus' followers become more like him, they see him as a "living stone," and themselves, similarly, as living stones in the world, "built up as a spiritual house, to be a holy priesthood, to offer spiritual sacrifices acceptable to God through Jesus Christ" (2:5). To be fit for this task, believers need to realize that, although they are "sojourners and exiles" on earth, they are to conduct themselves in such a way that others will see God's truth in their lives (2:11–12).

They should also understand that they will suffer in this life, as Jesus suffered (4:1). In suffering, it is important that they live to do God's will and not simply to satisfy their personal passions (4:2). Not knowing when Jesus will return, they must live in a way that honors God and is respectful of others, so that "in everything God may be glorified through Jesus Christ" (4:7–11).

"But you are a chosen race, a royal priesthood, a holy nation, a people for his own possession, that you may proclaim the excellencies of him who called you out of darkness into his marvelous light. Once you were not a people, but now you are God's people; once you had not received mercy, but now you have received mercy." (1 Peter 2:9–10)

Do you live in a way that encourages others to see God's truth through your life?

189. Faith Lived in Humility

[from 1 Peter 2:13–3:13 and 5:1–11]

Peter's second main point in his first epistle was that his readers needed to live with humility and in subjection to the authority of "every human institution" (2:13). Echoing 1 Peter 2:12, the point of humility is to live so that others see God's truth in their lives (2:15–17). This instruction obligates people to respect the government (2:13, 17). The teaching even applies to slaves, who have Jesus as their example of receiving unfair treatment yet trusting God as the ultimate judge and source of justice (2:18–25).

In marriage, wives are to be subject to their own husbands, while husbands are to honor their wives with understanding so that their prayers are not hindered (3:1, 7).

To make sure he did not leave out anyone, Peter exhorted everyone to "have unity of mind, sympathy, brotherly love, a tender heart, and a humble mind" (3:8). He wanted the followers of Jesus to be people of peace who give a blessing, rather than people of selfishness who seek revenge (3:9–12). Toward each other, they are to be clothed with humility; before God, they should trust his promises of provision and protection from the devil's attempts to control them (5:5a, 6–11). Peter instructed the church leaders in particular to be shepherds of the flock willingly, not for their personal financial gain or glory (5:1–4).

"For this is the will of God, that by doing good you should put to silence the ignorance of foolish people. Live as people who are free, not using your freedom as a cover-up for evil, but living as servants of God." (1 Peter 2:15–16)

How do you think we can live as "people who are free" yet at the same time "as servants of God"?

190. Faith Purified in Suffering

[from 1 Peter 3:13–22 and 4:12–19]

Peter's third main point was that believers will have their faith tested and purified in personal suffering. He urged them not to be fearful or troubled when the suffering comes. Rather, they should honor Jesus in their hearts and give an explanation for their faith in a respectful manner (3:13–15). Their suffering can be used as an opportunity to do God's will, following in the footsteps of Jesus, who suffered death so he could make our spirits alive to God (3:16–18).

Peter warned his readers not to be surprised when they suffer. Rather, they should rejoice, because this response reveals God's glory and shows that God's Spirit rests on them (4:12–14). Suffering for their faith is not a matter of shame, Peter explained, but rather an opportunity to praise God and trust him more deeply (4:16, 19).

"Beloved, do not be surprised at the fiery trial when it comes upon you to test you, as though something strange were happening to you. But rejoice insofar as you share Christ's sufferings, that you may also rejoice and be glad when his glory is revealed." (1 Peter 4:12–13)

How does the Christian faith help you make sense of suffering?

191. Anchors for True Gospel Living

[from 2 Peter 1]

Peter knew the importance of reminding Christians how they should live. He knew how easy it is to be influenced by others. And he knew that false teachers are a big problem—they want to turn God's people from his truth. In his second epistle, Peter gave some specific instructions.

First, Peter reminded his audience of God's great promise to give them everything they need to live in a way that honors him (1:3–4). Their response to this promise, he said, should be to "make every effort" to grow in their faith with virtue, knowledge, self-control, steadfastness, godliness, brotherly affection, and love (1:5–7). These qualities allow a believer to know God's truth in Jesus more deeply (1:8–9). Peter urged his readers to "be all the more diligent" in practicing these qualities in order to be proper instruments of God's work in the world (1:10–11). Peter's second reminder was an assurance that God will "always . . . remind [them] of these qualities" (1:12–15).

In addition to these reminders, Peter gave three main reasons they should rely on his teachings. First, he saw the majesty of Jesus as an eyewitness (1:16). Second, he heard the voice of God acknowledging Jesus as his Son (1:17–18). Third, he read the written Scriptures, which were inspired by the Holy Spirit and testified about Jesus (1:19–21).

"Therefore, brothers, be all the more diligent to make your calling and election sure, for if you practice these qualities you will never fall. For in this way there will be richly provided for you an entrance into the eternal kingdom of our Lord and Savior Jesus Christ." (2 Peter 1:10–11)

If we have God's promise to provide everything we need to live for him, why should we "make every effort" and "be all the more diligent" to live as Peter describes?

192. Peter Condemned False Teachers

[from 2 Peter 2:1–22 and 3:17]

Peter warned that false teachers will find their way into the church. These teachers secretly distort the gospel, and in greed exploit people. They manipulate people to follow them, but their teachings actually blaspheme God's truth and ultimately will lead to their condemnation and destruction (2:1–3). Peter cited the flood of Noah's time as an example of God's judgment on the earth; Noah and his family were saved, but everyone else was destroyed (2:4–10a; Pixels 8–10).

Peter described false teachers as "blaspheming about matters of which they are ignorant" while joining in eating feasts with those in the church (2:10b–13). These false teachers have "eyes full of adultery" and "hearts trained in greed" (2:14–16). They speak loudly as they promote "sensual passions of the flesh," but in the end, the content of their teachings is as fleeting in substance as mist (2:17–22).

Peter cautioned his readers not to be influenced by these ungodly teachers, who cause them to become unstable in their faith (3:17).

"For, speaking loud boasts of folly, they entice by sensual passions of the flesh those who are barely escaping from those who live in error. They promise them freedom, but they themselves are slaves of corruption. For whatever overcomes a person, to that he is enslaved." (2 Peter 2:18–19)

How do you recognize false teachers and false teachings?

193. Why Pursue Gospel Living?

[from 2 Peter 3]

Peter ended his second epistle with a great blessing of hope and encouragement. The "scoffers" who mock God for his apparently failed promise that Jesus will return deliberately overlook major facts, Peter explained. These people ignore the reality that God created all that exists through the words of his mouth. They ignore the fact that God has exercised his judgment in the past by destroying the ungodly (3:1–7).

Peter continued his theme of encouraging Christians to remember the past and "stirring up [their] sincere mind[s] by way of reminder" (3:1–2). While the scoffers overlook God's truth, those in the church should remember, and not overlook, that "with the Lord one day is as a thousand years, and a thousand years as one day" (3:8). They should be confident that God will not be slow to fulfill his promise that Jesus will return. They should realize God is being patient, wanting all his children to come to him. And when that happens, Jesus will return at a time no one expects (3:9–10).

Until Jesus' return, his followers should live holy lives and be diligent in their faith, Peter wrote (3:11–14). They should be on their guard against false teachers and scoffers (3:17). Most importantly, they should focus on growing "in the grace and knowledge of our Lord and Savior Jesus Christ" (3:18).

"Since all these things are to be dissolved, what sort of people ought you to be in lives of holiness and godliness . . . Therefore, beloved, since you are waiting for these, be diligent to be found by him without spot or blemish, and at peace." (2 Peter 3:11, 14)

Are you confident Jesus will come again? How are you living in light of that knowledge?

***

REFLECTION 19

Believers in Jesus Are Spirit-Crafted and Empowered to Love and Serve

God works to shape our character into the image of his Son (Reflection 15). This is God's work inside us.

But what about the exterior part of our lives—how we live in the world? Is our outward personal identity being formed by God, or by the desires we have for ourselves, the expectations of others, or what the culture tells us to be in order to be accepted and successful? If the latter is the case, then we will find ourselves striving to have more material possessions, accumulate more wealth, and impress others for our reputation.

If on the other hand our personal identity is formed by the blossoming of the character of Jesus in us, at least three goals will emerge in our lives: (1) being a living witness to the resurrection of Jesus (John 15:27; Acts 1:8; Reflection 12); (2) being a "living sacrifice" as an act of daily worship (Romans 12:1; Pixel 149); and (3) being a "living stone"—that is, spiritual offerings to God who make up God's new spiritual temple (1 Peter 2:4–5; Pixel 188).

God's intention is for us to find our identity in Jesus, not in ourselves, material possessions, or the opinions of others. Some speak of this way of living as living for an "audience of One." In other words, in everything we do, our first thought is how we will bring honor to God's name and advance his kingdom.

But Jesus said all of these things are only possible because of the Holy Spirit, who dwells in those who believe in him, teaches us, helps us remember truth, and witnesses to us about Jesus (John 14:26; 15:26–27).

***

194. Gospel Living as Kingdom Fellowship

[from 1 John]

In the first in a series of three letters, the apostle John defined kingdom fellowship and encouraged others to participate in it.

Fellowship with God, John explained, leads to proper fellowship with others. To have this fellowship, followers of Jesus must realize "God is light," and they are to walk in his light (1:5, 7). Furthermore, they are to know "God is love," and because of his love, he sent Jesus to be the propitiation for their sins (4:8b, 10).

With this love of God in them, Jesus' followers are to love others and believe God is life (4:11). Having Jesus means having life—eternal life—in him (5:11–12).

"That which we have seen and heard we proclaim also to you, so that you too may have fellowship with us; and indeed our fellowship is with the Father and with his Son Jesus Christ. And we are writing these things so that our joy may be complete." (1 John 1:3–4)

How would you define fellowship? Are you in fellowship with other believers?

195. True Fellowship with God

[from 1 John]

John called his readers into a life of fellowship with God and others. Interspersed throughout 1 John are indicators (tests) of how a person can know if he or she is experiencing this kind of fellowship.

John's main tests for evaluating whether or not a person is living a sinful life are based on whether that person is still living in darkness, loving the things of the world, hating others, and denying that Jesus is the Son of God. According to John, if a person realizes he or she is living a sinful life, the remedy is confession, because Jesus is the only advocate a person has before God, who wants to forgive and cleanse his children.

John made specific connections between a person's life practices and his or her faith and fellowship with God: abiding in Jesus, listening to the spirit of truth, and practicing the righteousness of God. John made clear that if and how a person loves others shows if and how a person loves God. Because Jesus made the ultimate sacrifice of love—dying—for those who follow him, believers are able to know and give genuine love to others.

John also helped his readers determine spiritual truths. First, a person should pay attention to his or her own heart for confidence of God's forgiveness. Second, a person should pay attention to the spiritual world, testing the spirits to determine which ones confess that Jesus came in the flesh. The spirits that confess this are "of God," while those that do not are of the "antichrist." Antichrist was John's term for anyone who does not believe that Jesus, as God, was also fully human.

"I write these things to you who believe in the name of the Son of God that you may know that you have eternal life. And this is the confidence that we have toward him, that if we ask anything according to his will he hears us. And if we know that he hears us in whatever we ask, we know that we have the requests that we have asked of him." (1 John 5:13–15)

Why is it so important for you as a follower of Jesus to test yourself and the spirits?

196. False Teachings Undermine Kingdom Fellowship

[from 1 John]

John knew there were already serious obstacles to realizing the fullness of a life in proper fellowship with God and other people.

The whole world, he wrote, is "in the power of the evil one," and many antichrists had already come, as evidenced by some people breaking off fellowship (5:19b; 2:18–19). These antichrists were trying to deceive with false teachings, prompting him to write this letter (2:26).

Some of the day-to-day results of being influenced by false teaching are: loving things of this world, hating others, living in a spirit of error, and denying the divinity of Jesus.

"And we know that the Son of God has come and has given us understanding, so that we may know him who is true; and we are in him who is true, in his Son Jesus Christ. He is the true God and eternal life." (1 John 5:20)

Why are false teachings so prevalent, and why is fellowship so hard to maintain?

197. John Defended Gospel Living against False Teachers

[from 2 John]

John wrote a second letter to emphasize that while those who are in Jesus should love each other, they also should be on their guard around those who attack the faith.

He commended those who walk in the truth, meaning their lives show their faith in Jesus because they obey his commands (verses 4–5). The clearest demonstration of this gospel living is for believers to "love one another" (verse 5).

But he sternly warned that deceivers who deny Jesus will actively attempt to undermine believers individually and as a church. He said believers should have nothing to do with these false teachers, and certainly not provide them any financial support (verses 10–11).

"For many deceivers have gone out into the world, those who do not confess the coming of Jesus Christ in the flesh. Such a one is the deceiver and the antichrist." (2 John, verse 7)

Why is it so dangerous to associate with false teachers?

198. John Explained Gospel Living

[from 3 John]

John wrote a third, personal letter to a dear friend, Gaius, about the intimacy of a relationship with Jesus. In this letter, John referred to Gaius as "beloved," exemplifying the close bond fellow believers in Jesus have with each other. In his message, John told Gaius that he prayed for Gaius' physical and spiritual health. John shared his joy in knowing that Gaius was "walking in the truth," meaning his life honored God (verse 3). John encouraged Gaius to give financial support to traveling teachers; this tangible form of encouragement to those who teach others about Jesus would demonstrate that he was living "in a manner worthy of God" (verse 6).

John cautioned Gaius not to follow a particular false teacher "who likes to put himself first" and who spoke disrespectfully of John (verse 9). When people put themselves first, they do not have proper respect for authority, John explained. Also, the false teacher was similar to others who oppose Jesus because he was "not content" and felt the need to control others (verse 10). John gave Gaius practical and wholesome advice when he said, "Do not imitate evil but imitate good" (verse 11).

The letter ends with John showing the reality of what it means to be part of the fellowship of people who acknowledge Jesus as their Lord. He offered peace and grace to his readers, from both himself and those with him, and encouraged them to offer greetings in the same way (verse 15).

"Beloved, do not imitate evil but imitate good. Whoever does good is from God; whoever does evil has not seen God." (3 John, verse 11)

How would you describe the difference between living for your personal interests and living for the gospel?

199. Contend for True Faith against False Teachers
[from Jude]

Jude, the half-brother of Jesus, wrote to the entire Christian church in his letter, which is the final epistle of the New Testament. He sounded the alarm about false teachers and the necessity of believers in Jesus to "contend for the faith" (verse 3). He stressed that false teachers had infiltrated the church and could be identified by their ungodly conduct, in which they followed their "sinful desires" and "ungodly passions" (verses 4, 16, 18). Their teachings perverted God's grace into sensual license, denied Jesus as Lord, rejected authority, blasphemed, and caused divisions (verses 8, 19).

Jude said this problem of false teachers should not come as a surprise, for God's prophets gave fair warnings for a long time about such teachers (verse 14). But God, in his sovereign power, is still in control, and these ungodly deceivers would, in due time, receive his condemnation, judgment, and destruction (verse 11).

In the meantime, believers should be ready to "contend for the faith" (verse 3). They should remember that the ungodly present a real problem, but eventually these unbelievers will be destroyed. Jude encouraged the church to keep itself in the love of God by building up faith, praying in the Holy Spirit, and waiting on the mercy of Jesus for eternal life (verses 20–21). Moreover, those in the church should have mercy on sinners and on people unsure of their faith (verse 22).

The book of Jude ends with its author encouraging believers to always keep this in mind:

"Now to him who is able to keep you from stumbling and to present you blameless before the presence of his glory with great joy, to the only God, our Savior, through Jesus Christ our Lord, be glory, majesty, dominion, and authority, before all time and now and forever. Amen." (Jude, verses 24–25)

How should you respond to false teachers and false teachings?

***

REFLECTION 20

God's Will—Walking in a Manner Worthy of Jesus

In Reflection 19 we discussed three specific ways believers are to live before others.

Now we see an overview concept in a beautiful mosaic of verses that directs how we should live before other people. Our lives demonstrate to others what it means to honor God as followers of Jesus. Conforming our character to the image of Jesus makes a difference in our daily lives, and in how other people see us and therefore God.

We should all ask ourselves: When I am with other people, do they experience my old nature, with all of its futile thoughts, beliefs, and actions? Or do they experience the thoughts, beliefs, and actions of Jesus as he lives in and through me? At all times, we are to "walk" and live in ways worthy of the Lord Jesus.

Here are some other important verses in the Bible that you might want to read that emphasize this calling: 2 Corinthians 8:21; Ephesians 4:1; Philippians 1:27; Colossians 1:10; 2:6; 1 Thessalonians 2:12; 4:1; 2 Thessalonians 1:11; and 3 John, verse 6.

***

PART NINE

Revelation Ended the Bible but Not the Story

Book of the Bible Discussed in This Part:

Revelation

Jude	John Wrote Messages to 7 Churches
63–68 AD	94–97
John Received a Revelation of Jesus Christ	John Saw Jesus and a Scroll

Jesus Opened the 7 Seals			THE EARTH REMADE!
			ETERNITY!
	Jesus at War with Satan; Jesus Won		THE NEW JERUSALEM!

CONNECTION 16

John Went to Prison and Jesus Spoke to Him

Late in the life of John the apostle, the Roman government arrested him because he kept teaching and preaching about Jesus. Roman emperors demanded devotion to the Roman Empire. They saw John as a troublemaker. John taught devotion to Jesus as a first priority; everything else, including the government, came after Jesus. The Romans sent him away to a prison on the small Greek island of Patmos.

While John was in prison, Jesus sent an angel to show John what would happen in the future. Then John had a vision of Jesus telling him to write what he saw and then send it to seven churches. This vision is the content of the book of Revelation, the last book in the New Testament.

Revelation is a complex book to read and understand. It was written as an exhortation to the worldwide Christian church, as represented by seven specific churches that received direct messages in the book.

The book has broad application to all Christians, emphasizing that God is in control of all of history. Before Jesus returns to complete the salvation of God's called and treasured family, trouble and persecution await his followers. Because of the disgusting wickedness of many people, God will pour out his righteous judgment, his justifiably great anger, and his final wrath. When he does, human history as we know it will end. Jesus, by his death and resurrection, already stands in victory over Satan and all the evil promoted by Satan. Jesus will one day return for God's children, and the earth will be made new in ways we do not fully understand. And then, God's family will live with him for eternity—forever and ever . . . and ever!

***

200. John Received a Revelation of Jesus Christ

[from Revelation 1]

The Roman government put John's body in prison but could not keep him from knowing and hearing God's Spirit and his Lord Jesus. When John heard a loud, trumpet-like voice, he turned and saw a vision of Jesus.

In this vision, Jesus assured John not to be afraid, but to write his message to seven churches. John was so confident of what he saw and heard that he told the seven churches that God would bless everyone who read aloud what he wrote, and those who heard and obeyed the words would also be blessed. He assured his readers that one day soon, Jesus will return. When he does, he will come in a manner so that everyone will see him, even the people who killed him.

"When I saw him, I fell at his feet as though dead. But he laid his right hand on me, saying, 'Fear not, I am the first and the last, and the living one. I died, and behold I am alive forevermore, and I have the keys of Death and Hades. Write therefore the things that you have seen, those that are and those that are to take place after this.'" (Revelation 1:17–19)

Why did Jesus appear to John?

201. John Wrote Messages to Seven Churches
[from Revelation 2–3]

Jesus' message to each church, given through John, addressed specific circumstances, problems, and issues of the church. Jesus also gave important instructions about what each church needed to do.

These are the seven churches along with the instructions Jesus gave to each:

1. Ephesus. "Remember therefore from where you have fallen; repent, and do the works you did at first. If not, I will come to you and remove your lampstand from its place, unless you repent" (2:5).

2. Smyrna. "Be faithful unto death, and I will give you the crown of life" (2:10b).

3. Pergamum. "You have some there who hold to the teaching of Balaam . . . So also you have some who hold to the teaching of the Nicolaitans. Therefore repent. If not, I will come to you soon and war against them with the sword of my mouth" (2:14a, 15–16).

4. Thyatira. "Only hold fast what you have until I come" (2:25).

5. Sardis. "Remember, then, what you received and heard. Keep it, and repent. If you will not wake up, I will come like a thief, and you will not know at what hour I will come against you" (3:3).

6. Philadelphia. "I am coming soon. Hold fast what you have, so that no one may seize your crown" (3:11).

7. Laodicea. "I counsel you to buy from me gold refined by fire, so that you may be rich, and white garments so that you may clothe yourself and the shame of your nakedness may not be seen, and salve to anoint your eyes, so that you may see" (3:18).

Jesus confirmed that those who follow his directions will be "conquerors," and he will reward them (2:7, 11, 17, 26; 3:12, 21).

Is there something you need to conquer in your life? If so, what is it, what are you doing about it, and who can best help you with it?

202. John Saw Jesus and a Scroll

[from Revelation 4–5]

In his vision, John saw a door standing open in heaven. An angel told him he was about to see "what must take place after this" (4:1). He then saw an overwhelming vision of Jesus on his throne. Over the throne was an enormous rainbow, and around it were twenty-four elders worshiping Jesus, praising him, and casting their crowns before him. Lightning, thunder, and seven torches of fire appeared (4:3–5). There were four living creatures around the throne who never stopped praising God.

Jesus held a scroll with writing on both sides and sealed with seven seals. No one but Jesus could open this scroll. Only he was worthy to open it because only he died to pay for the sins of people from every race and nation, so they may be "a kingdom and priests to our God" who will "reign on the earth" (5:10).

"Worthy is the Lamb who was slain, to receive power and wealth and wisdom and might and honor and glory and blessing!" (Revelation 5:12b)

In John's vision, why was Jesus the only one who could open the scroll?

***

REFLECTION 21
God's Big-Picture Plan

The remainder of Revelation reveals the next and final stages of God's plans for people and the earth. People will be judged and Satan will be defeated totally—the victory of Jesus will be decisive and severe. The earth will be remade in a form suitable for those who seek and believe in God to spend eternity with him.

In the introduction to this book, and throughout it (for example, Reflection 8), you have read about God's big-picture plan: his wide-angle perspective as he seeks to establish for himself a special family for his treasured possession—a kingdom of priests, a holy nation of people who desire to live with him forevermore and by his grace will do so.

This grand plan began to crystallize after Jesus' resurrection and in the early days of the church. In the first few chapters of Revelation, you will see even more about this plan and how God fulfills it; after Jesus died, rose from the dead, and defeated Satan's power of evil and death, we see him opening a scroll with seven seals (6:1).

***

203. Jesus Opened the Seven Seals of the Scroll

[from Revelation 6–11]

In John's vision, when Jesus opened the first four of the seven seals of the scroll, four horses, each of a different color with a rider, appeared in power to execute God's judgments. After the fifth seal was opened, "the souls of those who had been slain for the word of God and for the witness they had borne" appeared under the altar (6:9). After the sixth seal was opened, there was a great earthquake, and John saw four angels holding back the four winds of the earth, and before the throne "a great multitude that no one could number" (7:9).

When Jesus opened the seventh seal, there was silence in heaven for half an hour. Then John saw seven angels with seven trumpets of judgment; one-third of four physical elements were destroyed, four angels killed one-third of the people, and two witnesses of Jesus appeared.

Finally, heavenly voices announced that the kingdom of Jesus had come, and the temple in heaven appeared.

"Then the seventh angel blew his trumpet, and there were loud voices in heaven saying, 'The kingdom of the world has become the kingdom of our Lord and of his Christ, and he shall reign forever and ever.'" (Revelation 11:15)

The prophet Nathan told King David that his throne would be established forever (Pixel 55). Is this the fulfillment of his prophecy?

204. Jesus Won the War with Satan

[from Revelation 12–20]

After the last of the seven angels blew his trumpet of judgment, John saw more of what would happen in the future.

There was war in heaven when a dragon came and attacked a woman who had just given birth to a son. When God defended the mother and son, the dragon attacked her other offspring—those who kept his commandments and remained true to the testimony of Jesus (12:17). A beast, in cooperation with the dragon, made war against God's children wherever they were. Another beast—whose number was *666*—came out of the earth, causing people to worship the first beast (13:1–18).

Then John saw the Lamb of God (Jesus). With him were 144,000 of his people. They had the Father's name on their foreheads and sang the "new song" from heaven (14:1–5).

At that point, three angels appeared with messages from God. Jesus, the Son of Man, appeared for the purpose of bringing the final judgment. Then there were seven angels with the last seven plagues of God's final wrath (14:6–15:1). Jesus came as the victor over everything evil. Satan's defeat was permanent when he was thrown into the "lake of fire and sulfur" forever (20:10). Finally, a throne in heaven appeared with books of life and judgment.

"And I saw the dead, great and small, standing before the throne, and books were opened. Then another book was opened, which is the book of life. And the dead were judged by what was written in the books, according to what they had done . . . And if anyone's name was not found written in the book of life, he was thrown into the lake of fire." (Revelation 20:12, 15)

Where are you in this picture?

REFLECTION 22
How We Live and What We Do Matters

For the Old Testament, we might summarize God's message as this: God is faithful to you, so be faithful to him. For the New Testament, we might summarize his message this way: Jesus is faithful to the point of death, so you should live as a faithful witness to his resurrection. In other words, what you do and how you live your life here on earth really matters.

Seven times in Revelation, *witnesses* to the *testimony* of Jesus are affirmed for their steadfastness and designated as conquerors and overcomers:

1. John "bore *witness* to the word of God and to the *testimony* of Jesus Christ, even to all that he saw" (1:2).

2. "When [the Lamb] opened the fifth seal," John "saw under the altar the souls of those who had been slain for the word of God and for the *witness* they had borne" (6:9).

3. "And when they have finished their *testimony,* the beast that rises from the bottomless pit will make war on them and conquer them and kill them" (11:7).

4. "And they have conquered [the accuser, Satan] by the blood of the Lamb and by the word of their *testimony,* for they loved not their lives even unto death" (12:11).

5. "Then the dragon became furious with the woman and went off to make war on the rest of her offspring, on those who keep the commandments of God and hold to the *testimony* of Jesus" (12:17a).

6. John was told not to worship the angel because the angel was "a fellow servant with you and your brothers who hold to the *testimony* of Jesus"; instead, John should worship God, "for the *testimony* of Jesus is the spirit of prophecy" (19:10b).

7. "Also I saw the souls of those who had been beheaded for the *testimony* of Jesus and for the word of God" (20:4b).

God's calling for each of us is clear: live as faithful witnesses—living testimonies—to the resurrection of Jesus!

***

205. The Earth Remade

[from Revelation 21–22]

With Satan thrown into hell for eternity, John saw a vision of the earth remade. In his vision, the earth he knew "passed away" and the "new Jerusalem" came down from heaven. This New Jerusalem was the bride of Jesus, the invisible, worldwide church from across all of human history, and the dwelling place of God with his children. From his throne, God said he is "making all things new," and that the "one who conquers will have this heritage, and I will be his God and he will be my son" (21:1–7).

Then one of the seven angels who had one of the seven final plagues showed John "the Bride, the wife of the Lamb." It was "the holy city Jerusalem coming down out of heaven from God," having no temple, "for its temple is the Lord God the Almighty and the Lamb." The city had no need for a sun or moon because "the glory of God gives it light, and its lamp is the Lamb." Nations will come to the city, but nothing unclean will enter it—"only those who are written in the Lamb's book of life" (21:9–27).

The angel also showed John the "the river of the water of life . . . flowing from the throne of God and of the Lamb through the middle of the street of the city" (22:1–2a). The angel said God had sent his angel to "show his servants what must soon take place." Then Jesus said, "I am coming soon. Blessed is the one who keeps the words of the prophecy of this book." And he promised "to repay everyone for what he has done" (22:6–12).

John ended the record of his vision with this short prayer:

"The grace of the Lord Jesus be with all. Amen." (Revelation 22:21)

Isn't John's prayer a fitting and dynamic way for the New Testament to end?

Concluding Reflection

God's Family Will Live with Him Forever

Who is entitled to live with God for all eternity? The answer to this question is one of the main themes in the Bible. In Psalm 24, David asked, "Who shall ascend the hill of the Lord? And who shall stand in his holy place?" (24:3). David's answer: "He who has clean hands and a pure heart, who does not lift up his soul to what is false and does not swear deceitfully" (24:4).

This might make for nice reading, but as a practical matter, who on earth has clean hands, a pure heart, never falls for what is false, and always tells the truth with sincerity? The answer, if we're honest, is *no one*!

To solve this problem, the Bible from start to finish shows us God's answer. And the answer is not a program, a plan, our performance, or our persistence. It is a person. God came to live on earth as a human named Jesus. The Bible speaks of Jesus as the only mediator between us and God, the only way to have a personal relationship with God (1 Timothy 2:5–6).

Jesus described himself as "the way, and the truth, and the life" (John 14:6). He came to show us the way: the way to new life; the way for our character to be transformed from people of sin to people of faith; and the way of being God's children who will live with him forever, rather than enemies who offend and reject Him.

If you want to be at home with God, both now and for eternity, then you and God are in agreement—he wants the same for you!

Do you hear God calling you? Jesus said, "My sheep hear my voice, and I know them, and they follow me. I give them eternal life, and they will never perish, and no one will snatch them out of my hand" (John 10:27–28).

Are you ready to ask Jesus, as your mediator with God, to make your hands and heart clean, to lead you in his true way, and to use your words and deeds for his purposes? If you are ready, now is the time: ask him!

Appendix of Timelines

• *Old Testament* •

Part One: God Created the World and Began His Special People

Books of the Bible Discussed in This Part:
Genesis, Job, Exodus, Leviticus, Numbers, Deuteronomy

Creation		Noah and the Flood				Job (Approximately)		Isaac as Sacrifice
Before Christ (BC)	U	N	D	A	T	E	D	2091 (1915)*	2050 (1874)

	Adam and Eve		Tower of Babel		Abraham Moved to Canaan	

	Jacob Moved to Egypt		Ten Commandments, Tabernacle, and Sacrifices		Moses' Death	

1898	1876	1446	1445	1433		1406
(1722)	(1700)	(1270)	(1269)	(1267)		(1230)

Joseph Sold as a Slave		Moses as Leader to Canaan		40 Years in Wilderness		Israel Entered Canaan

*Some scholars hold to more recent dates for events in Genesis–Deuteronomy; these dates are shown in parentheses.

Part Two: A Homeland for God's People

Books of the Bible Discussed in This Part: Joshua, Judges, Ruth, 1 & 2 Samuel, 1 Kings, 1 & 2 Chronicles, Psalms, Proverbs, Ecclesiastes, Song of Solomon

Israel Entered Canaan		Samuel's Birth		David Killed Goliath		Solomon as King	
1406 BC (1230)	1375	1105	1050	1025	1010	970	959

	Judges Ruled		Saul United the Kingdom		David as King		Solomon's Temple Completed

1 Samuel...........................II 2 Samuel................II

1 Kings.........................

1 Chronicles..............II 2 Chronicles..........

Part Three: God's People Rejected Him and Went into Exile

Books of the Bible Discussed in This Part: 1 & 2 Kings, Jonah, Amos, Hosea, Joel, Micah, Isaiah, Nahum, Zephaniah, Habakkuk, Obadiah, Jeremiah, Lamentations, Ezekiel, Daniel

Solomon's Temple Complete		*Prophets to the Northern Kingdom (Israel)*				
		Elijah	*Elisha*	*Jonah*	*Amos*	*Hosea*
959 BC	930	875		760	750	
						735

Israel Divided		*Joel*			*Micah Isaiah*
				Prophets to the Southern	

1 Kings..|| 2 Kings..
2 Chronicles..

Israel Fell to Assyria					**2nd Captivity: Ezekiel to Babylon**	
722				605	597	586
	660	635	625			

Nahum, Zephaniah, Habakkuk, Jeremiah			*Obadiah, Ezekiel, Daniel*
Kingdom (Judah)	**Judah's 1st Captivity: Daniel to Babylon**	**3rd Captivity: Temple Destroyed; Judah Fell to Babylon**	

2 Kings..||
2 Chronicles..||

Part Four: God Restored His People to the Homeland

Books of the Bible Discussed in This Part: Daniel, Ezra, Haggai, Zechariah, Esther, Nehemiah, Malachi

3rd Captivity: Temple Destroyed; Judah Fell to Babylon		Cyrus's Decree for Jews to Return to Judah		Temple Construction Stopped		
Daniel					*Haggai*	*Zechariah*
586 BC	539	538	536	530		520

	Babylon Fell to Cyrus		Second Temple's Construction Began			Temple Construction Continued
Temple Completed		Ezra to Jerusalem			Jerusalem's Walls Rebuilt	*Malachi*
	Esther	*Ezra*	*Nehemiah*			
516	479	458	445	444		430

	Esther as Queen of Babylon		Nehemiah to Jerusalem		Malachi as Prophet

• *New Testament* •

Part Five: The Coming of Jesus

Books of the Bible Discussed in This Part: Luke, Matthew

John the Baptist's Birth	Jesus' Birth		Jesus Age 12 at the Temple	Jesus' Baptism
6/5 BC	5/4	Anno Domino (AD; in the year of our Lord)	7/8	27/30

Part Six: Jesus' Earthly Ministry

Books of the Bible Discussed in This Part: Matthew, Mark, Luke, John

Jesus' Baptism	Jesus Began His Ministry	Jesus Chose 12 Apostles	Jesus Fed 5,000	Jesus Was Crucified and Raised, Then Appeared and Ascended
27/30 AD	27/30	28/31	29/32	30/33

Part Seven: God Sent His Spirit and Established His Church

Book of the Bible Discussed in This Part: Acts

Jesus Was Crucified and Raised, Then Appeared and Ascended		Holy Spirit Power Unleashed at Pentecost		Paul's Conversion
30/33 AD	30/33	30/33	34/35	34/35
	Matthias Replaced Judas as an Apostle		Stephen Killed; Paul Helped!	
Peter Baptized Cornelius			Paul as a Prisoner in Caesarea	
37/40	46/57		57/59	60/64
	Paul as a Missionary			Paul a Prisoner in Rome

Part Eight: God Taught His Family How to Live

Books of the Bible Discussed in This Part: Romans, 1 & 2 Corinthians, Galatians, Ephesians, Philippians, Colossians, 1 & 2 Thessalonians, 1 & 2 Timothy, Titus, Philemon, Hebrews, James, 1 & 2 Peter, 1, 2, & 3 John, Jude

Paul a Prisoner in Rome		1 & 2 Corinthians		Ephesians		Colossians	
60–64 AD	55–58	53–57	48–55	60–63	55–63	60–63	49–53
	Romans		Galatians		Philippians		1 & 2 Thessalonians

1 & 2 Timothy		Philemon		James		1, 2, & 3 John	
62–67	62–66	60–62	64–68	45–50	62–68	85–95	63–68
	Titus		Hebrews		1 & 2 Peter		Jude

In Part Eight, the date of the written epistle refers to the approximate time of the writing of the epistle.

Part Nine: Revelation Ended the Bible but Not the Story

Book of the Bible Discussed in This Part: Revelation

Jude		John Wrote Messages to 7 Churches	
63–68 AD	94–97		
	John Received a Revelation of Jesus Christ		John Saw Jesus and a Scroll
Jesus Opened the 7 Seals			THE EARTH REMADE!
			ETERNITY!
	Jesus at War With Satan; Jesus Won		THE NEW JERUSALEM!

Recommended Reading

The Bible

When you look for a Bible, have in mind that there are two main approaches to translations. One is word-for-word, while the other is thought-for-thought. Three modern translations that are word-for-word are the English Standard Version (ESV) published by Crossway, the New American Standard Bible (NASB) published by both Zondervan and Tyndale House, and the New King James Version (NKJV) published by Thomas Nelson.

Crossway's *ESV Study Bible* is a particularly valuable resource and is the source for all Scripture quotations in *The Panoramic Bible*. In addition to notes about the text, this study Bible has substantive articles on issues such as the origin and history of the books of the Bible, doctrinal matters, and the application of biblical concepts to personal and social life.

The Life Application Study Bible edition of the NASB is an excellent resource, focusing on helping readers understand how the Bible applies to their lives.

The Reformation Study Bible edition of the NKJV (Reformation Trust Publishing, a division of Ligonier Ministries, 2016) was edited by renowned Christian theologian R. C. Sproul (general editor) and contains notes and substantive articles in the tradition of the Geneva Bible and Reformed theology.

An excellent study Bible that is thought-for-thought is the *New Living Translation Study Bible* published by Tyndale House.

Spiritual Growth and Formation

I recommend the following resources, each focused on gospel living and personal spiritual growth in different ways.

Dr. Kenneth D. Boa's *Conformed to His Image* (Zondervan, 2001) explores twelve approaches to Christian spiritual growth and helps readers develop a biblical perspective of their lives. E-book, audiobook, and print versions are available at www .kenboa.org. Dr. Boa's website offers a wealth of other resources as well that can help you explore the Christian faith, grow in faith and understanding of the Bible, and understand the reasons behind what Christians believe. I recommend his *Handbook to Prayer* and *Handbook to Scripture* as two resources to help you pray using God's Word.

Dr. Boa's *Life in the Presence of God: Practices for Living in Light of Eternity* (IVP, 2017) is (in the author's own words) "a contemporary guide to practicing the presence of God."

The Knowledge of the Holy (Harper, 1961) by A. W. Tozer explores the attributes of God, giving deep insight into the nature of God.

Tozer's classic *The Pursuit of God* (WingSpread, 2006), first published in 1948, opens readers to what it means to pursue and live for God.

Concise Theology: A Guide to Historic Christian Belief (Tyndale House, 1993) by J. I. Packer provides summaries of ninety-five topics in Christianity alongside related Scriptures.

Reasons to Believe

Do you wonder if God really exists and if the Christian faith makes sense? Here are some suggestions for books that might help you.

Dr. Timothy Keller's *The Reason for God: Belief in an Age of Skepticism* (Dutton, 2008) addresses (in the author's own words) "how faith in a Christian God is a soundly rational belief, held by thoughtful people of intellectual integrity with a deep compassion for those who truly want to know the truth."

In *20 Compelling Evidences That God Exists: Discover Why Believing in God Makes So Much Sense* (Victor, 2005), Dr. Kenneth D. Boa and Robert M. Bowman Jr. discuss the reasonableness of the Christian faith, tackling questions from philosophy and science to psychology and history.

Josh and Sean McDowell's *Evidence That Demands a Verdict: Life-Changing Truth for a Skeptical World* (Thomas Nelson, 2017) is a current and comprehensive compilation of historical evidence and thoughtful insights into the intellectual and philosophical reasons that Christianity is the only credible religious faith.

For those who wonder about the reality of Jesus, the Son of God, who became a human, died, and rose from death, I urge you to read Lee Strobel's *The Case for Christ: A Journalist's Personal Investigation of the Evidence for Jesus* (Zondervan, 2016).

In *Total Truth: Liberating Christianity from Its Cultural Captivity* (Crossway, 2004), Nancy Pearcey provides a readable and challenging discussion of what it is to understand and live a Christian worldview.

Index

A

Aaron, 35–36, 41–44, 47, 69

Abel, 14–15

Abraham (Abram), 19–25, 33, 35, 37, 39–40, 45; journeys, map of, 20

Adam, 10–14, 124

Ahab, 76

Amos, 75, 80

angels, 11–13, 114–117, 154–155, 228, 230–232, 234

antichrists, 222

Assyria, 75–76, 79–81, 86–87, 100

apostles, 124–126, 148–149, 155–156, 160, 162–164

ark of the covenant, 43, 63, 66

atonement, 44, 177, 210

B

Babylon, 57, 82–83, 88–91, 93–96, 100–106, 109, 148

baptism/baptize, 121, 125, 167

Bethlehem, 58, 85, 118–120

big-picture plan (God's), 5, 124, 230–231, 233, 237

Boaz, 55–56, 58

C

Caesar, 118

Cain, 14–15

Caleb, 47, 52

calf god, Aaron's golden calf, 41–42; Jeroboam's golden calves, 69

Canaan, 20–21, 25, 30, 32, 39, 45

captivity, 57, 73–97 *passim*

Carchemish, battle of, 86

census, 118

church, 158–230 *passim*

Cornelius, 167–168

Covenants, with Noah, 17–18; with Abraham, 21–23; at Mount Sinai, 40–41; with Phinehas, 47–48; with David, 63–64; new with Israel and Judah, 93; new by Jesus' death, 148–149; old covenants fulfilled by Jesus, 205–209

Covenant promises, to Adam and Eve, 13–14; to Israel in Egypt, 37–40; by Moses, 48; judgment, 84, 87–91, 108; Malachi and God's messenger, 108; John the Baptist, 114; Jesus the Messiah, 114–116; Jesus' birth, 119; coming of the Holy Spirit, 155, 161–162; Jesus defeats Satan, 232

Cyrus, 57, 96, 100–102, 104

D

Daniel, 90, 94–97, 100–101, 109

David, 58–63, 101, 114, 118

Darius, 96

Deborah, 55

devil. See Satan

disciples, the Twelve. *See* apostles

dream(s), 24, 28, 94

E

Edom, 88–89

Egypt, 27–38, 41, 46

Eli, 56

Elijah, 57, 75–77, 141–142

Elisha, 57, 75, 77–79

epistles, themes of, 174

Esau, 24, 89

Esther, 103–104

Eve, 10–14, 124

exile. *See* captivity

expiation, 177

Ezekiel, 90, 93–94, 109–110

Ezra, 90, 100, 102, 104–105, 107, 109

F

false teachers, 188, 193–194, 200, 202–203, 219, 222–225

fiery furnace, 95

G

Gabriel, 114–116

Galilee, 82, 118, 128, 138, 155; map of, 118

Garden of Eden, 11–13

Gentiles (non-Jews), 20, 79, 87–88, 117, 167–178

Gideon, 55

Goliath, 59–60

Good Samaritan, the, 82, 129, 136

Gospels (books), 117

H

Habakkuk, 87–88

Hagar, 21

Haggai, 90, 102, 107, 109

Hannah, 56

Haran, 20, 23–24

Holy Spirit, 155–202 *passim,* 221; gifts of, 180–181, 220; fruit of, 188–190

Hosea, 75, 81

I

idolatry, 69, 175

Isaac, 21–25, 35, 37, 89

Isaiah, 85–86

Ishmael, 21

Israel, family of Jacob, 33, 35–40, 45–46, 52–53, 145

Israel, nation of, 55–64, 66, 69; divided kingdom, map of, 75

Israel, Northern Kingdom, 69–93 *passim,* 100; map of, 75

J

Jacob, son of Isaac, 24–46 *passim,* 89

James, half-brother of Jesus, 174, 212–215

Jeremiah, 89–91, 93, 101, 141, 148

Jericho, 52, 136

Jeroboam, 69, 76

Jesse, father of David, 58, 60

Jesus, 32, 38, 40, 45, 55–56, 63, 82, 85, 109–229 *passim*; new covenant by Jesus' death, 148–149; crucifixion of, 151–153; resurrection of, 154–157, 175, 183–184; resurrection appearances of, 155–157; return of, 195–197, 229; the mind of, 192; walk worthy of, 194, 225; fulfills Old Testament covenants, 205–209; Lamb of God, 232–234; brings judgment, 232

Jew, origin of word, 103

Job, 19

Joel, 83–84

John the Baptist, 110, 121, 125, 141–142, 155

Jonah, 75, 79–80

Jonathan, 60-61

Jordan River, 52, 121

Joshua, 47, 52–54

Joseph, father of Jesus, 114, 116–120

Joseph, son of Jacob, 27–33

Judah, post-exile community, 100, 102–108

Judah, son of Jacob, 27, 30–32

Judah, Southern Kingdom, 69–93 *passim*, 100; map of, 75

Judah, tribe of, 46, 63

Judas Iscariot, 146–150

Jude, half-brother of Jesus, 174, 212, 224–225

Judea, 82; map of, 118

Judges, 54–56

justification, 176–177

L

Lazarus, 143

lions' den, 96–97, 101

M

Malachi, 90, 107–110, 114–115

Mary, mother of Jesus, 114, 116–120, 126, 152, 160

marriage, 11, 41, 81, 107–108, 127, 129

Micah, 84–85, 120

midwives (Israelite), 33, 35

Moab, 47, 55

Moses, 33–52 *passim*, 127, 130, 142, 145, 207

N

Naaman, 77–79

Nahum, 86

Naomi, 55–56

Nehemiah, 90, 105–107, 109

New Commandment, 148–149

Nicodemus, 127–128, 132

Nineveh, 79, 86

Noah, 16–19

Northern Kingdom. *See* Israel, Northern Kingdom

O

Obadiah, 88–89

Obed, 56, 58

P

Passover, 37–38, 145, 148–149

parables of Jesus, 135–138

Paul (Saul), 117, 129, 164–215 *passim*

Pentecost, 161–162

Peter, 141–142, 149, 160, 162–164, 167–168, 181, 212, 216–220

Pharaoh, 28, 30, 33, 35–39

Pharisees, 127, 142–143

Philistine(s), 59–60

Phinehas, 47–48

plagues, 36-37, 83, 232, 234

prayer, 56, 64, 76, 89, 105, 114, 133, 145, 160, 163, 167, 169

Promised Land, 43, 45–48, 52–53, 57, 207

propitiation, 177

R

Rachel, 25, 27

Rebekah, 24, 89

Red Sea, 38–39

Rehoboam, 69

religious leaders, 127–167 *passim*

repentance, 76, 79–80, 84, 87, 104, 121, 144, 160, 229

Reuben, 27, 31–32

resurrection (of believers in Jesus), 183–184, 195–197

Ruth, 55–56, 58

S

Sabbath, 39, 41, 131, 154, 207; rest, 207

sacrifice(s), 22–23, 44–45, 177, 210

Samaria, southern portion of Northern Kingdom, 81–82, 100, 128–129, 136, 215; map of, 118

Samuel, 56–59

sanctification, 178

Sarah (Sarai), 19–23

Satan, 11, 124–125, 142, 232, 234

Saul, king of Israel, 57–61

Saul of Tarsus. *See* Paul (Saul)

Simon Peter. *See* Peter

slave/slavery, 33, 35–36, 38, 77–78, 80, 205, 217

sexual purity/impurity, 41, 81, 127, 175–176, 182, 188–189, 200, 204, 219, 224

Solomon, 57, 63–70

Southern Kingdom. *See* Judah, Southern Kingdom

sovereignty, 32, 67–68

spies, 46–47, 52

Stephen, 164

T

tabernacle, 43–44, 46, 63

temple, 63, 66, 90–92, 100–104, 146, 153, 163; of the Holy Spirit, 181–183

Ten Commandments, 40–43, 130–131

Tower of Babel, 18

tribes of Israel, 46, 53–54, 74; map of, 54

U

Ur, 20

W

wilderness, 38–45, 53

wise men (magi), 119–120

Z

Zechariah, father of John the Baptist, 114–116

Zechariah, the prophet, 90, 103, 107, 109

Zephaniah, 87

Zerubbabel, 101–105, 109

Acknowledgments

Just about every married writer thanks his or her spouse, and I want to do the same. Shirley is the most important person in the world to me. I am thankful for her role in *The Panoramic Bible*. Not only has she been patient and encouraging during this project, but her consulting and editing made a great contribution.

I have spent many years teaching and participating in Sunday School classes. My teachers, my interactions with those whom I have taught, and my relationships with fellow travelers along the way have sharpened my focus.

The careful teaching and thoughtful wisdom of Dr. Kenneth D. Boa has given me a vision for the depth, beauty, and practical relevance of God's kingdom. Ken directed me to an excellent editor, Jenny M. Abel, whose intensity for knowing and teaching God's Word rivals my own. My political theory professor at Georgia State University, Dr. William D. Richardson, helped expand my use of the beneficial tools of close reading. Catherine C. Anderson's illustrations reflect what artists do; they take words on a page and open new vistas into what can be seen and experienced. John Köehler and his talented colleagues at Köehler Studios provided skilled design insights for the cover, presenting the text in an engaging manner, and bringing together this work you now are reading.

My ultimate thanks are to Jesus, the most important person in the universe to me. He enables the new covenant for us, sent the Holy Spirit who empowers the new covenant in us, and is one with our Father God who makes an eternal provision for us.

About the Author

WILLIAM HOLLBERG practiced law in Atlanta, Georgia, for more than forty-five years.

Bill is a native of Griffin, Georgia. After graduating from Wheaton Academy in Illinois, he earned a BA in political science from Wheaton College (1968), a JD from the University of Georgia (1971), and an MA in political science from Georgia State University (1987). Bill served as a legislative assistant to U.S. Senator David H. Gambrell (D-Ga.) in Washington, D.C., in 1972. Since 1973, Bill and his wife, Shirley, have lived in Atlanta, which is also home to their two adult sons and three grandchildren.

During his career as a lawyer, Bill was recognized as one of Georgia's Super Lawyers in General Litigation (published by *Law and Politics* and *Atlanta Magazine*) and as one of Georgia's Legal Elite in Family Law (*Georgia Trend Magazine*). He is rated by Martindale-Hubbell as one of "America's Most Honored Professionals–Top 1%," a "Top Rated Lawyer" in Litigation and Family Law, an AV Preeminent Attorney, and an AV Preeminent Attorney, Judicial Edition.

Bill is a member of Christ Church of Atlanta, a parish in the Anglican Church of North America. Previously, Bill was a member of ChristChurch Presbyterian in Atlanta, a congregation in the Presbyterian Church in America, where he served as a ruling elder for more than fourteen years.

About the Illustrator

CATHERINE ANDERSON enjoys many forms of art, but she specializes in graphite photorealism. Her technique for *The Panoramic Bible* was a blend of realism and symbolism, striving to convey a gritty sense of the earthly and the heavenly in every image.

Catherine plans to pursue a degree in medical illustration. For several years, she has owned and operated an online Etsy store, where she sells her art. In addition, her work has been displayed in a gallery in New York City, and she was employed as a sketch artist on a pilgrimage to Israel to document the Holy Land.

When she's not drawing, Catherine enjoys reading Agatha Christie novels, listening to Needtobreathe, and hiking in Shenandoah National Park near her home in central Virginia.